The Art of
Global Thinking

The Art of
Global Thinking

Integrating Organizational
Philosophies of East and West

Donald Cyr

Ichor Business Books
An Imprint of Purdue University Press
West Lafayette, Indiana

Printed in the United States of America

Library of Congress Cataloging-in-Publication Data
Cyr, Donald, 1949–
    The art of global thinking : integrating organizational philosophies of
East and West / Donald Cyr.
        p. cm.
Includes bibliographical references and index.
    ISBN 1-55753-244-3 (cloth : alk. paper)
    1. Corporate culture. 2. East and West. 3. Social values. I. Title.

    HM791 .C97 2002
    302.3'5--dc21
                                                        2002004472

Contents

For Ruth

Introduction

The Art of Global Thinking describes ways to improve the chances of success in your corporate and personal life by recognizing and employing fundamental assumptions from both Western and Eastern cultures. As East meets West, understanding these seemingly divergent cultures allows individuals and corporations to deal more effectively with each other—not only cross-culturally but from within one's culture as well.

The Art of Global Thinking provides new perspectives you will need to operate in a global environment, to cope with change, and to respond to the escalating demands of modernization. We know only too well the problems facing us. In the Western world, corporate restructuring has brought efficiencies, but we also recognize that restructuring based on mechanical rules rather than on human bonds has created an acute sense of cynicism. Characterized by a significant loss of trust in leadership, this down-sized environment fosters feelings of lost participation in decisions affecting our lives. Modernization brings affluence, but with it comes disconnection of human communities as people become increasingly alienated from each other. In the West, excessive individualism further accentuates the sense of social isolation. This book provides a strategy to restore the sense of participation essential for corporate success and personal fulfillment.

I use the term *Western* to reflect the traditional cultural values generally found in North America and Europe. In the same way, the term *Eastern* resonates with those dominant cultural values found in the Far East. North American and Japanese cultures serve as the foci for my examples, not only because there is a wealth of data about them but also because both enjoy great success in socioeconomic, political, and cultural spheres. I trace core values and principles from both traditions as they have developed through time, showing how they are relevant for us today. What can we learn from the practitioners of these contrasting cultural traditions? How can understanding cultural values guide and influence our lives?

In exploring success stories from both Japan and North America, this book links our two contrasting but complementary capabilities for logic and intuition, individualism and collectivism, and distinctiveness and harmony. *The Art of Global Thinking* exposes common psychological impediments to our perceptions of the world and identifies cultural stumbling blocks that hinder effective leadership. It further explores how the search for our individuality sometimes competes with our need for participation in the collective, and it suggests how the Western pursuit of individualism can be complemented rather than conflicted by Eastern notions of collective participation.

Through these comparisons, you will begin to understand and place into perspective your culture's fundamental assumptions. You will learn to recognize not only how these assumptions shape your beliefs and values but how they influence what choices you make and the way you live in the world. *The Art of Global Thinking* provides a foundation for changing and enriching your personal life and your business practice.

Focusing on the themes of Eastern wisdom and Western understanding, I have used an interdisciplinary approach to the topic. I combine the work of respected authors in the business world with the insight from unconventional business sources like philosophy, history, and psychology to help us Westerners learn to unpack our cultural baggage and find relevance for conducting business in today's environment of innovation and uncertainty. Different disciplines have much to offer business, as do the thoughts and experiences of various individuals—from the armchair philosopher to the corporate executive.

Through this study, I show how value systems have influenced the structure of institutions and the way we view ourselves and others. In turn, our institutions have influenced our value systems. Although value systems, institutions, and individuals are inevitably interrelated, the nature and expression of these relationships are manifested differently from culture to culture and from time to time. A change in view or institution will not necessarily lead to a particular new institution or a particular new view. For example, in Japan the existence of advanced calculus in the Tokugawa period or the introduction of science during the Meiji period did not mechanize the Japanese mind as it did in the West. Because these three factors are interrelated but lend themselves to separate explorations, I have divided the book into three corresponding sections: value systems, institutions, and the individual.

Value Systems: Foundations

Chapter 1 is an introduction to ideas at the foundation of Eastern and Western value systems and their influence on contemporary business environments. Chapters 2 and 3 touch on the formation of the major belief systems in the East and in the West and their relationship to early global population surges. Chapter 4 deals with the mechanization of the Western mind. Chapter 5 explores the collective *we* and the relevance of harmony in Japan.

Institutions: A Means of Organization

Tools and how we organize our world have a profound effect on our means of production, our institutions, and our quality of life. To underline how value systems influence institutions, Chapter 6 compares modern Eastern and Western business practices and relates the corresponding belief systems' and institutions' effects on the individual. Chapters 7 and 8 discuss Western organizations and the advantages of integrating elements from the East and West. Chapter 9 looks at strategy through time as it relates to people and business enterprises.

Individuals: The We and Me of the Self

Chapter 10 deals with the Western penchant for the logical and our need for developing emotional competence, and relates benefits to the individual that have evolved from the concepts of Western duality and Eastern oneness.

The goal of *The Art of Global Thinking* is to demonstrate how being aware of Eastern collectivism and Western individualism can nourish our personal and business lives. Thinking in global terms means being aware of cultural differences and their powerful influence on the way we think, feel, and act. The integration of Eastern collectivism and Western individualism is not about a melting pot of values but about the recognition and acceptance of the differences between cultural values and how this can enhance different parts of our being.

The Art of
Global Thinking

1
Integration

An iceberg moving along the calm waters of the ocean is a sight to behold. Its peak can rise an impressive 400 feet (120 meters) high above the water. Its shape can resemble a mountain, a palace, or a church spire. The visible tip of the iceberg draws our attention, but if we consider only the obvious without considering that 70 to 90 percent is hidden below the water we have a limited picture of the iceberg's real size and its full strength. So it is with people: by paying attention only to the visible we ignore concealed aspects of ourselves and limit our potential.

In the same way, your values—your emotions and the Self—have a hidden yet tremendous influence on your leadership style. I reveal those hidden values by linking Eastern and Western value systems and treating them as complementary, thereby improving your ability to enhance your leadership, performance, and peace of mind. In so doing, I link our contrasting but complementary capabilities for logic and intuition, individualism and collectivism, and distinctiveness and harmony.

Today, a great number of programs are offered to help individuals and corporations meet new challenges. Unfortunately, even though some of those programs offer sound direction, many result in disappointment. We need to address not only what needs to be done but also what prevents us from doing it. Paying attention solely to our visible characteristics means we ignore hidden characteristics that, if accessed, would contribute greatly to our success.

As Westerners, we focus on values such as individualism, distinction, and independence. We admire the person who takes action, we respect those with confidence, and we pride ourselves on our logical approach. Easterners emphasize collectivism, harmony, and accord. They see themselves as connected to others, and they respect those who demonstrate restraint and establish ties with others. Each of these two different value systems offers strong advantages, but each by itself is limiting. Unaware of their full influence on what we think and how we act, we allow our values to become stumbling blocks to attaining our full capabilities.

We need to bring to light those concealed but powerful influences as they shape our thoughts and actions. An awareness of their influence is the essential first step toward understanding and enhancing our personal development. When applied, this awareness will help you in your personal relationships, in your community, and in your career. It is the basis for the success of leaders and professionals concerned with increased corporate performance.

The Visible Values

In contemporary North America, clarity, individualism, taking charge, independence, and measurable accomplishments are taken for granted as a way of life. Being confrontational, competitive, and assertive is not only acceptable but desirable. Independent thought and individualism are highly valued, and we reward high achievement and individuals who distinguish themselves. We see the evidence for these values throughout Western culture: in the workplace, in our families, in our sports, and in the arts and popular culture. The media extol these values in the thousands of advertisements to which we are exposed each day. Contemporary examples reflecting these cultural values abound:

> Taking charge: *Just do it.* (Nike)
> Assertiveness: *Satisfaction guaranteed or your money back.*

Measurable: *Buy one, get one free.*
Confrontational: *Lead, follow, or get out of the way.*
Clarity and delineation: *Two out of three say they prefer brand A.*
Individualism: *"I Did It My Way"* (Paul Anka)
Independence: *Financial Freedom at 55* (London Life)

One way to understand the cultural uniqueness and influence of our own value system is to compare it to others. For example, North Americans champion the rugged individuals portrayed by Clint Eastwood and John Wayne. Whether it's Dirty Harry or the renegade gunslinger, the character takes charge, singularly courageous in responding to confrontational situations fraught with danger as he ingeniously solves dilemma after dilemma. These characters epitomize our value of individualism.

Traditional Asians who value collectivism view these characters in quite a different way. In a Japanese context, the characters we typically associate with Clint Eastwood would symbolize tragedy, exile, and misery. In Japan, movie heroes epitomize the Samurai duties to the lord and the clan. Comparison between the Eastern and Western views brings into perspective the powerful influence of cultural values and principles that shape our lives and our institutions.

Individualism pushed to the extreme denies a part of our humanity. By combining elements of collectivism with individualism, we can enhance our personal competence and our chance of corporate success. Before exploring that topic, however, I want to introduce two principles: duality and oneness. They derive from ancient societies and have shaped fundamental assumptions—the value systems and principles—integral to the thinking and actions of contemporary North American and Asian people.[1]

Duality

The seeds for the value system that shaped Western thinking flourished in ancient hunting societies.[2] From the hunting society came the notion of duality, a notion that puts the accent on separation and division and the belief in the uniqueness of all things with the accent on the individual.[3] Hunting is dangerous and violent. In hunting societies, the individual impulses were not to be subdued.[4]

Individualism

Where survival depended mainly on finding meat, individual risk-taking was highly valued. In contemporary Western society, we also place a high value on individualism, aggressiveness, and distinguishing ourselves. Taking charge characterizes the corporate manager who provides direction, motivates the troops, and makes decisions.[5] As evidenced by abundant seminars, programs, and books dealing with assertiveness, self-esteem, and self-improvement, individualism flourishes as an ideal in the West. Individuals recognize the maximization of their individualism as the pathway to affirming self, as the key to improving their chances for success and, ultimately, their quality of life.

> The squeaky wheel gets the grease.
> —American saying

Mechanical Order

With the advent of science and industrialization in Western Europe being added to the concept of duality, a mechanical order evolved that sought to explain everything with mechanical accuracy. Industrialization brought mass production that, in turn, brought improved economic conditions. Through understanding nature scientifically, people came to believe that they could gain dominance over the environment, control society, and thus change and improve their situation. For the masses, science and industrialization inspired hope for the future as the world became more accessible and, ultimately, more predictable. As I will discuss in Chapter 4, with increased predictability also came the mechanical order.[6]

The introduction of the scientific method into the corporate world gave rise to bureaucratic organizations that appropriated a step-by-step decision-making process and divided work tasks into tangible, measurable, manageable segments. Sophisticated systems of rules and procedures to define the responsibilities, rights, and duties of each part of the production were instituted. As we shall see, this gave rise to an unprecedented growth in productivity and wealth, as well as transparency, accountability, and discipline in management. But the logic of a system approach to production likewise resulted in mechanical institutions that, in the extreme, disconnect people, detract from meaningful human relationships, and neutralize some strong Western assets: commitment and initiative.

Oneness

In the East, the value system was shaped by the ancient planting societies. From the planting society came the concept of "oneness," with an emphasis on interrelations, interdependence, and harmony. Being in tune with nature was critical to survival of the society, for until the advent of science and its applications in horticulture and agriculture, individuals could do very little to influence the different growth cycles of crops. Therefore, cooperation and collective effort, which harmonized and aligned with nature's own cycles, were required when the time came for planting, harvesting, and storing crops. With the emphasis on collective effort, the concept of self, surrendered to the concept of *group*.[7] From a planting society perspective, individual impulses are subdued for the betterment of the group.

Collectivism

Asians see the individual person not as independent but rather as connected and aligned to the group. Oneness took on a variety of meanings in different planting regions. For the Chinese, alignment was to the family, while in Japan it was to the group.[8] In Japanese corporations, consideration for harmonious relations favors values such as attunement, participation, and integration with one's surroundings. In corporations, the Japanese are not governed so much by rules as by obligations based on personal relationships. Relationships are voluntary and take time to develop. Once good

By nature men are nearly alike. By practice they get to be wide apart.
—Confucius

relationships are established, every effort must be taken not to disrupt them. Japanese corporate managers take pride in being attuned to their surroundings, sensing the mood, and acting on gut feelings. Managerial intuition is valued. I will say more on this later.

At the personal level, collectivism and harmony favor accommodation, appeasement, compromise, softness, conformity, moderation, and order.[9] In the West, American corporate executives act individually to provide direction, motivate the troops, and make

I'm opposed to millionaires, but it would be dangerous to offer me the position.
—Mark Twain

decisions. In the East, however, Japanese corporate executives primarily function to maintain harmony within the company and foster good relationships outside the company.[10] Group consensus, bottom-up decisions, consultation, and the integration of input from different corporate units drive the Eastern decision-making process.

There are exceptions, but in general value systems have a tremendous influence on what we do, how we see things, and how we make judgments and choices. It must also be remembered that the application of those value systems varies greatly within any given culture. Here I have emphasized our differences, but although we have different value systems, it is important to recognize that we have much more in common, nonetheless.

To summarize, the Eastern concept of oneness, where the self resides in the group rather than in the individual, contrasts with the Western notion of duality.[11] In the West, the self relates to *Me*, the individual. It is interesting how the Western saying, "the squeaky wheel gets the grease," apparently contrasts with the Japanese axiom, "the nail that protrudes gets hammered in." But does it?

As just discussed, our values strongly influence how we think as well as how we shape our organizations. In turn, our institutions influence our values and our personal well-being. I will first discuss how our values influence our personal competence and then how they shape our corporate approach. In addition I will show how seeing Western and Eastern values as complementary can enhance your personal competence and chance of corporate success.

Personal Competence

Whether you look at Olympic medalists, accomplished musicians, or respected executives, they all have in common what has come to be known as emotional intelligence. Daniel Goleman's book, *Emotional Intelligence,* provides a wealth of research demonstrating that, with emotional competence, people do better at work, at home, in personal relationships, and in their community. A lack of emotional competence has been linked to failures in life ranging from school dropouts to management disasters. We know that children not accepted by classmates are up to eight times more likely to drop out of school.[12] When looking at the effects of technical skills, IQ, and emotional intelligence on performance, Goleman states that "emotional intelligence proved to be twice as important as the others for jobs at all levels." Comparing star performers with average ones in senior leadership positions, Goleman's research indicates that "nearly 90% of the difference was attributable to emotional intelligence rather than cognitive abilities."[13] The West's focus on scientific logic should not be surprising given the importance we assign to the tangible and measurable. The interest in IQ or SAT scores, which measure one's ability for calculation or geometric design, conforms very well to the value the West puts on the observable. Yet despite the popularity of IQ testing, an IQ score by itself is a poor indicator of success.[14] At its extreme, it denies intuition, emotion, empathy, creativity, judgment, common sense, and quality of relationships. However, this "soft stuff," as some people call it, is as much a part of our identities as logic. We need to balance all of these faculties. Albert Einstein once said, "I never discovered anything with my rational mind."[15]

How does this soft stuff work? You may think of it as the human touch that gives you the ability to successfully communicate and empathize with others and to achieve desirable outcomes. Emotional competence gives you the ability to control your impulses and keep on going in the face of challenge. Simply put, emotional competence is grounded in the ability to:[16]

- Comprehend your own feelings
- Control and manage your impulses
- Identify and assess other people's feelings

Self-awareness channels our abilities to change conditions through gaining mastery over ourselves while the ability to deny impulses in the pursuit of goals determines how well or how poorly people conduct their lives. Finally empathy, the ability to read other people's feelings, provides the foundation for effective interaction.[17]

Heeding only the observable takes away some of our greatest assets, those that come from emotional competence. This is not to deny the importance of logic or technical skills but to suggest adding the advantages of emotional competence to our present repertoire of capabilities. In part the high value we put on logic denies the advantage that comes from intuition, from knowing what to say and when to say it. Let's look at some other values that at times limit our full capabilities.

Courage is resistance to fear, mastery of fear, not absence of fear.
—Mark Twain

Merging Duality and Oneness

It seems the evolution of the human psychology gave us the dual but complementary needs for *attachment* and *autonomy*. I will discuss this in greater detail in Chapter 10; suffice it to say for now that the need for *attachment* ensures the infant gets the adult protection needed to ensure survival, and later in life it favors working in groups. The need for *autonomy* means that we are motivated to acquire the skills, knowledge, and proficiency to support ourselves and the ability to contribute to the group. Combined, these two basic needs give us the essential survival tools to gain personal proficiency and the ability to work with and gain from the advantages of the group.

I have explained how the concept of duality from the West and the concept of oneness from the East put different but complementary values on the nature of our being. It seems the importance we put on the Western "Individual Self" emphasizes *autonomy*. It means we look at the person as independent from the group and value self-sufficiency, self-fulfillment, and distinctiveness. We look for personal validation, for distinction, for importance. When it comes to emotional intelligence, emphasis on individual self and distinction, the West stresses being in touch with and comprehending oneself.

Although Western values put less emphasis on being in tune with others, we recognize the need to be liked, to be attractive, to be appreciated. The Eastern "Civic Self," on the other hand, emphasizes *attachment*. In this context the person is seen as interdependent and connected to others. Putting a high value on alignment, integration, and accord demands an ability to sense what is going on. To move with the flow requires you to be in touch with and assess the feelings of others. In this way the West and the East are very different, but if we can view their approaches as complementary rather than contradictory, we can enhance our emotional competence. The Spiritual Self discussed in Chapter 3 relates to traditional religion. Although some of the doctrines discussed may seem irrelevant to modern time, many of the values that came from religion still exert a tremendous influence on our everyday life. Christian values of self-restraint or Buddhist virtues such as patience and freedom from pretense and from anger support the management of one's impulses. Combined they allow for emotional competence and the ability to gain the knowledge and skills needed for personal competence.

Corporate Success

There is a strong relationship between a culture's value system, its individuals, and its institutions. In keeping with individualism,

Americans reward individual effort, while in keeping with oneness, the Japanese reward group effort. Our inclination for a mechanical order means American corporations have a system approach, while the Japanese' sense of duty means their corporations take a paternalistic approach. We favor big risk taking, while the Japanese favor continual improvement (*kaizen*). In business, Americans play poker, while the Japanese play chess.

Together with a number of factors such as industrial practice, market demand, and leadership style, our value systems have a strong influence on our corporate approach. In turn the corporate structure influences what individuals can do, their level of satisfaction, and their self-esteem. This offers an interesting analogy between personal emotional competence and corporate competence. Likewise Western and Eastern values as they relate to the corporate world are complementary. And similarly, there is a parallel for emotional competence. I will discuss this in more detail, but for the time being, I would like to discuss the three factors essential for successful corporate strategy.

Corporate strategy is about creating a fit between your business strengths and marketplace demands. In this context, management roles are central to the integration of functions, activities, and interactions that fit corporate strengths to the market situation. Successful corporations must have three essential factors:

- Knowledge of the company's strengths and limitations: corporate structure
- Control and management of resources: leadership style
- Identification and assessment of the market: marketing demand

In Chapters 5 and 6, I compare Western and Eastern management practices. Then, in Chapters 7 and 8, I show how we can use the best of both practices to complement each other. Let's take a brief look at each factor and how, by understanding its influence of our value system, we can improve corporate performance.

Corporate Structure

Your corporate structure represents the systems that govern employee incentives and discipline, and the procedures, rules, and regulations that direct your operation. Depending on the flexibility of your corporate structure, systems govern how people relate to each other inside and outside the organization and how they do business. When it comes to corporate structure, the complementary difference between the West and the East can be stated:

> The West negotiates a contract.
> The East negotiates a relationship.

In the West the mechanical order means we like contracts—that is, systems that define our obligations and duties. In balance, systems provide focus, accountability, and transparency. In the East, obligations are first and foremost based on personal relationships and ties. In balance, such personal obligations provide flexibility, commitment, and a sense of belonging. Three areas that our corporate structure influences are the level of commitment, the means to the end, and the quality of information.

Level of Commitment

Undue attention to systems results in a corporate approach governed by the demands of the corporate system rather than by market demand and the business situation. Contractual obligation requires us to pay sole attention to the tangible and the measurable. We focus on administrative procedures, rules, and economic utility at the expense of loyalty, commitment, and relationships. At its extreme, a system creates cynicism and a sense of helplessness, disconnects people, and saps productivity. If employees feel they do not count, they likewise treat customers with indifference. A number of other important factors relate to employees feeling indifferent, but if 68 percent of your customers who leave go elsewhere because they are treated with indifference, it makes for an expensive system.[18]

The Means to the End

A second problem with mechanical order is that it frames the answer. The means dictates the end. Emphasis on the inner workings subordinates the individual to the system and stifles flexibility and innovation because it prevails upon people to look inside the organization rather than outside to the market. Peter Drucker says, "In fact, approximately 90% or more of the information any organization collects is about inside events."[19] This would be like spending 90 percent of your time while driving your car looking at the dials rather than paying attention to the road.

Quality of Information

Our Western inclination for mechanical order, for cause and effect, for negotiating a contract, makes us look for the one right answer, the one right structure, the one right process, the one right rule.[20] In balance, the mechanical order puts more weight on clear and explicit information. Negotiating a relationship, on the other hand, puts more weight on judgment, intuition, and experience. It relies more on implicit information with emphasis on the circumstances surrounding the present situation. In combination, these two different approaches give us the advantage that comes from clarity and flexibility, logic and intuition, and give us direction with purpose. In brief, they give us working knowledge.

Do not underestimate the powerful appeal of the mechanical order on the Western mind. This is not to say you should banish all forms of systems, but you must recognize their powerful influence on your decisions about your corporate approach. Negotiating a contract has costs, but that does not mean you should switch to just negotiating relationships. Likewise negotiating a relationship has costs. Negotiating a relationship for the sake of fitting in can be very stifling and destroy creativity and innovation. Personal obligation makes it very difficult to let people go and is in large part responsible for costly excessive layers of Japanese distribution. The lack of system transparency and patronage fostered through relationships is in part responsible for the great number of nonperforming bank loans of the Japanese' burst economic bubble and the Asian debt crisis of the late 1990s. While contracts offer transparency and accountability, relationships offer flexibility and commitment. In balance, each approach has much to offer toward how we conduct business. I will discuss this in more detail in Chapter 5.

People must feel they count and make a difference in the destiny of the business. By now, a number of us have heard about the need for functional integration, shared vision, empowerment—in short, creating a partnership where employees are committed to solving customer problems. An optimum corporate structure helps, but for this to happen you need leadership. You must now ask, "What do we stand for?"

Leadership

When it comes to leadership, the complementary difference between the West and the East can be stated:

The West focuses on the individual.
The East focuses on the relationships among individuals.

Innovation by itself will go nowhere without the commitment of all involved. Individual as well as group effort is needed when it comes to corporate performance. Many companies recognize that the quality of input and performance is greater if they treat their employees as business partners. People need to feel they can make a difference. For many managers, this has become clearly evident, and they take great care to communicate their intentions. But although more than 60 percent of managers believe they treat their employees as business partners, only 27 percent of employees believe they are treated as business partners.[21]

At its extreme, the Western ideology of rugged individualism favors the confrontational manager; that is, the individual who takes charge, who knows the answers, who sets direction, who makes key decisions, and who motivates the troops. Taking charge and exercising control is easy to justify because you can always point to a fundamental of Western culture: individual initiative. But there is no justification for taking charge to the point where no one else can take initiative. That hurts the organization because it does little to motivate others or to encourage informed options. In today's educated environment, people are skeptical and are quick to distinguish between the essential and the irrelevant. Because we accept individualism in the West, we readily accept heroic pursuits. If we push these heroics to the extreme, though, we pay the price of excluding participation. The management of knowledge requires a different leadership style than the management of skills. Employee participation can no longer be excluded. It is difficult to extract knowledge without the consent of the employee.

> *A Synergy:*
> *Knowing others is under-standing. Knowing self is wisdom.*
> —Zen proverb

The role of the Japanese executive is one of maintaining harmony within and good relationships without. This is consistent with focusing on relationships among individuals. It promotes a sense of participation where people feel they count. But taken to the extreme where no one is accountable, it likewise has its cost. Leadership is not about position but responsibility. Leaders need to be honest about what they stand for, as well as to respect what others stand for. Your ability to articulate a shared vision and provide a framework that motivates commitment requires very much that you be in touch with your own inclinations as well as the aspirations of others. This requires you to focus both on the individual and on the relationships among individuals.

Marketing

When it comes to marketing, the complementary difference between the West and the East can be stated:

The West talks.
The East listens.

The West values autonomy and distinction. We pride ourselves on having unique views and distinct opinions and find it easy to talk about them. In business, this offers great advantages when it comes to product differentiation and positioning ourselves against our competitors. However, your company may be different, but that does not mean customers will buy from you unless you give them what they want. New products fail for a number of reasons. Poor timing, competitor strength, technical problems are but a few of the logistical problems a company faces with marketing a new product. But the number-one reason why a product or service fails is the company's inability to determine the needs of the market. What you are good at is important, but you must also ask what the market is willing to pay for. Listening with the intent to understand the customer's needs is a critical step to the launch of many goods. Talking with customers and doing a market survey is a good start but by itself is not sufficient. Yes, in America we do listen to customers, but our emphasis on the individual self is out of sync with attuning ourselves to our customers. Unaware of our values, we often listen and respond as if looking at ourselves in a mirror. The East, in contrast, values harmony and alignment. Listening is important to attune one's response to the situation. This gives you great advantages in understanding your customer. Although customers will not buy from you unless you listen and give them what they want, at the same time they also want something unique. Each approach by itself has limitations, but in combination they offer great advantages.

Most managers claim if you don't satisfy the customer you're out of business. In the end, as Peter Drucker contends, it is the customer who pays your salary. Not surprisingly, everywhere you look in business reports, vision statements, and advertising you see the claim, "Service to our customer is our number-one priority." Yet, 68 percent of customers who leave, go elsewhere because they were treated with indifference. The best market plan won't work unless your employees are committed, and to be committed, employees need to feel they can make a difference. This is a marketing issue that can only be resolved through integrating your corporate approach and leadership style. How do we get commitment from

	Autonomy	Attachment
Myth	Duality	Oneness
	Differentiation	Attunement
	Heroism	Passivity
	Achievement	Collectivity
Religion	Moralistic theology	Philosophical wisdom
	Separation from body and soul	Oneness with body and soul
	Law and God	The way and godliness
	Ego development	Ego dissolution
Civic	Individualism	Collectivism
	Priority to self	Priority to group
	Self-fulfillment	Self-restraint
	Distinctiveness	Harmony
	Autonomy	Connection
	Independence	Interdependence
	Self-reliance	Loyalty
	Linear thinking	Circular thinking
	Either/or	What/if *(ki)*
	Universal application	Situational application
	Abstract principle	Social consensus
	Rationalism	Practical
	Time-related	Space-related
	Content	Context
	Telling	Listening (sensing)
	Verbal	Nonverbal
	Explicit	Implicit
	Direct	Indirect
	Problem solving	Affirmation
	Challenge	Stability
	Confrontation	Pleasing
	Convert the order of things	Conform to the order of things
	Law of book	Law of customs
	Accountability	Saving face

Table 1. Characteristics of Western autonomy and Eastern attachment.

	Autonomy	Attachment
Civic (*cont.*)	Legislation Transparency Ideology of rights	Propriety Diffusion Duty and obligation
	Predictable efficiency Process Principles Performance	Positional expediency Norms Conformity Commitment
	Leadership Active and dynamic	Stewardship Reticent and dignified
	Government Service	Governance Order
	Horizontal Equality Life and liberty	Vertical Hierarchy Order and security
	Importance of truth Obligation to principles Rules and concepts	Importance of social expectation Obligation to people Significant others
	Divine approval Ambition Astuteness	Good karma Humility Diligence
Business	Big breakthrough First one out Market differentiation Branding	Kaizen (continual improvement) Beat the competitor Market share Reliability
	Transparency Systems Arm's length Contractual	Alignment Personal connections Inclusive Interpersonal
	Me Economic bond Individual rewards	We Social bond Group rewards

Table 1— *Continued.*

employees? Many good solutions are proposed but most fail to bring the desired result because we are not aware of the powerful, but concealed, influence that makes us act counterproductively.

The concepts of duality and oneness emphasize entirely different parts of our being, as summarized in table 1. I am not implying you should either embrace or deny the full spectrum of Eastern or Western cultural values or behavior. Both concepts have their benefits and both, at the extreme, have their costs. But each concept can put into perspective different parts of our nature. Wisdom comes when you understand those perspectives limiting your ability to achieve your full potential. In this way, the West and the East are very different, but if we view these differences as complementary rather than incompatible, we can develop a new approach that will enhance the whole being of the person, and similarly, the success of the corporation (chart 1).

This book is not about dropping one system or favoring the other; rather, it is about how to incorporate advantageous elements of each cultural paradigm. Adaptations need to be made with pragmatism. Eastern traditional acceptance of hierarchy, absolute loyalty, and deference to superiors is frowned upon by Western culture. In America, nepotism is a dirty word. Hiring should be based on tangible and measurable achievements. For Asians, as in many other cultures, hiring a relative helps ensure trustworthiness. For Asians, dealing at arm's length is cold.

Our culture is an integral part of who we are and provides the springboard from where we start. Let's look at an example: what Chrysler did to adapt Japanese practices consistent with American values. In the 1980s the bid system at the Chrysler corporation prevented suppliers of automobile parts from participating in car design. Chrysler engineers provided detailed contracts outlining design specifications and the supplier who came in with the lowest bid got the contract. With continuing erosion of its market share in the 1980s, Chrysler studied and adapted certain Japanese practices. Chrysler kept the American practice of dealing with suppliers at arm's length but integrated the Japanese practice of having a number of departments, including outside suppliers, working together at the

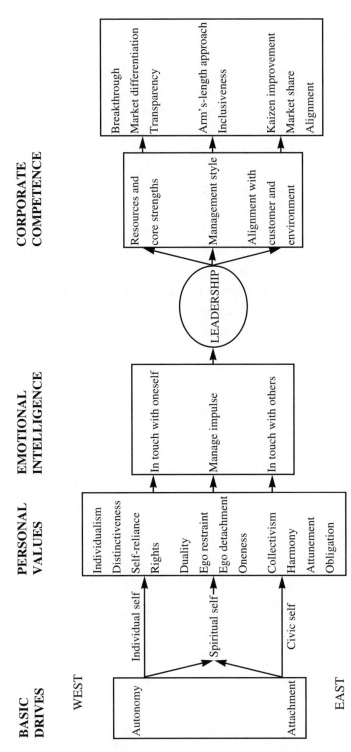

BASIC DRIVES	PERSONAL VALUES	EMOTIONAL INTELLIGENCE	CORPORATE COMPETENCE

Chart 1. This chart summarizes the concepts in this book. The items above and below the centerline represent the extremes of the Western emphasis on autonomy and the Eastern emphasis on attachment, respectively. The chart can be used as a quick reference throughout the book.

design stage. This benefited both suppliers and Chrysler. Chrysler's profit rose from $250 per car in the 1980s to a record $2,110 in 1994. Suppliers appreciated being listened to by Chrysler, and Chrysler got a better product. But more critically, both were able to find ways to cut costs and increase profitability.[2]

To seek either individualism and distinction or collectivism and harmony is not a problem. The problem occurs when one notion is pushed to the extreme. Then we deny a part of who we are. The dichotomy of our needing to be distinct as well as to be part of a group is not contradictory. We have the dual need for autonomy and attachment. In search of autonomy we stress self-sufficiency, distinctiveness, and independence. In search of attachment we stress accord, integration, and harmony. Our values make us attend to one need, but at its extreme this denies us the benefits gained from paying attention to both. Oneness and duality may be opposite, but these opposites generate, define, and enhance each other.

2
Foundation of Our Cultural Values

A Journey into the Past

Journeying into the ancient past, we can examine the factors that have shaped some of the core values in both Western and Eastern cultures and that influence the way we think and act today. We know that throughout time values have evolved and changed to reflect new circumstances. Our emphasis on certain values has taken thousands of years to evolve. These changes have come gradually and differ in velocity from culture to culture.

Looking at values cross-culturally, we tend to notice and pay attention to contrasts, and although there are differences between cultures, they are not overwhelming. The full range of human attitudes is present within any society, but a culture favors certain attitudes and behaviors over others. In this chapter I discuss how we came to put different emphases on different values. To do this we will travel in time and look at what cultural environments, accomplishments, and mythologies tell us about ourselves and about others.

Stories throughout the world relate people to animals, plants, and the supernatural. Although these stories have their local flavor, ancient myths from different cultures share common themes. The universality of human psychology and the commonality of peoples' experiences give rise to shared themes in many of the myths across the world. Although they may be interpreted differently, in all societies people share such universal experiences as birth, puberty, suffering, old age, and the polarities of light and dark, male and female, life and death.[1]

In ancient times, people told stories about memorable events that inspired them, and from such stories we have inferred much about the way those ancient people saw their world. Early myths were not about dogma but rather were an expression of people's explanations, knowledge, relationships, and beliefs about their social, natural, and supernatural worlds. Today as in the past, myths, like stories, help communicate the relationship between an identity or image and the environment. They relate individuals to the group, illuminating their connections to society and, ultimately, to their place in the universe.

In an extensive study of world mythologies, the eminent mythologist Joseph Campbell observed a recurrence of two major themes in the myths and beliefs of ancient people. One theme was linked to an economy dependent primarily on hunting animals and the other to an economy dependent primarily on harvesting plants.[2] Both themes shared many common beliefs as well as similar explanations for the mysteries of life. In this chapter, I focus on the different significance given to certain beliefs and values as revealed in the mythologies from hunting societies and from planting societies, and I show how these came to be emphasized and featured in modern cultures.[3] To better understand today's corporate boardroom, I will start with antiquity and trace the evolution of some of our present beliefs and values from organic myths.[4]

Organic Myth

Until 7000 B.C., people's view of the world was determined mainly by the natural environment.[5] With their essential reliance on nature, ancient people saw the natural world with reverent wonder, and their organic myths associated the realities of human experience with the natural environment. People's dependence on nature largely dictated society's economic, political, and social well-being. Surrounded by the unseen, people assigned special forces and spirits to things in nature. These natural spirits were perceived to reside in animals, plants, humans, whole environments, and even in inanimate objects.[6] This provided our distant ancestors with a link to their surroundings and likely with some comfort in an awesome world. By pleasing the spirits, people believed they could gain certain favors and perhaps achieve a sense of control over their domain. Over the millennia people's perception of supernatural forces evolved into diverse beliefs as reflected in various value systems.

Duality and Hunting Myths

To begin explaining the differences in hunting society and planting society beliefs, let's start with a story. Analyzed in Campbell's book *Primitive Mythology,* the story of the Bear ritual comes from the Ainu people who live on the northernmost Japanese island.[7] Unlike the mainstream Japanese, the Ainu were from a predominantly hunting and fishing society, ancient descendants of the great eastern migration of tribes from Asia across the Bering Strait into the Americas. Although this story relates specifically to the Ainu, the Bear ritual was commonly found in hunting societies from Northern Europe throughout Russia and North America.[8] The Bear ritual represents a typical myth found in a society dependent on the hunting of animals.

The Bear Ritual

On occasion deities would pay a visit to the Ainu people. One of their most divine visitors was Bear, a mountain god.

When a young black bear cub was caught, it was jubilantly taken to the village where it would then be nursed by a woman. When the cub was too big to be safely around humans, it would be put in a wooden cage, where it was well treated and fed for two years. On a September day, after two years of being extremely well cared for, the young bear was taken to a joyous festival where it was sacrificed in order to release its soul.

Prayer sticks were brought to the cage. Women and children danced while men approached the cage and

explained to the bear that it would be released. The men
would then ask the bear to speak well of them and tell
others of how well it had been treated. After the sacrifice,
the bear's head was taken to a house where again it was
honored with a speech. There the bear was asked to tell
his parents and others of how well it had been treated.
Then they asked the bear to come back again, when it
would be honored a second time.

Hunting is violent, whether it takes place in the land of the living or in the land of the spirits. In a world populated by many spirits,
it was appropriate for the hunter to believe that only the animal's
body died, not its soul.[9] Superficially one might say this could have
served to alleviate guilt and anxiety over killing another living crea-
ture. But, as we have seen in the Bear cult, respectful treatment of
animals would ensure kind words about humans from the soul of the
slain animal and would assuage supernatural forces who might take
offense at the killing of the natural animal. Treating the hunted well
in life and in death would ensure the success of present and future
hunts and thus ensure the continuity of human life.

Hunting societies survive by killing animals. In ancient times,
the hunting of game was a precarious business because the hunter
could also be injured or killed. A hunting economy did well not to
subdue individual impulses but rather to support the heroic individual who took charge and initiated the hunt. As opposed to planting
societies, individual risk-taking was largely responsible for the success of the hunt. As Joseph Campbell states, "the advantages of the
group lay rather in the fostering than in the crushing out of
impulse."[10] Successful hunters were adorned with symbols of prestige and rewarded for their skillful achievements.[11] In societies that
were largely dependent on hunting, the individual status of a hunter
was elevated with each successful foray. In time these values gave
rise to the concepts of duality and individualism.[12]

According to Campbell, then, the hunting myth was based mainly on a hunting economy, and hunting myths gave rise to the notion
of duality.[13] Duality in turn favored individualism, heroism, aggression, and distinction.[14] Our Western culture thrives on ideals that

accentuate the individual, and today this notion is repeatedly reflected in the popular media. Examples of our own mythology are continually played out in television and movie scripts that champion the individual who, through heroic initiative and action, reveals or upholds the truth. We see it, too, in our corporations that reward individual effort and in business seminars with titles such as "Self-Assured and in Control."

Western culture puts a high emphasis on values such as individualism and distinction. To be sure, individualism evolved over time and took on its full flavor after the Renaissance. With the advent of science, the West reinforced the notion of control over nature. North Americans see situations as problems to be solved by individual initiatives. Embedded in this notion are Western values: human mastery of the world; human dominance over nature; the ability to control and change situations through taking action. On a daily basis, advertising in America extols the virtues of individualism and tells what is needed to gain the competitive edge. Nike says, "Just do it." Advertisements cleave to our cultural values and their messages for the products of our lives, from perfume to sporting equipment, from beverages to mutual funds, drive home the concept of duality: "This Bud's for you," and "To be what you are."

Oneness and Planting Myths

Along the equatorial zone, we find many myths such as the story of the Jaguar and the Serpent. The Serpent story is a very old myth and is presented here in an adaptation from Joseph Campbell's *Primitive Mythology*.[15]

The Serpent Myth

One day while walking in the forest, a young woman was approached by a serpent who asked her to marry him. The young woman said, "You are a serpent, who would have you?" The serpent said, "My body is indeed that of a serpent but my speech is that of a man." The woman agreed to the marriage, and soon she bore a boy and a girl.

> The children grew. One day the serpent noticed they
> ate their fish raw and bloody. The Serpent said, "If you
> eat your food raw, perhaps one day you will eat me." The
> serpent then asked the boy to come and get the fire from
> his belly and give it to his sister. The boy was afraid but
> after more encouragement from the serpent, the boy
> entered the belly of the snake and brought out the fire.
> The Serpent then asked them to get some coconuts, yams,
> and bananas.
>
> After cooking the food and eating it, the Serpent
> asked, "Which food is better? What you had before or my
> kind of food?" They answered, "Your kind of food."

The conclusion that the cooked fruit tasted better would be expected in this story. Cooking food is a cultural activity, one that becomes a primary distinction separating the natural world of animals from the cultural world of humans. Equally important to notice in the Serpent myth is the scary journey the boy has to undergo to get the fire within the serpent's belly. Basic to the planting myth is the sacred notion that the energy from the fire is the soul or spirit within oneself. The world of the spirit or the divine is not external but rather resides inside people. In the Bear story from the hunting world, the spirit is extolled—like magic—in order to ensure future favors from the natural and supernatural worlds; in the Serpent myth from the planting culture, the spirit is believed to reside in all things. In hunting society death is considered a matter of accident or chance, whereas in planting society death is considered, as Campbell states, "a natural phase of life, comparable to the moment of the planting of the seed, for rebirth."[16] In planting society the spirit came to be associated with transformation and continuity; a oneness found in all.

In planting societies, people ate by growing food, and it was the combined effort of men and women with skills attuned to nature that provided the essentials of subsistence. Foraging for seeds and knowing when and where to plant and when to harvest all require being in touch with the environment and in tune with the cycles of nature. Planting and harvesting the crop can be critical and require the collective cooperation of every individual in the group. As Joseph Campbell states, "the planter's view is based on a sense of group participation."[17] The

planting societies' concern "has been that of suppressing the manifestations of individualism."[18] Planters are as subject to and as dependent on
the elements and seasonal varia-
tions as they are subject to and   *Sitting quietly, doing*
dependent on the cooperation of   *nothing, spring comes, and*
the group. People's intimate rela-   *grass grows by itself.*
tionship with nature, their   *—Zen saying*
understanding of agricultural
processes, and their needs to move with nature and for coordinated
efforts gave rise to the concept of oneness and collectivity.

The planting myth, then, was based mainly on a planting economy, and it gave rise to a notion of oneness that favored collectivity,
harmony, passivity, and attunement. Today, that notion is personified
in Japanese movies that accentuate the Samurai devotion to the clan.
We see examples of oneness in every part of Eastern culture: in the
corporation rewarding group effort; in the social phobia called *taijin
kyofusho* typified by individuals who have an intense fear of being
offensive to others; and in mass media advertisements stressing the
value of collective effort.

Eastern culture puts a high emphasis on values such as collectivism and harmony. Easterners are more likely to emphasize continuity, complementarity, and connectedness. Change is accommodated
because it is the result of personal initiative coordinated with the situation and conditions. In Japan, as in China, harmony, unity, and
loyalty are fundamental cultural values. For example, in a Japanese
beer advertisement, four men run to catch an escaping hot air balloon,
then work together as a team to bring down the balloon. The ad then
shows the four men together enjoying a beer after their collective
effort to save the balloon. Similarly, corporations in Eastern cultures
reward groups rather than individuals for successful outcomes.

Duality and Oneness: A Comparison

People, like cultures, share much in common. But there are differences. In many hunting societies and planting societies, males were

the hunters, and females were the planters and harvesters. Joseph Campbell contends that hunting societies gave rise to a patriarchal system. On the spiritual side, the early patriarchal societies developed a concept of duality that favored rigid division of male and female labor and a correspondingly clear division between gods and humans.[19] Planting societies, Campbell says, gave rise to a matriarchal system. In early matriarchal societies, the concept of oneness was expressed in the idea of complementarity between males and females and their work. Similarly, there was little distinction between humans and gods. These differences would, in time, influence the way people looked at the Self, the way they related to others, and the way they perceived their place in the universe.

Many of the major tenets of today's religions were formed during the time when people were intimately related to the earth. Planting myths provided the foundation for Eastern religious beliefs, and hunting myths gave rise to Western religious beliefs. As tribal groups evolved semisedentary life styles, world populations grew and found more complex economic bases. Village life grew and required alliances in aggregates of communities; and eventually cities and city-states formed. With the advent of civilization and its attendant higher levels of sociopolitical and economic organization, new views of the supernatural and the cosmos evolved. Before being written down, organic myths underwent major transformations as cultures grew more sophisticated. Whereas the ancients believed gods resided on the earth and in nature, with the advent of civilizations, people moved their gods to the sky.[20] How have these changes influenced our present culture?

Civilization and the Transformation of the Ancient World

It is hard to imagine, but the formidable Sahara Desert was once covered with lush vegetation and inhabited by elephants and giraffes. Between 14,000 and 10,000 years ago, high annual rainfall created expanses of wild grains that encouraged large groups of people to form at different places where they could collect the grains. However, over the next millennia, as the last ice age retreated, the climate became drier. With it, some people transported the wild grains to nearby lowlands, where water was abundant, and started to grow the grain artificially. Different types of plants and animals were domesticated at different times and places in the world. From around 8000 B.C. onward, the domestication of plants and animals started a process that would bring tremendous social, economic, and political change. With the invention of agriculture, people increasingly formed large communities and committed to a particular plot of land on a permanent basis.[21]

As the climate became drier, large irrigation schemes were instituted and marginal land was brought under cultivation. The introduction of the plow pulled by an animal was further improved when a hoe blade replaced the plow's pointed stick. This great laborsaving device was augmented by technological inventions such as the copper tools that influenced greater productivity among the agriculturists. The combined impact of planned irrigation, improved plowing techniques, improved tools, new husbandry techniques, and the domestication of livestock created an enormous increase in food surplus. Whereas hunting and gathering lifestyles required from 100 to 1,000 acres of land to support one family, approximately 25 acres of land could support one farming family.[22] The resulting surplus of food allowed a great increase in population, and perhaps more importantly, the development of specialists who traded skills and products for food they themselves did not produce. Food surpluses also led to the creation of leisure time and the development of new skills and activities.

New specializations and innovations found expression in the arts as well as in the invention of written languages and advances in technologies such as pottery, carpentry, and metallurgy. The dawning of civilization brought the first large-scale architecture: cities were born and, with them, states. From around 3500 B.C. onward in the Near East Mesopotamian regions of the Euphrates and Tigris Rivers now occupied by Iran and Iraq, the first true cities with major public buildings and complex administrations appeared. The creation of cultural and economic centers combined with the diversity of technologies brought substantial increases in trade. People developed a taste for different products from distant parts of the world. With civilization came inventions and organizational structures that brought new economic wealth, higher standards of living, and more reliable food production. Population growth continued. The formation of larger governments, the building of cities and related infrastructures brought increased needs for cooperation, organization, and the planned protection of territory.

With the growth in those activities came the need to keep records. As early as 3500–2350 B.C., the Sumerian priests of Mesopotamia kept cuneiform records of business transactions as well as land sales in a pictographic writing system. By 3100 B.C. Egyptians had developed hieroglyphic writing to make similar records and calculations. Knowledge could be accumulated and preserved—an essential feature in the foundation of civilizations. In addition, these information specialists of ancient times served another important function. In ancient Sumer the high priests, recognizing the critical significance of being able to chart dates and seasonal activity, turned to the study of the sky. With the formation of larger communities, logistics and the planning of events had become increasingly important. Understanding the movements of the planets and the length of the moon cycles provided essential information for such activities as timing the harvest or planning flood control.

As we have seen, with the surplus of food came surplus time that, in turn, promoted specialization, differentiation, and eventually, the prototype for a new social hierarchy. The invention of written languages, tools and technology, the specialization of labor, the discipline offered through sociopolitical organization, and the new approach to modes of production forever changed standards of living.

The cooperation and discipline brought about by civilization gave new dimension to the quality of living; people had greater security and protection from the elements, diversity in food production, and the proliferation of art. The invention of writing systems began an era when information could be accumulated and preserved. The tenets of today's major religions were written down. The growth of cities and the development of monumental architecture required an even greater amount of planning and organizing populations than was needed in early agricultural communities. Monument building imposed order and timing on societies governed more by cultural than natural goals.

With civilization also came a new form of territorial defense based on the formal development of armies and the systematic waging of wars. With the growth of cities, the defense of territory and of the trade routes between them became essential, as did the mounting of expeditions to look for raw materials and the competition for resources and land. Civilization brought great benefits to human populations, but it was also a time of great changes, some of which carried tremendous conflict and turmoil.

Manmade Institutions Add a New Order to Organic Myths

During these times of development and change, foundational cultural values were modified and slowly transformed.[23] With the advent of civilization, organic myths underwent modification. No longer regulated solely by nature, people focused on cultural institutions that in time gave rise to new orders and directions. Revised institutional orders and mythologies augmented and transformed the existing organic myths. With these new belief systems, statehood and manmade institutions began to supplant nature as the inspiration behind fundamental concepts of organic order and movement.

The world was changed forever as the age of emerging civilizations accentuated cultural variations. The next major global change would come with the advent of science. In the Western world, this new age revolved around a mechanical view and a dissociation from the natural environment. As we continue our journey through time, however, we will see how strongly some fundamental cultural values and the corresponding notions of duality and oneness have been maintained—relatively unchanged—in different parts of the world.

3
Principles People Live By

Our principles shape our perceptions, guide our actions, steer our decisions, and give meaning to our experience. Like many of our basic emotions and instincts, cultural principles once internalized exercise a powerful, sometimes subconscious influence on all our experiences and our thinking. Culture gives context to our personal experiences and social interactions. We find different practices from culture to culture because individuals generally behave according to their cultural values. For example, Islam prohibits charging interest on loans, and in Islamic countries, running a Western style bank would be difficult. In traditional Chinese society the imperative of Confucianism is family obligation, and sending parents to a Western-style nursing retirement home would be considered disgraceful. With modernization and exposure to other cultures, some of those values are changing. Although modifications are taking place, the basic tenets of a culture usually take a considerable time to change.

In this chapter, I review some of the fundamental assumptions of the major world religions. Many of our basic ideologies, the things we do, the shapes of our institutions, have come from religion. Beginning in prehistoric times, worshipping the forces of nature through magic, totems, ritual, and taboo was a human response to those awesome forces. People sometimes personified the elements into deities and gods to provide what today might be called a sense of control in their relationship with the supernatural.[1] Later, with the advent of civilization, people merged gods and spirits into one or a few deities who occupied a cosmic realm. It was during this time that the main doctrines, ideologies, and principles of the major religions of the world were written down.[2]

In Western societies, some people view religious beliefs as mere opinions or simply other points of view that can neither be proved or disproved. In today's technical environment, many people assume they are no longer surrounded by the unseen, and for them many religious concepts seem irrelevant.[3] But are they? In many cultures, the church interrelates with all aspects of society. In the West, the church has to compete for legitimacy with other institutions. Studies have shown most North American Catholics do not agree with and sometimes even deviate from the Church's teaching on such issues as divorce, birth control, and the need to celebrate mass. However, even though many will digress from some doctrines, a study found most Catholics believe they are good Catholics by virtue of the fact that they adhere to the core

Although some elements of religion are changing, many religious tenets and ideologies still provide the core of the principles that shape our values, color our perceptions, and determine our actions.

principles.[4] Principles such as self-restraint in Christianity and patience from Buddhism serve to enhance our ability to manage emotion and as such still provide significance to our spiritual self.

Throughout history and in every part of the world, men have sought to understand the meaning of existence. Until the advent of modern science, stories, myths, and later, organized religions, provided understanding of the forces found in nature, the supernatural, and the meaning of existence. Religion's success was not so much because it provided a viable explanation for existence but rather because it was effective, according to Karen Armstrong, author of *A*

History of God, in preventing human despair and promoting individual hope.[5]

The brief description of the major religions or philosophies is presented here to provide some of the core ideologies governing many contemporary societies. Ideologies from the major religions are presented for comparison purposes and are not meant to be comprehensive. That would be another book. Whether or not one supports or disagrees with a particular church, sect, or doctrine, one must acknowledge that religions have been influential in shaping and mirroring societal values, reflecting and providing many of the principles by which we live today.

Judaism

From its early beginnings Judaism represented a way of life thatevolved into a religion. The body of Jewish literature and oral traditions—the Torah—contained laws, teachings, and divine knowledge of the religion. This biblical account of the Old Testament was written about the eighth century B.C. and collated into the final text in the fifth century B.C. Judaism gave birth to Christianity and Islam, which together comprise more than half of the world's believers.[6]

Judaism, a monotheistic religion, was a religion of the prophets. The first of its prophets was Abraham, born approximately 4,000 years ago in the city of Ur in Mesopotamia.[7] Although Abraham likely adapted many of the beliefs from his heritage, Judaism considers Abraham the first man to renounce idolatry and to recognize from the multitude of gods the existence of the one true God, *Yahweh.* Abraham made a covenant or contract with Yahweh that all of his descendants would be loyal only to Him, love Him, revere Him and obey His laws. A sound spiritual life in Judaism is important. Some have speculated that after the dispersal of Jews during the Babylon captivity and later under the Roman subjugation, the Jews compensated for their suffering and loss of prosperity by concentrating on their spiritual life.

From the beginning, Judaism stressed living an ethical life based on social justice.[8] Jews accepted competitiveness and private property, but were expected to act with justice toward the state, institutions, and the individual. Although social customs were expected to conform with religious purposes, many customs took their roots when Jews were nomads in the desert.

One of Abraham's descendants, Moses, brought down from Mount Sinai the tablets containing the Ten Commandments or laws of God:

1. I am the Lord your God.
2. You shall have no other Gods before me.
3. You shall not take the name of the Lord in vain.
4. Remember the Sabbath day to keep it holy.
5. Honor your father and your mother.
6. You shall not kill.
7. You shall not commit adultery.
8. You shall not steal.
9. You shall not lie.
10. You shall not covet.

Although through the millennia Judaism has reexamined the nature of God and people's relationship with God, many of the basic tenets have remained the same since the Jewish philosopher Philo Judaeus of Alexandria (30 B.C.–45 A.D.) described Judaism. Jews believe in only one God, who created the world and cares for the world and its creatures. Yahweh, who some believe originated as the ancient god of war, became the one and only God to be revered by the Jews after Moses' triumphal exodus from Egypt.[9]

Inherited from old Judaism—and different from Eastern religion—is the concept of a God with human characteristics and feelings such as love and hate, mercy and compassion. The Bible states that "God created man in his own image." In time the concept of a corporal God give way to a noncorporal God who was omnipotent, omniscient, and eternal. However, the early portrayal of God in human terms, and the constant reminder of man's dependence on God imparted to Judaism a high regard and need for God's justice and social concern. After the Renaissance, in Christian Europe, that notion of justice became a matter of civic right instead of a divine decree.

Throughout the centuries, Judaism has undergone changes; there are variations in many rituals and traditions depending on whether the believer practices Orthodox or Reformed Judaism. Some fundamental beliefs in Judaism are:

- The one God is the Creator and Preserver of the universe.
- God the Creator will judge mankind.
- Man has a mortal body and an immortal soul.
- Man is driven by both good and evil impulses.
- Man is free to choose between good and evil.
- Life is to be revered because it is a gift from God.
- Justice is a cardinal virtue, for God is just.
- Truth is discovered so justice can be done.
- The Ten Commandments were revealed to Moses as guidance and laws for all people.

Christianity

Christianity was founded by Jesus of Nazareth. The Nazarenes, whom the Greeks called Christians, were followers of the Messiah Jesus. For many Christians the mere repetition of the word *Jesus* (like repeating the word *Rama* for Hindus) evoked a flood of emotions and brought blessings. The Christian Bible was written around 70 A.D., forty years after Jesus's death. Jesus was born in Judea, a state under Roman rule. He was raised in Nazareth where, as a Jew, he learned the Holy Laws of the Pentateuch. Very little is known of the historical Jesus except for what was written after his death. His spiritual life and teachings were recorded in the New Testament beginning with the synoptic gospels of his apostles John, Matthew, Mark, and Luke. Jesus's teachings took place at a time of great unrest, amid the promise and speculation of a Messiah coming to redeem the Jews from the ruling Romans. At the age of thirty, after his hidden years in the desert, Jesus's preaching immediately attracted disciples, with whom he traveled to preach to the poor, the sick, and the oppressed. Virtues commended by Jesus included self-sacrifice, forgiveness, and nonviolence. His Sermon on the Mount contains some of the essential parables and teachings of Jesus:

- Blessed are the poor in spirit, for theirs is the kingdom of heaven.
- Blessed are the meek, for they will inherit the earth.
- Blessed are the merciful, for they will be shown mercy.
- Blessed are the peacemakers, for they will be called the children of God.
- Blessed are they who are persecuted for righteousness sake, for theirs is the kingdom of heaven.
- Think not that I have come to destroy the Law or the Prophets; I have come not to destroy but to fulfill them.
- Give to the one who asks from you.
- Love your enemies, and pray for those who curse you.
- Judge not, or you too will be judged; forgive, and you will be forgiven.
- Do not store up for yourselves treasures on earth. But store up for yourselves treasures in heaven. For where your treasure is, there your heart will be also.
- Therefore do not worry about tomorrow, for tomorrow will worry about itself.
- Ask and it will be given to you; seek and you will find; knock and the door will be opened to you.
- So in everything, do to others what you would have them do to you.

After Jesus's crucifixion, many of His disciples went on preaching. Paul, after preaching from synagogue to synagogue, concluded that the Gospel was meant not just for Jews, but for gentiles as well, indeed for all humankind. In Greece and Rome the new religion was opposed and bitterly persecuted until the emperor Constantine of Rome, was converted to the Christian faith in the year 312 A.D.

Though Christianity was grounded in Judaic beliefs, it also absorbed some pagan practices of the indigenous European religions, was shaped by Greek philosophy, and influenced by Roman institutions. In keeping with Judaism's beliefs, consistent with duality and different from the East, God was conceived as being from a different essence than that of humans or nature. Consistent with duality, there was a clear separation between man and soul, between man and nature, between what is right and wrong. Today, most Christians share a fundamental set of beliefs:

- God is the creator of all things.
- The Trinity consists of God the Father, the Son, and the Holy Spirit.
- People are born as sinners with the original sin.
- Jesus was the Messiah who brought redemption for original sin.
- Jesus came to earth for the redemption of mankind.
- Belief in a personal God and the divinity of Jesus.
- Belief in the existence of Satan or the devil.
- Baptism is a remission from the original sin.
- Man's immortal soul is accountable to God.
- In the kingdom of heaven there is a life hereafter.
- The Kingdom of Heaven is for those who follow the teachings of Jesus Christ as recorded in the Bible.[10]

Buddhism

Buddhism in its pure form is more of a philosophy or a system of ethics than a religion.[11] As Joseph Campbell said of Buddhism, the aim is not the satisfaction of a supernatural father, but an awakening of the natural man to truth.[12] Buddhism is not about punishment for something done but about one's nature and reaching one's bliss.

Well-versed in Hindu scriptures, Prince Siddhartha instituted Buddhism in the fifth century B.C. Buddhism arose in a period of high contrasts between the literate and the illiterate, the poor and the rich, and subjects and princes. The privileged high castes were growing as fast as the number of lower castes and outcasts. The prince was moved by the sight of illness, old age, and death, and by people's experience of pain and suffering. Upon seeing the tranquillity on the face of a monk, Siddhartha, at age twenty-nine, decided to seek enlightenment through meditation without human distraction. The night he left his home was known as the Night of Great Renunciation. There are two major divisions in Buddhism, and the beliefs of Buddhists are many, depending on the sect, its geographic location, and historic affiliations. But there are shared beliefs, many of which go back to those originally delineated by Prince Siddhartha, the Wise Man of the Sakyas. There are Four Noble Truths:

- Life is suffering.
- Suffering comes from desire and ambitions. The desires for immediate gratification, pleasure, or power are all sources of suffering.
- Desire can be eliminated and dissolved.
- Cessation of desire—detachment from desire—requires one to follow the eightfold path of right belief, aspiration, speech, behavior, livelihood, effort, contemplation, and concentration.

The body is ruled by passion, desire, and meaningless earthly ambition. The soul, bonded in the body, is ruled by serenity and the search for truth. The wise—the enlightened—try to live their lives, not controlled by physical desires or the deception of their senses, but rather by the serenity and tranquillity of their souls. As long as the body is controlled by desire and passion, the soul's serenity remains concealed and will be reincarnated or reborn in bondage in another body. To traditional Buddhists Nirvana is reached when the individual soul is released from the bondage of reincarnation of the body and is joined with the World-Soul.

The Western mind should recognize that, for Buddhists, the soul or the gods did not carry the same meaning as in Judeo-Christian and Islamic religions. Hindu gods were more like sages or symbols who functioned to impart knowledge and provide mystical illumination to help people attain enlightenment. In keeping with the notion of oneness from the planting society, the soul was conceived as a universal spirit. A Hindu saying, "Like the salt dissolved in water everywhere the taste is the same," provided the analogy to explain how humans were not conceived as being apart or different from the World-Soul, or made up of a separate essence from that of the gods. In Judeo-Christian thought, the notion of gods evolved as being of a different essence than humans.

As Christianity came from Judaism, so Buddhism came from Hinduism. Buddhism did not agree with the Hindu Vedas—the oldest sacred writings—that Brahma created the caste system, and outcaste. But Buddhists, like the Hindus, believed that from good must come good, and from evil comes evil. The central belief in Hinduism and Buddhism was that there is one Universal Spirit or Eternal Essence with no beginning or end. Both believed Nirvana was reached when the individual soul was released from the chain of rebirths and was joined with the World-Soul. Individual existence on earth was like a prison that must be renounced in order to be released. The prison was desire, the ambition that prevented a soul from joining the World-Soul. Enlightenment came when wisdom allowed release from the earthly bondage—from what the West called the ego or one conscious.

Confucianism

The Chinese and Japanese concept of worship did not fit either the Western concept of individual salvation through the intervention of a divine being or the Indian search for the ultimate purpose. For thousands of years Chinese worshipped the elements of nature and the spirits of their ancestors. The Chinese developed a rich variety of folklore, rituals, and ceremonies appropriate to their deities and ancestral spirits. Chinese ancestor-worship is not a matter of charity or morality but of justice. In traditional Chinese society, a privileged person is believed to have made his fortune by drawing from the blessing of his ancestral family, and is expected to share with members of his family. To be greedy with the privilege of your blessing might jeopardize the well-being of your descendents. But Chinese life is above all a code of ethics based on a hierachy of civil obligations and social harmony.

In the Chinese feudal state of Lu in the sixth century B.C., wars were being fought between lords. In the ensuing poverty, despair, and hopelessness, many traditional beliefs and rituals began to lose their meaning. In this atmosphere of flux, Ch'iu K'ung (551–479 B.C.), who was born and raised in the state of Lu, resigned his government post as supervisor of the granary and began teaching. His teaching attracted a large number of students, and in time he began to be called the K'ung Fu-tse—the Philosopher—from which came Confucius. Confucius taught the value of education, the need for courage, reverence for elders, filial piety and loyalty, respect for tradition, regard for justice, the principles of good government, and appropriate human relationships. For Confucism following your *tao* meant doing the right thing, and consistent with oneness, living in accordance with the natural distinction. Confucius said, "May the prince be a prince, the subject a subject, the father a father, the son a son." Confucism is not so much a religion as a system of politics, good order, and social ethics. For Confucius, harmony related to proper civil order.

A century after the Great Teacher died, Mencius gathered the discourse and sayings of Confucius, organizing them into books. Mencius went among the people to teach about the essential goodness of human nature. The principles of Confucius were founded on the concept of Jen, a term for goodness. Jen meant practicing the five virtues, and showing consideration and understanding for others by your conduct. The core of the Jen teaching revolved around six principles and five virtues.[13]

The Six Ethical Principles:
1. Human nature is good, evil is unnatural.
2. Exercise reciprocity, that is, what you do not want others to do to you, do not do unto them.
3. A man has five duties: to his ruler, to his father, to his wife and her to him, to his older brother, and to his friends.
4. Man is free and master of his choice.
5. A man should strive to become a superior man.

6. Virtue should be done for its own sake, not for fear of punishment.

The Five Virtues:
1. Benevolence: kindness, humility, and goodwill toward others
2. Respect: loyalty, honor, and diligence
3. Propriety: righteouness, courtesy, and regard for the proper order
4. Courage: performance of one's duty and sincerity with one's inner nature
5. Wisdom: to be guided by understanding and knowledge

From the time of Confucius to the present day the core ideologies of the Chinese people came from Confucius. As Confucius said: "it is man who makes the Way great, and not the Way that can make man great." Confucius's interest was not so much in the spiritual world, but rather in the practical world. For Confucius knowledge was "to know men" with ethical standards based on the natural order of things and the proper functioning of society. The fabric of Confucianism was, and still is, the social obligations and relationships, with a moral imperative on duty. Confucianism is concern with how men can best learn to live together in harmony and good order. This was very much in alignment with the demand for collective effort that came from the notion of oneness.

Taoism

In the sixth century B.C., when Ch'iu K'ung became known as Confucius, Lao-Tze was expounding the doctrines that later became known as Taoism. Lao-Tze, the person, is now generally thought of as representing the personification of a philosophical movement that may have taken place in a later century. But it is reported that Confucius requested an audience with Lao-Tze to ask questions about ancient history. Lao-Tze was annoyed by his questions as well as by Confucius's polite mannerisms and the vain display of his fine robes. When his questions were challenged, Confucius explained new knowledge must be based on old knowledge. To that Lao-Tze replied, "It is not bathing that makes the pigeon white." Thus, their conversation came to an abrupt end.

Lao-Tze was known as the "old philosopher" who lived like a hermit, immersed in his ancient manuscripts. Lao-Tze did not seek students, honor, or personal gains. In his old age Lao-Tze wanted to retire to the province of Chou. According to the story of this event, a guard named Yin Hsi refused to let Lao-Tze cross the border until he wrote down the essentials of his teachings. Later a little book was handed to Yin Hsi. Lao-Tze crossed the border and was never heard of again. Taoism was established almost two centuries later by Chuang-tze (369–286 B.C.). Based on his teaching of Lao-Tze's sayings, Chuang-tze wrote fifty-two books.

Buddhism was introduced in China in the first century A.D. and over the years some Buddhist concepts, influenced by the Chinese mentality, were incorporated into Taoism. Taoism was believed to have been a quiet revolt against Confucius's stern rites and beliefs. Taoists tended to ignore the state, tradition, and the rule of laws emanating from the Confucian convention that, according to Taoism, distorted the Way of true human nature. Taoism and Buddhism overshadowed Confucianism for a thousand years until the arrival of the Sung and Ming dynasties. Although Confucianism formed the basic fabric of the Chinese ideology, by the fourth century Taoism had become part of the Chinese values. Sayings from Taoism illuminate some of these fundamental values:

- He who overcomes others is strong, he who overcomes himself is mighty.
- What gives a clay cup value is the empty space its walls create.
- Good implies the idea of evil; beauty implies the idea of ugliness, and existence the idea of nonexistence.
- The wise reject all extremes.
- The best instruction is not in words.
- In serving Heaven and in ruling men, use moderation.

- Those who are motivated by desire see only the outer shell of things.
- Man takes his law from the Earth, the Earth from Heaven, and Heaven from the Tao.

The law of the Tao was "being what it is." In keeping with the planting society notion of the fire or spirit within oneself, the Tao was conceived as a force, "the prime mover and the order" that pervaded everything. As such the aim in Taoism was for the "Te" within the individual to connect with the Way of the Tao. An individual's Te represented those virtuous characteristics contained within the person. When the Te connects with the Tao, people live harmoniously within the bounds of the natural order, allowing the individual to unfold with circumstance as well as influence the ordering process.[14] For the individual to connect with the Tao, one needed a blank mind, empty of aggression and ambitions—characteristics fundamental to planting societies and opposite to those found in hunting societies. Taoism, consistent with the notion of oneness of being, was attuned to nature. To the Taoist, the highest value was individual freedom that was achieved through being harmonious with Natural Law.

Shintoism

Shintoism, the aboriginal religion of Japan, was characterized by the veneration of nature spirits and of ancestors. In keeping with the Eastern concept of oneness, Shintoists believed a life force called the Kami flowed in everything. People, like all the elements in nature, were part of the Kami. Shintoism provided a strong cultural base for the Japanese people's profound love of nature, purity, and reverence. There is no teaching about original sin, eternal punishment, or heaven. Evil has to do with tipping the balance and immoderation.

The early gods of these ancient Japanese practitioners were divided into opposite but complementary male and female spirits. Shintoism promoted a strong sense of ethics based on the Code of the Knight, which placed a high value on courage, loyalty, cleanliness, and a loathing for cowardliness. Shintoism played a significant part in Japanese history, and until 1946, when forced by the U.S. government to deny his divinity, the emperor of Japan was believed to be descended from the Sun-Goddess.

Shinto sayings and precepts provide an insight into the concept of oneness:

- Faith is just like filial obedience to parents.
- Both heaven and hell come from one's heart.
- One should not be mindful of suffering in one's own life and unmindful of suffering in the lives of others.
- Do not forget your obligations to ancestors.
- Do not forget the limitations of your own person.
- Be loyal to the ruler.
- Be diligent in business.

Religions have never been static. The great religions and the meanings of their ideologies have evolved throughout time and in different contexts and places. In the West, there has been a high interest in Eastern ideologies and religions. Zen Buddhism, a religion introduced in Japan in 1190 A.D., provides a good example of a doctrine that amalgamated different religions from different parts of the world and subsequently was modified and adapted to local conditions and values.

Zen Buddhism: A Brief History

Zen Buddhism has its origins in Ch'an, a religion formed in China. Ch'an combined the history and philosophy of Chinese Taoism with the beliefs and theology of Indian Buddhism. Hui-neng (638–713 A.D.), credited with founding Ch'an, urged his followers to take refuge in their own individual natures. But the indigenous Chinese traditions of filial piety were in conflict with Buddhist concepts of earthly renunciation. According to Chinese tradition, nature is good and life on earth is not to be abandoned but to be made valuable. Relationships with parents and siblings and harmonious relationships within the community are to be fostered and developed, not renounced. Thus, the meeting of Taoism with Indian Buddhism merged the speculative with the practical and the metaphysical with the earthly.[15]

Ch'an was introduced to the Japanese in 1190 and there became known as Zen. To the ideas of Ch'an, the Japanese added simplicity.

What is the sound of one hand clapping?

Zen was consistent with Shintoism's high regard for intuition and respect for nature. The Zen concept of detachment from one's personal ego suited and appealed to the newly established military class of the Kamakura Era. The military interpretation of detachment was transposed to mean fighting without fear.

In the 1950s and '60s, Zen was introduced to North America, where it was again adapted and transformed to suit Western culture. While the West found it difficult to accept Japan's vertical social structure and the requirement of absolute loyalty to a master, the Zen approach to aesthetics and its emphasis on "personal experience" were consistent with the Western pursuit of "individuality."

What is Zen? Zen Buddhism shies away from any system of understanding—it cannot be called a dogma or religion. As such, Zen is instructive rather than sacred. Zen has often been described by

The more you know the less you understand.
—Taoist saying from the Tao Te Ching

what it is not. Noted contemporary Western thinkers have resorted to the method of defining something by describing its opposition. For example, Pablo Picasso once said "Art is a lie that makes us understand the truth." Albert Einstein, who formulated the laws of relativity had three rules for work:

1. Out of clutter, find simplicity.
2. From discord, find harmony.
3. In the middle of difficulty lies opportunity.

A saying in Zen used this same style to define itself: "Everything the same; everything distinct." Zen was not something one talked about but something one experienced. Zen's goal was to provide the individual with a clear awareness, uncluttered by rationalizations and intellectualizations. Zen's approach was to help one see the nature of one's true being by pointing the way out of one's conceptualizations. Zen valued and sought naturalness, spontaneity, and inner freedom.

According to Zen, knowing was false understanding; not knowing was blind ignorance. A system was required for all learning, but Zen practitioners taught that once learning took place the system for learning should be dropped. To reach clear awareness, Zen teachers asked questions, avoided logical demonstrations, and used a rich repertoire of metaphors, analogies, and paradoxes to help the individual gain firsthand experience distinct from preconceived concepts. In the East, Zen was understood more as being one with the Tao. Using meditation, self-contemplation, and intuition, the individual achieved detachment from the ego and reached enlightenment to live in accordance with the Way of the Tao.

Enlightenment in Zen Buddhism and Buddhism shared a common meaning but was sought for a different purpose. Both Zen and Buddhism believed one reached enlightenment by cultivating the ability to detach oneself from the ego. However, the purpose of detachment or separation from ego was different in Buddhism and in Zen. For Buddhists, separation from this world was an objective in itself that resulted in becoming one with the World Soul or reaching enlightenment. In Zen, enlightenment was reached when one's ego was dissolved to reconnect back to the nature within oneself. Both Taoism and Zen looked inward for wisdom but applied it outwardly. Zen sought simple clarity through the cultivation of the inner life to engage in the physical existence of this world. In keeping with its Taoism roots, Zen Buddhism had a kind of disregard for imposed limits that prevented individuals from reaching inner freedom and being one with the natural way. A famous Zen saying explained this idea: "Get rid of the self and act from the Self." From another Zen saying, the concept of being one with the natural way was illustrated: "Sitting quietly, doing nothing, spring comes, and the grass grows by itself."

Religions and the Self

The brief descriptions I have provided were chosen to illustrate some of the ideologies that affect and govern a great number of people. Other great religions such as Islam, Hinduism, Zoroastrianism, or Jainism were not covered for the sake of brevity. From even these brief descriptions we can see how over time, most religions and philosophies have been modified or absorbed new concepts as they were exposed to other cultures. Yet in the majority of religions, the core ideologies have remained largely consistent through time. A large number of shared beliefs characterize the great world religions. For example, the belief that life has a purpose is common to all major religions but differs only in how it is expressed. Buddhism, like Christianity, has commandments prohibiting murder, stealing, lying, and adultery. Although the world's great religions have a great number of similarities, there are some differences. And, went adopted to modern demand, each in balance contributes much to our Spiritual Self and aids in the management of our emotions.

In his book *What the Great Religions Believe,* Joseph Gaer divided the great religions and philosophies of the world into three major groups: (1) the religions that originated in India such as Hinduism, Buddhism, and Jainism; (2) those from the Near East such as Judaism, Christianity, and Islam; and (3) those from the Far East such as Confucianism, Taoism, and Shinto. I have divided the three major groups of religions in terms of how we relate to the Self as one's center of responsibility. To the Far East the center of responsibility is the group such as the family or one's association. To the West the center of responsibility is the individual, and to the Indian the center of responsibility lies outside one's ego.

Indian Religions: The Spiritual Self

The Indian religions can be viewed as introspective. A well-lived life is achieved through a personal indifference toward the temporal existence and the control of your ego, desires, and fears. The Self in Indian religions represents a spiritual ideal reached by detachment from temporal needs. As stated by the Hindu mystic and leader of modern Hinduism, Ramakrishna (1834– 86), temporal existence is dissolved "like a salt doll that has walked into the ocean," by detachment from the ego so the Self becomes one with the World-Soul.

In contrast, in the modern Western mind, duality makes a clear separation between spiritual and temporal existence. The Self represents the psychology of being realized through temporal existence. The purpose of a well-lived lifetime is not to dissolve personal temporal existence or detachment from the ego but rather to experience the psychology of temporal being. To Westerners, civic rights are sufficient justification for temporal pursuits.

Western Religions: The Individual Self

The Western religions often referred to as the Near East religions, can be viewed as moralistic. In the Near East the relationship between man and God the Creator is based on a covenant as given through the prophets. In the Near East religions, God is a separate identity from humans. Their covenant with God is to do His will as taught by the prophets.

The basic tenet of Judaism is based on a twofold affirmation: (1) Man shall seek to know and love God, revere Him and do His will; and (2) Man shall love his fellow man and deal with him in a righteous way. Judaism is very much a religion concerned with social justice. Contrary to Indian religions, Near East religions consider the idea of humans as being of the same essence as God as blasphemy.

Christianity as it spread to Europe is influenced by its Jewish heritage, Greek philosophy, and Roman culture. The Greeks and Romans, as well as the Celtic and Germanic tribes, believed the laws regulating human interactions were derived by people even though they were inspired by Judaic Law. The separation of law and God— or body and soul—resulted in the concept of Self as an individual, and it is thus consistent with the hunting society concept of duality. In early Christianity the soul was to subdue the body. In Europe this suppression of the body by the soul changed after the Renaissance, when the Self as related to the body came to dominate.

In the Western world the concept of Self is related to man himself as the center. The Self is related to the psychology of being in the temporal world within the bounds of moral laws and is not concerned with becoming one with the World Soul. The West accepts only one God and makes a clear distinction between people and God. As I will show in Chapter Four, Western science added the mechanical view to this concept.

The Far East Religions: The Civic Self

The Far East religions and philosophies can be viewed as being concerned with propriety. Confucius's emphasis was on civic participation. An individual's conduct had to show consideration and understanding of others, and to recognize the proper social order. In the Far East the concept of oneness gave rise to the notion of harmony and collectivism. The Self is not centered on the individual, but rather on proper civic behavior that is synchronous with the family, the group, and society. The concept of Taoism and Zen demands for harmony with the natural way were, with time, aligned with the Confucian notion of civic participation and social harmony.

Far East religions' acceptance of ancestor-worship should not be confused with Western or Indian asceticism. Transcendental and supernatural considerations have little to do with the proper social order. As Confucius said, "Knowledge is to know man," and ancestor-worship provides justification for a hierarchy of obedience and obligation within the family.

Oneness in Indian religions became associated with becoming one with the essence of the World-Soul permeating all. In Hinduism, deities are not the cause or source in themselves, but rather vehicles to help you attain World-Soul. This is in contrast to the Western God, who is the cause and creator of all things.

Oneness in the Chinese religions relates to being one with the Zen or the Way of nature. Confucius's strong influence expressed collectivism as driven by the need for harmonious relationships within society. Civic concern means living within the consciousness of proper social relationships.

Social Implications

In the West, individualism, heroism, personal ambition, distinction, and the pursuit of a strong independent ego are the heritage of a hunting society's concept of duality and the willingness to take risks. Starting with self-consciousness of the Renaissance, individualism took on its full flavor in modern time.[16] In the West, the individual is perceived as being autonomous and independent of the group. Driven by one's beliefs, self-fulfillment, where one gives priority to self-interest in order to accomplish one's goal, is acceptable. In the East, collectivism, passivity, harmony, accord, and indifference to an independent ego are consistent with the heritage of a planting society's concept of oneness. In the East, the individual is perceived as being connected to others in the group. Driven by norms and obligations, self-discipline demands that you attune yourself to the collective interest and show loyalty, respect, and regard for it. The spiritual self from Indian religions favors serenity, humility, purity, and right conduct. At a social level it favors patience, freedom from pretense, anger, and malice and demands self-mastery.

As I shall discuss in later chapters, how you view the Self has a tremendous influence on your beliefs and actions. For example, rewards in the West are based on personal performance while in Japan rewards are given for group performance. I will return to this but for the time being I would like to correct a few misperceptions.

To the Western mind, the Eastern indifference to an independent ego should not be interpreted as having no ego or not being concerned for oneself. Indian religions are concerned that individual desire and fear prevents becoming one with the World-Soul. In Chinese culture, the ego is to be subdued to the proper civic behavior.

To the Western mind, Eastern passivity must not be interpreted as being taken advantage of by others or be conceived as the opposite of aggressiveness. Passivity is more about being in touch with and in accord with your surroundings. Indeed, individual characteristics such as aggressiveness and passivity are found in both the Western and the Eastern societies. Ideologies promoted by a given culture make the expression of some characteristics more acceptable and others less desirable within a given society.

Group consensus should not be interpreted by Westerners as lacking a personal opinion. Based on Japanese civic ideologies, there is a proper place and time to express individual opinions or disagreement. Likewise, standing out and pointing a finger Western-style should not be interpreted by Easterners to mean that Americans are rude and do not care about what others think or feel or that they are indifferent toward their family, their group, or their surroundings. Harmony does not mean Easterners love their neighbor more than Westerners.

In the West, the word *harmony* has been romanticized. Harmony in the East is about recognition of one's nature, and the complementarity of roles and duties. It also implies that you need to take the time to listen carefully and maintain proper public decorum. Although Easterners are less likely to point figures or insult others in public, this does not preclude aggressive business strategy.

Religious ideologies have shaped many of the values that influence our perceptions. As humans, we share similar experiences, though we may express those experiences differently to reflect our cultural contexts and the ideologies we live by.

Discussion

As I discussed in Chapter One, emotional competence is one of the key factors responsible for success in our personal development. Emotional competence requires that we develop the ability to: (1) comprehend our own feelings; (2) identify and assess other people's feelings; and (3) control and manage our impulses.

With the emphasis on the Individual Self, today's North Americans put high value on self-sufficiency, independence, and the right to pursue one's distinct individuality. With emphasis on the Civic Self, today's Chinese, Koreans, and Taiwanese put a high value on propriety, respect, and obligation; while the Japanese demand for harmony puts importance on accord, conformity, and courtesy. With emphasis on the Spiritual Self, self-restraint is highly valued. The upper caste Indian Brahmin values serenity, self-mastery, and purity. The prevalence of Buddhist values in today's Thailand puts emphasis on virtues such as patience and gentleness, concentration of effort, and freedom from pretense and anger.

I believe that each emphasis—the Individual Self, the Civic Self, and the Spiritual Self—evolves values that are different from each other but at the same time are complementary. When brought together as a whole, they provide us with the means to greater personal development. The Individual Self with its focus on your distinctiveness fosters the comprehension of your own feelings. The Civic Self with its focus on propriety and alignment demands that you be able to assess others' feelings. The Spiritual Self with its focus on qualities like patience, self-restraint, and concentration supports the management of your impulses.

4

Institutionalization of a Mechanical View

Here's an all-too-familiar scenario. You are browsing in a store and you see an item you like. You decide to buy it, but are told they don't have one in your size. No trouble. You put in an order and are told that it should arrive within two days. Four days go by and you decide to follow up on your order. You call the store, and within fifteen minutes you have been transferred to five different people. You call a salesperson who, after sending you to numerous other people, finally transfers you to the manufacturing department.

> Do not seek to follow in the footsteps of the men of old; seek what they sought.
> —Basho

"Yes," a distracted person in manufacturing tells you, "your goods have just left the plant for the packaging department." You are transferred to the packaging department, and they are pleased to tell you the goods have been forwarded to the shipping department for delivery. You call the shipping department, and they tell you they have your goods but are waiting for the billing papers from finance. No problem; you call finance and you are told that the clerk in charge of your district is away for the week. You are then asked if you could call at a later time. "It's not our fault," they say, "it's the system." You immediately lose half of what is left of your hairline. But it's not all bad. You discover that, yes, the human body does produce steam—it comes out of your ears. You wonder if you really need to put up with this frustration or if someone else might do things differently. You start looking for another supplier.

It is not the case that people are indifferent, but rather that the mechanical bureaucracy they serve is indifferent. And in mechanical bureaucracies such as the one I've just described, people serve the system rather than the system serving them. In bureaucracies run by mechanical systems, employees are more concerned about the rules and procedures than about the work that needs to be done. This is not to say that rules should not exist or that systems are all bad. Rules can provide direction and discipline, and systems can improve performance. But when rules, systems, and the bureaucracies they serve become an impediment to performance, they have gone too far.

When we think of bureaucracy, we often think of government. Although I've seen contracts between government and consultants that are thicker than the reports they produced, governments do not have a monopoly on bureaucracy. As the above example demonstrates, bureaucracy also exists in business and, yes, in all forms of organizations from charitable associations to universities—even management faculties that teach entrepreneurship. I've used business examples mainly because I find it easier to demonstrate the effect bureaucracy has on business, which is governed by a bottom line. In certain situations, corporate bureaucracy has its place, but for the most part, many businesses that remain bureaucratic simply go bankrupt. Thus, the costly implications that self-imposed rules and procedures have on business are more readily measured (my Western habit of measuring).

The New Reality

Governed by the ever-present bottom line, today's business cannot afford to become rule-bound, especially if it means customers will perceive the company to be indifferent to customer needs. Rules and procedures created during the Industrial Revolution gave rise to impressive results. Those who developed mass production adapted to a changing social and economic environment; they met the challenge of a new reality. But today many of the rules, procedures, and theories created during that earlier era have given rise to a mechanistic approach—a mechanistic order that impedes rather than advances productivity. This mechanistic approach brings compliance but negates commitment and participation; it promotes the rationale of cost control but negates the power of insight and innovation. In a global environment, we again face a new reality—a reality that once again will demand that business change and adapt.

As business guru Peter Drucker has said, "The assumptions on which the organization has been built and is being run no longer fit reality."[1] Those assumptions emerged with the Industrial Revolution, and in order to understand how they became the foundation of Western thought, I find it useful to review some of the ideas and events that formed them. This is not to say we need to push aside all of our assumptions, but some of them incline us toward a

> Life can only be understood backward, but must be lived forward.
> —Kierkegaard

mechanistic application and deny the advantage of a more fluid approach. To understand our modern approach to business, I first turn to the advent of the scientific age and its influence on the way we think and approach solving problems. I will get back to business, but first let me introduce the concept of mechanical order.

Knowledge: A Change in Method, a Change in Meaning

The scientific method of understanding can be attributed largely to major thinkers of the sixteenth and seventeenth centuries such as Descartes, Bacon, Galileo, and Newton. Their combined notions of observational procedure, patterns of argument, and methods of presentation and calculation became the foundation of modern science.

René Descartes (1596–1650) has been called "the father of modern philosophy" and the archetype of the modern rationalist. Seeking to discover an objective system of knowledge through reason based on precise, mathematically measurable quantities in the external world, Descartes inspired a new model for human understanding and changed the way we understand work and manage our business affairs.[2] The scientific approach, based on the idea that careful observations and calculations could illuminate all problems, brought a new kind of discipline to our thinking—one that alleviated superstition and fear, augmented logic and bypassed metaphysical speculation, and inspired hope that the universe was not only intelligible but available to all reasoning thinkers. Francis Bacon (1561–1626), concerned with the prejudice of the subject, stressed the need for deduction from the measurable. Descartes emphasized the separation of the subject (the person or the object) from the phenomenon being studied. This Cartesian approach to understanding—this vital new spirit of scientific inquiry and mathematical rigor—appealed to the European mind in a rush to reexamine all that was known or could be known in the world.

The idea of knowledge itself began to change. From antiquity until the pre-Industrial Age, knowledge had been associated with *being.* Socrates equated knowledge with virtue.[3] In his search for objectively valid definitions of the outer world and the inner person (or truth), Socrates paid little attention to how things should be done. Work, after all, was not considered a noble enterprise. Two millennia later, Bacon equated knowledge with power. With time, knowledge came to be equated with the idea of *doing.*

Another important thinker of the time was Sir Isaac Newton (1642–1727), who altered modern science by his careful application of empirical principles based on experience and perception. Newton's law of gravity expressed in mathematical terms meant you could predict the speed at which an object would fall or the motion of the celestial bodies. It meant you could isolate the different factors believed to be responsible for the occurrence of natural events and measure them. Until challenged by Bohr, Einstein, or Heisenberg principles in modern times, Newton's law of physics lent support to the notion that nature was governed with a machine-like regularity. The early evolution of scientific thought was consistent with its Christian context. After all, Saint Thomas Aquinas had said, "With a greater understanding of the world, would come greater knowledge and reverence for God." Thus we can see Western ideas about God, nature, and man evolved largely within a Christian context, and from that perspective we can understand how the scientific method came to be developed and accepted.[4]

In the West, God and nature were conceived as separate entities. Traditionally, Western thinkers thought of nature as being devoid of any spiritual properties. In contrast, Eastern thinkers traditionally thought of the individual self as part of nature and expected to live in harmony with the way of nature; for them, to question nature was futile. In the West, to study the mechanics of nature became acceptable because it did not constitute a separation from God. After all, by understanding God's creation, the more you would appreciate the beauty and the order in the world, and the more you would revere God.[5] But within Western scientific thought it was all right to think of the relationships between God and nature—and God and man—as being of different essences. Hence, knowledge of nature was not to be gained through the examination of oneself; nature was to be understood through impersonal means using quantitative experimental investigation. With the scientific age, it became possible to design experiments that could isolate, measure, and observe a natural phenomenon independently of one's personal view. In a nutshell, the world—and all that it held—was conceivably measurable and therefore knowable.

> *Men argue, nature acts.*
> —Voltaire

According to the philosopher Richard Tarnas, Charles Darwin's theory of evolution did for the world of biology what Newton's law of physics did for the physical cosmos.[6] Before the scientific age, man was understood to be part of God's creation having a special purpose. People were thought to be endowed with mystic qualities, emotions, and spirituality and to live in a world designed to respond to human values. After Darwin, this idea changed. Humans were now understood to be an evolutionary product of nature competing for biological success.[7] Newton's eloquent explanation of the law of gravity gave impetus to seeking the same level of understanding in the laws that governed the actions of individuals. With Darwin's explanation of the survival of the fittest, the world could be understood as impersonal. The cosmos, nature, and humans could now be explained according to a mechanical order.

In all fields of endeavor from biology to psychology, from cosmology to medicine, science brought unprecedented advances and understanding.

Bacon was right, of course, about knowledge and power. With knowledge came greater power to produce. As Peter Drucker contends, "In both the West and the East, knowledge had always been seen as applying to *being.* Then, almost overnight, it came to be applied to *doing.* It became a resource and a utility. Knowledge had always been a private good. Almost overnight it became a public good."[8] Knowledge, once the domain of virtue and the understanding of the inner *being,* was now turning to the relationship between the power of *doing* and the outer being. Starting with science and the Industrial Age, interest turned to the application of knowledge to the external, active worlds of technology and nature.

From Craftsmanship to Mass Production

In the preindustrial age, goods were produced by skilled craftsmen. By performing a variety of tasks, craftsmen could produce a small number of goods that were well suited to a small number of consumers. The quantity and quality of goods produced depended directly on the individual craftsman's skill and motivation. Although craftsmanship meant the goods complied with customer specifications, only the wealthy could afford them.

Industrialization brought the construction of manufacturing plants, developments in machinery, and new forms of organization that defined a whole new way of doing work. Industrialization was synonymous with mass production—the creation of goods in bulk for the masses. Mass production made goods affordable and avail-

able, and it brought change to more than the way things were done—
it brought tremendous change to the scale in which they were done.
The survivors of the Industrial Age are those who made the transition from craftsmanship to mass production. As we progress through
the Information Age we must again find a new way of doing things.

In times of uncertainty, people attach themselves to what they
know, to the familiar. Solutions that were responses to past problems
often provide a sense of security. Despite its seductive pull, however,
we need to detach ourselves from the past if we are to become creative when conditions change. Henry Ford (1863–1947), an early
entrant in the age of automobile design and manufacturing, separat-
ed himself from the old ways of doing things and adopted a new
mode of manufacturing that shifted guild-bound ideas of craftsmanship to concepts of mass production. When industrialization took
hold in the early part of the twentieth century, 485 companies
entered the U.S. automobile manufacturing industry.[9] Ford survived
by changing and adapting to the demand of the new reality.

What are the new demands on organizations and how can they
best adapt to the information age? What can be learned from those
who adapted to the emerging reality of the mass production age
brought on in the Industrial Revolution? Let's first review how old
corporate assumptions formed in the dawning scientific age influenced our Western management style, shaped our preference for a
mechanical view, and favored a systems approach to problem solving. Then let's look at how these assumptions affect today's businesses and what we need to change.

Mass Production: A New Age

Changes that took place during the scientific revolution in Western
Europe represent the cumulative and interactive effects of a series of
social and cultural changes that occurred over several centuries.
Whether it be European fragmentation, rival states competing for
novelty, or the dual authority between the church and the secular, to
fairly treat the relevance of change in Western thought requires the

attention of a full book. Instead, I will briefly summarize several of the factors that led to some of the more significant changes in Western culture, concentrating mainly on the changes brought about by the development of the scientific method and its effect on our Western way of thinking and managing that has evolved into what I describe as our mechanistic world view.

In Europe the very first "preindustrial revolution" is thought to have taken place in the twelfth century—the latter part of the Middle Ages—when wind and water mills spread throughout Europe.[10] The addition of wind and water power to muscle or horse power, paralleled by the formation of the guilds as an urban social class and the revival of long-distance trade, represented a transformation in European economies.[11] Craftsmanship standards set by guilds dominated European ideas about modes of production until the advent of the Industrial Age. Throughout the centuries marking the Renaissance and the Reformation up to the Industrial Age, changes in how goods were produced took place slowly.

This is not to underestimate the new spirit of inquiry brought about by Renaissance thinkers who valued invention, exploration, and discovery, ushering in an atmosphere of confidence in human ability.[12] Clearly, the printing press bolstered the power of the written word; revolutionized the production, storage, and dissemination of knowledge; and fostered major social changes during this period in Europe.

The Renaissance spirit of inquiry and rebellion justified individual pursuit, and in politics, literature, science, and business, personal aggression and even rebellion became an acceptable means to an end. People hustled to be the first to discover, to publish, to create an original artwork, or to gain wealth. In this new milieu, individual personal experience and the determination to win individual gain became acceptable. Mistrust of authority, freedom of thought, and the victory of intellectual education over privileged birth became part of the European culture. Continuing with the Reformation and on through the Enlightenment, criticism of authority, revolution, and challenges to existing beliefs and dogma continued unabated. In the process, loyalties shifted away from king, lord, and Church, to the nation, and libertarian ideals demanded that people be judged on ability rather than heredity. Not inhibited by an environment where the winner-takes-all, independent men are more likely to take risks. The new order gave people confidence in their ability to understand and to change things. Turmoil was in the air, and entrepreneurship took place in all fields of endeavor.

> *Never, never, never, never give up.*
> —Winston Churchill

Working knowledge applied to technology brought impressive gains. The development of the scientific age and the Industrial Revolution are inextricably bound to each other as advances in scientific knowledge served to further industrial technology, and vice versa. Changes in thinking and in entrepreneurship, along with the development of new institutions, created unprecedented wealth and advancement. Supported by notions that valued individual initiative and effort, the Industrial Age sprouted as many new factories as new products. The new economy opened trade and brought access to high standards of living once thought available only through heredity or warfare.

The scientific approach fostered changes in every aspect of Western culture and society. Working from our business perspective, we must understand these changes in terms of (1) technology and investing in mass markets, (2) society and the emerging middle class, (3) division of labor, (4) finance, and (5) the evolution of a management class.

Technology and Investing in Mass Markets

Until the mid-1700s, the day-to-day life of ordinary people in Europe changed very little from ancient Roman times. People tended to live in small, isolated rural communities, producing their own shelter, food, and clothing. Roads were bad, trade limited, and the production of goods slow and expensive.

With the perfecting of the steam engine by James Watt in 1776, things changed. The success of the Industrial Age was predicated on a series of inventions, not the least of which were electric power and the internal-combustion engine. These inventions paralleled innovations in agriculture and transportation, as well as new labor techniques and management practices. The introduction of the railroad in the 1830s unified markets over large areas and provided the market size essential to mass production.

The expanding markets created by the railroad made large investments more desirable and less risky. These favorable conditions were further facilitated by the blossoming communication industry that sped the exchange of information. Rules and laws on property rights and contractual obligations—which started in the fifteenth century and evolved sufficiently over the next centuries to facilitate arm's-length transactions—flourished in the early twentieth century.

Science and technology, together with innovative ideas in investment, the formation of mass markets, and a new spirit of entrepreneurship, evolved as cumulative and integral parts of a whole. Technological innovation—such as developing a new iron-casting method or replacing steam engines with internal-combustion or electrical engines—brought impressive gains in productivity. But there are consequences associated with technological innovations. Inventions required capital investment for new tools and equipment as well as expensive modifications to existing plants or, sometimes, the creation of new plants. Consequently the concept of investments changed to align with new ideas about predicting the market place. Investment of capital dollars requires a willingness to accept future returns at a risk. The risk, however, can be minimized—and thus justified—if the goods produced can be sold to a large number of buyers. Mass production, therefore, requires large markets.

The development of new modes of production in response to the formation of adequate markets was built on factors such as improved means of communication, cheaper energy, the availability of capital, and growth and shift in population. Together, all these elements set in motion a series of consequences that would lead to the realization of economies of scale made possible with mass production and the concept of the open economy.

Mass production was a great departure from manufacturing by craftsmen who produced very few products at any one time. During the Industrial Age, those who continued in the craft production mode all but disappeared. In 1896, the first gasoline-powered vehicles were sold in the United States. The Duryea Motor Wagon Co. of Springfield, Massachusetts, built thirteen cars that year, and an industry was born. By 1929, a record 4.5 million cars were produced.[13] The automobile industry was a growth industry, already exceeding the wagon and carriage trade in terms of value traded, and many sought the promise of success by becoming pioneers in the industry. Between 1900 and 1908 in the United States alone, 485 companies entered automobile manufacturing. First Ford, then General Motors and Chrysler, not only adapted the new mode of production but improved on it—and were successful.

The application of mass production by the likes of Ford and Sloan increased productivity and gave us wealth and choice. Today, we must not seek to follow in the footsteps of the Industrial Age, but rather, we must seek to foster the emergence of a new reality.

Society and the Emerging Middle Class

Mass production brought impressive increases in productivity that created unprecedented wealth. As a result of growth, the average blue collar worker's real income in the 1980s was about twenty-five times more than it was in 1907.[14] Before mass production, the distribution of wealth looked like a pyramid with a wide base, with few people at the top, a few more in the middle, and the great majority at the bottom. Today, the distribution of wealth looks more like a diamond with a few people at the top, a much greater number of people in the middle and fewer people at the bottom.

Before 1910, the average American worked 3,000 hours per year. Now the average American works 1,850 hours per year. Early in this century, a Model T Ford car cost $750, and only the wealthy could afford one because, for the average worker, $750 represented the equivalent of three to four years' salary. Today, although we work fewer hours per year, the cost of an average car represents the equivalent of only three to five months' salary.[15] This tremendous increase in productivity means that, starting in the 1960s, the majority of people could afford what was once available only to the wealthy.

In the past, most people were content to buy what was affordable and reliable. With affluence, however, people start looking for products that suit their lifestyle. Today, an affordable and reliable watch, for example, is taken for granted. People don't just buy watches anymore; rather, they buy jewelry that gives the time—and signals their lifestyle. Jewelry must, like a signature, be unique to the individual and consistent with the customer's self-image. This means that in addition to reliability, quality, and price, a watch must match the wearer's particular lifestyle and image.

Before the affluent 1960s, manufacturers depended on engineering specifications to make a reliable product and sell it at an affordable price. Starting in the sixties, however, manufacturers began depending on the customer for product specifications as they started to focus on customer-driven marketing strategies rather than on product-driven strategies. Success belonged to the firm that could meet a customer's preferred lifestyle. As Peter Drucker contends, lifestyle is now a determinant, while income is more of a restraint. This created a whole new way of doing business.

Division of Labor: A New Organization Skill

Adam Smith (1723–1790) first enunciated the economic basis of nineteenth-century *laissez-faire* theories, outlining ideas about the division of labor and the principles at work in a free-enterprise economy. Smith observed that by dividing the process of making safety pins into eighteen different specialized tasks, a factory could increase its productivity by many hundredfold. Smith's analysis showed that ten people with specialized tasks, aided by specialized tools and machines, could produce 48,000 pins per day compared to only a few pins per person using the hand-crafted methods.

Division of labor and mass production first made their most noteworthy inroads in the textile industry and then eventually spread to other industries. For example, in 1913, the Henry Ford Motor Corporation innovated on Smith's division-of-labor concept and applied it to the manufacture of a product much more complex than pins. The company developed the innovative idea of mounting the chassis of cars on a moving belt. The assembly work for each car was divided into a series of repeatable tasks performed on each car as it traveled down an assembly line of workers. As each car moved from workstation to workstation, workers performed specialized and simplified tasks. Before, one craftsman would perform a combination of tasks. Now, the assembly line broke production into specific tasks, each performed by a specific person. This specialization and division of work into simple, repetitious tasks ensured efficiency and speed of performance. This innovation reduced the time required to make a Model T from 12.5 hours to 1.5 hours.[16]

Dividing jobs into simple and repeatable tasks represented a major shift from the working assumptions of craftsmen who previously had done all the tasks necessary to complete a whole job. When combined with major capital investments in manufacturing plants and improved technology, this new innovation in work organization brought unprecedented and astonishing increases in productivity.

Finance: A Measuring Tool

After a decade of growth, in the mid-1920s General Motors added a new and higher level of competency to its manufacturing process: financial control. As Drucker said, "As a result, GM invented modern cost accounting and the first rational capital-allocation process."[17] By the late 1920s, systems such as *Return on Investment, Flexible Budgeting,* and *Cost Measure Financing* were introduced in response to organizations' need to make more complex decisions.[18] Cost accounting provided standardized business communication and measurement, and therefore allowed for comparative analysis and improved decision-making in the world of business. Like labor division, management specialization, and measurable standards, cost accounting brought focus, discipline, accountability, and greater productivity.

Impressed by this new system's success, management relied on more and greater divisions of authority. Specialization and standardization procedures were rapidly developed as management's reliance on numbers, rules, and procedures grew. As we shall see, that development was consistent with our mechanistic view and preference for logic; however, in excess, it pushes decision making away from the reality of the situation and denies intuition, participation, and insight—musts in today's new environment.

We are again in a period that requires us to change the way we do things. By integrating the best of Eastern and Western management practices, we can gain greater commitment and performance. This will come from adopting the Eastern sense of participation while retaining the Western focus that comes with accountability, and from combining the Eastern astuteness for intuition with the Western discipline for system transparency.

> *Imagination is more important than knowledge.*
> *—Albert Einstein*

Our new environment demands integration just as the environment in the industrial age favored mass production. A few hundred years ago, our predecessors faced a great challenge, adapted to their new environment, and produced impressive results. We now face a different situation. But as the Industrial Age represented an adaptation to a multitude of factors brought on by a series of social changes from the previous centuries, it in turn brought on its own changes, which we now must recognize.

A Management Class Is Born

One hundred and twenty-five years ago, emerging enterprise adopted the hierarchical, command-and-control reporting model that had been characteristic of the military and of the growing railroad industry. This hierarchical and autocratic style was not unlike the structure found in the Catholic Church and was consistent with the prevalent concept of many people working for a few masters.

Specialization in labor as well as in management produced unprecedented gains in efficiency and productivity. This was consistent with principles Frederick Taylor (1856–1915) set out in *Principles of Scientific Management*. Taylor, an industrial engineer, introduced the concept of specialized labor and measurable standards, but he is best known for his time-and-motion studies that sought increases in productivity.

Dividing the job of making a complex thing like a car into a series of simple tasks requires complex and detailed coordination of people and skills—and that requires management. With more division and more specialization, the formation of organizational platforms to coordinate the various components of a large job became critical. The seeds for such managerial coordination already had germinated in the railroad industry, where trains operating on single tracks needed well-defined procedures to prevent head-on collisions.[19] Management developed and enforced rules of conduct describing contingencies, lines of authority, and reporting requirements that ensured railroad safety.

Companies were growing, and by the 1920s Du Pont executives had developed multidivisional structures to cope with diversification. In the car industry, Alfred Sloan, the successor to the founder of General Motors, is best known for creating the prototype of our present management system.[20] As we have seen, the division of labor in manufacturing had produced impressive gains in productivity. Sloan applied the same concept to divide management functions. As labor was divided into tasks and specialization, management was likewise divided in terms of knowledge, level of authority, and responsibility. With time the division of different management functions expanded and created different functional departments such as marketing, production, acquisition, and finance. These in turn were divided into further subdepartments. This management structure was well suited to mass production and provided the specialization, control, and planning required to ensure high levels of performance.

A Mechanical Order:
The New Environment

As we have seen, with the invention of motorized pumps, mechanical clocks, measuring devices, and scientists' ability to explain nature with mathematical accuracy came the notion that the universe was governed in mechanical terms. Newton's law of gravity may not have been understood by all, but the slide rule used for calculation, the thermometer's daily gauging of temperature, and the compass that gave precise directions provided constant visible reinforcement of the new concept. With understanding of the workings of nature came improvement in the standard of living. With greater understanding came the sense of control by individuals over their own destinies.[21] This appealed to the emerging new class and the growing pursuit of individual self-fulfillment.

In time, science evolved a new mechanical order that displaced the awe and reverence associated with nature. Mysticism, with its emphasis on emotion and imagination, essentially vanished. People thought everything, including human behavior, society, and nature could be mechanically explained.[22] Conversely, the glory attached to rationalism sometimes undermined the great benefits offered by intuition and insight so important to creative thinking and innovation.

How, then, has this mechanized world view affected business?

For all the criticism that some may have about past management practice, mass production brought wealth for the masses. Greater wealth resulted in an increasingly educated middle class as well as a more affluent society in general. In the West, Karl Marx's so-called abused workers became the ruling proletariat. Investment was once the sole province of the wealthy, but now the wealthy have to share control with affluent workers who, through institutional investors (estimated to provide close to 50 percent of the common stock capital), exercise a substantial influence on the distribution of investment.[23] Education of the masses opened the door to a large pool of talent once reserved for the established elite. Opportunities for innovation and organization opened to a wide spectrum of the population.

This rise in education and affluence created an unprecedented broadening of horizons. Today's more educated workers and customers are demanding greater participation in the creation and distribution of goods and services. With advancing technology, information, and travel, many people have been exposed to other cultures and to alternative ways of doing things. This exposure has produced an extraordinary rate of exchange between all nations of the world.

One of the most striking features of the modern age is the way in which people in most countries of the world are aware and conscious of each other. This new level of consciousness has increased people's expectations in terms of standards of living and their demands for personal growth and participation. More and more, the educated populace, with its tendency to look across cultural boundaries for innovative business ideas, is pushing corporations to achieve new levels of sophistication in terms of what they produce and how they produce it.

But what are the obstacles to business in this mechanized world view? I want to examine two areas: (1) the mechanization of modern bureaucracy, and (2) the mechanical order and management. Against that backdrop, I will show how our cultural assumptions have played out in the evolution of business practice and discuss some of the consequences. I will demonstrate how changes in our mechanical world view are slow and sometimes detrimental to our personal and corporate growth.

The Mechanization of Modern Bureaucracy

Productivity gains translated to bigger markets, and with bigger markets came bigger corporations. Division of labor and specialization of tasks had proved efficient, just as division of management functions seemed logical and reasonable. Corporations were growing, as were the number of regulations that governed the marketplace and the interactions between labor and management. Technology, formerly specific to production, started to gain a greater role in organizational management. With the growth of corporations, more departments and subdivisions were added as increasing complexity required more specialists and greater coordination among those departments and subdivisions. With more functional specialization, more rules and procedures were added to define levels of responsibilities and authority. In addition, employee contracts, safety requirements, and employee benefits added still more rules and procedures. Under the banner of efficiency, more specialists and an increasing number of levels of management and white collar workers were justified.

This, of course, suited the rising star of the new class of managers who gained status and value as they ascended through the extra levels of management. But more specialists, more managers, more rules, and more complexity meant a greater separation of the decision makers from the users and producers. Fitting the scientific notion, systems of measurement were added to help make decisions. So with the growth of organizations, new financial systems were added. By the 1960s, "management by numbers" was well entrenched. Thus organizational performance came to be measured according to a series of indicator numbers. In government, for example, cost-benefit analysis came to be used to prioritize public projects. In business, management calculated return on investment to determine how much an organization would invest in a venture—and, indeed, if it would invest at all. Spreadsheets provided the tools to prepare a myriad of analyses, helping management assess the level of risk and set the cutoff point. It seemed that all management needed to ensure an organization's success was to understand what the numbers meant and to allocate resources accordingly. To handle the necessary intense analysis, companies added still more systems and still more management layers.

But trying to make decisions based on numbers alone is akin to trying to describe a cornfield by examining corn starch—knowing something about corn starch does not mean you know something about corn plants. Adding layers of management removed decision-makers from the customers and from production. Knowing the customer, the product, or how the product was produced was left to specialists. This situation was not so critical when business catered to homogeneous market demands where manufacturers understood pretty well what customers wanted. But the marketplace was becoming more segmented. While spreadsheet analysis, rules, and procedures helped focus our business efforts, their use became too much of a good thing.

Operating an organization on a routine diet of financial analysis is similar to feeding your family a steady diet of broccoli. Most of us know that broccoli can be good for our health, but a diet comprised only of broccoli is not complete and is ultimately even detrimental to our health. The steady diet of analysis served up to many Western organizations began to adversely affect their health. The market was about to change.

Spreadsheet analysis with its series of numbers, rules, and procedures makes us look inside the organization for answers. Although the answers lie outside in the marketplace, rules and procedures provide a standardized step-by-step way of getting information. The information is then evaluated, based on a series of bottom-line numbers. While there is nothing wrong with systems that provide discipline and focus, we must be aware that when the mechanics determine what gets done and how, they likewise determine the results—results that have nothing to do with reality. Is that what business wants: action that does not correspond to reality?

Management: A Mechanical Order

With the prevalence of the mechanical view, the scientific principles of management enunciated in the early twentieth century reflected the prevailing beliefs of the time. Dividing a phenomenon into measurable parts made sense, just as dividing management and labor or dividing a job into different measurable tasks was consistent with the scientific approach. For example, from Taylor's scientific approach to management also came the notion of a clear division between labor and management and the development of the ideology of the manager as a *thinker* and the laborer as a *doer.*[24]

In separating *thinkers* from *doers,* labor was freed from the business of thinking and was paid for doing. A carrot-and-stick approach brought increased productivity, confirming the economic and psychological theory prevalent at the time that individuals respond primarily to narrow self-interest.[25] Initiative, innovation, planning, and control were the domain of management and specialists—the thinkers. It was a notion well suited to the Western scientific preference for defining clear and measurable functions and separating roles. In time, this approach evolved into the highly legalistic "box approach" that operated with detailed rules and procedures, clear assignments, and specified responsibilities.

Taylorism was consistent with the Western scientific method because it employed a sequential, step-by-step, linear, deductive approach. Later, with increasing organizational complexity, financial indicators were added. The prevailing wisdom was that just as lines of degrees indicated temperature on a thermometer, financial numbers could accurately indicate business activity.

The rise in bureaucracies with their highly structured organizational models provided a step-by-step decision-making approach. Function and duties delineated the rights and obligations of each member of an organization and, furthermore, defined relationships within the organization. Following a sequential, linear, and deductive process provided for predictable, measurable, and it was believed, relevant results.

This concept fit well with the common belief in a mechanical order. Problems could now be divided into parts and work assigned according to function. Specialists studied operations and made recommendations. The impersonal nature of rules and regulations and of rights and duties suited the impersonal nature of a mechanical order.

Today we are in a different environment, and clear distinctions between thinkers and doers are not suitable where the doers are required to solve the problem. You learn by doing. In a competitive dynamic environment you need to move with market demand. Market sophistication means you need to be able to read customer needs and respond to their specific demands.

Where technology, reliability, and quality used to represent an advantage, they are now your price of entry. In Chapter 7, I will discuss how to integrate some of the best Eastern and Western practices to gain a competitive edge. But before you can do that, you need to be aware of how our predisposition to fundamental cultural assumptions and our slowness to change those assumptions can block our adaptation of management practices more suitable to the Information Age. The following examples from the automobile industry offer dramatic lessons of our mechanical view's impact on business.

Old Assumptions vs.
Market Reality

In the 1960s, General Motors operated under the assumption that the U.S. was still a homogeneous car market interested only in style and gadgets. GM thought that the U.S. car market corresponded to four or five different socioeconomic groups.[26] A man with a Buick was better off than a man with a Pontiac, but not as well off as a man with a Cadillac.[27] Detroit was very good at setting the fashion but poor at following it. Different categories of cars were produced for each socioeconomic group by simply varying the style and the number of gadgets appropriate to its status. Meanwhile the characteristics of the U.S. market were changing, but the assumptions of what the market wanted remained the same.

The 1960s gave rise to a youth culture that rejected authority and wanted to do its own thing. Arrogant or maybe simply naïve, overprivileged, pretentious, and self-righteous, the noisy nonconforming sixties generation constituted a tremendous change from the silent conformity of the fifties generation. Falafel, cheese fondue, and flower power were in. The stink of the Depression that had affected their parents was gone. Food and accommodation were taken for granted, and life was there to be "experienced." Rejecting Detroit's implied status ladder, the Volkswagen Beetle made its debut, appealing to youth in pursuit of a carefree lifestyle. Starting in the sixties, lifestyle became a key determinant of choice.[28]

The 1973 energy crisis gave a boost to the energy-efficient Japanese car. Their critical dependence on imported fuel forced the Japanese to produce cars offering 30 miles to the gallon, versus 10 miles to the gallon for American cars.[29] In the 1960s, an American car running four miles a gallon was a nonissue, whereas in Japan, the price of fuel did not allow for such luxury.

The superior steel-belted radial tires adopted in Europe in 1946 were not adopted in United States until the late 1970s. American companies were slow to introduce such features as disc brakes or fuel-injection technology.[30] While the Japanese and German car companies were busy working on reliability and quality, the American companies were busy making gadgets even as market demands were changing. John DeLorean, an ex-GM executive, worried "that there hadn't been an important product innovation in the industry since the automatic transmission and power steering [in] 1949. Year in and year out, we were urging Americans to sell their cars and buy new ones because the style had changed."[31]

American auto manufacturers kept operating under the old market assumptions that meeting a predetermined socioeconomic style and offering gadgets were sufficient to entice buyers. These outdated assumptions were costing American auto manufacturers tremendous losses in market share. The combined Japanese and German portion of the U.S. auto market rose from near 0 percent in the early 1960s to almost 38 percent in 1986.[32] In terms of worldwide motor vehicle production the U.S. market share fell from 52 percent in 1960 to 13.8 percent in 1989.[33] Not until the late 1980s was the American mode of production realigned with the new business reality to save the ever-eroding market share. By 1996, the U.S. producers' share of the world market for motor vehicle production had risen to 22.7 percent.[34] The American car producers' comeback in the 1990s indicates the caliber of their vitality and ingenuity once they realigned their assumptions with market demand and business reality.

Old Assumptions vs. Production Reality

James Flinks, in his book *The Automobile Age,* claimed that work rules in American automobile plants limit the tasks that a given worker can perform. In contrast with the usual 400 to 500 work rules in American automobile factories, Japanese plants have only 4 or 5 work rules.[35] Japanese workers are free to perform a wide variety of tasks, and that results in greater labor productivity. Detailed work rules and job classifications hampered the U.S. teams' work and flexibility in production.[36]

In 1980, workers in the United States produced approximately one car for every two or three cars produced by the same number of workers in Japan.[37] A 1982 study by the National Academy of

Engineering and the National Research Council reported that the productivity gap was due not so much to automation as to management practices.[38] With the introduction of new management practices, the gap in productivity between the United States and Japan, as measured by the number of hours per vehicle taken to produce one vehicle, has been getting smaller. Now, although the Japanese facilities are still more efficient, approximately one American car is produced for every one and one-half Japanese cars.[39]

Many other comparisons have shown tremendous productivity loss caused by the rigidity of rules and regulations. Initially, division of labor brought specialization and gains in productivity. To ensure compliance, the system became regulated and subsystems were formed for monitoring. Although this provides consistency, problems arise when the system feeds other systems that feed other systems that in time only serve to fuel exponential growth of systems. Further divisions create further specialization that has nothing to do with the end product. Bureaucracy, with its system of rules, specializations, and measurable outcomes based on procedures, alleviates fears created by the unknown, but it may have little to do with the production of value.

As some executives have complained, the "finicky customer" may be difficult to understand. But the certainty provided by procedural outcome has nothing to do with customer service. The road to success starts with the customer's willingness to buy your goods. Clearly, rules and regulations are required—just as a driver needs dashboard instruments to show the amount of gasoline left or if brake fluid is low. The instruments become a problem, though, when the bulk of the driver's time is not spent looking at the road.

The Psychology of Bureaucracy: Fallacies in the Mechanical View

Bureaucratic behaviors that evolve into dogma hold people prisoner. They shut down development. If people start to think of assumptions as facts, they cannot challenge existing problems or find effective alternatives. However, bureaucratic behavior is not limited to corporate rules and procedures. In many small businesses, a forceful management style creates the same environment produced by rules and procedures. Once you believe you have the answer—and you believe it is the *only* answer—critical and creative thinking disappears and you close yourself off from alternatives.[40]

In balance, there is virtue in those values of scientific thought. However, pushed to their extreme, they deny a part of the Self. The concept of achievement applied to all facets of life demands tangible, observable, and measurable outcomes, but taken to the extreme it denies intuition, creativity, and imagination. Later I will look at individualism and its implications in more detail as I demonstrate how the individual "hero king," seeking distinctiveness solely through confrontation, lacks empathy, flexibility, and emotional perspective. In the extreme, the mechanical order disconnects people from each other and, when combined with other social transformations, facilitates and amplifies the lost sense of participation.

This last idea leads into a problem many corporations are experiencing: low creativity coupled with poor critical-thinking and problem-solving skills. No wonder—our rules have shut us down. How many books and seminars and workshops are out there now, all trying to teach people how to be creative? But workshops will do little to help, once you return to a bureaucratic environment.

The Frog Assumption

Businesses, like individuals, need to be wary of taking their knowledge base for granted and short-changing development of the organization's principles, modes of operation, and ideas. The point is, personal or business assumptions can become uncritical, uncreative, habitual responses to the world. Habits are those actions that have become a reflexive and automatic response. Habits feel comfortable and are difficult to break. Similarly, an organization's principles, assumptions, and ways of doing things—if left to uncritical thinking or unimaginative responses—can become ingrained habits, difficult to break.

This kind of situation points to the fact that too often we are not even aware of our assumptions. Instead, we are oblivious to our surroundings if they change gradually or appear to evolve comfortably. Let me give an example. Biologists tell us that if a frog is put in a pan of warm water on a stove, the frog will sit there very contentedly. Even if the heat under the pan is turned on, the contented frog just sits there until it boils to death.

Many businesses are content with the way they have always done things even when the environment around them is gradually changing. Moving with change often requires radical rethinking of the way we do things; failure to rethink, or at least reevaluate, our business assumptions could result in our becoming someone's dinner instead of providing it.

Here is a sample of some dangerous business assumptions:

- Customers will buy our product because it is technically the best.
- Everyone wants our product.
- The product will sell itself.
- The competition is no match for us.
- We have no trouble attracting and retaining the best staff.
- All staff is on board.[41]

Mastery of our assumptions is about developing sensitivity to new ideas, and development is an ongoing process. We know that, more often than not, today's problems can often come from yesterday's solutions. We also are aware of the value of direct experience as a most valuable source of learning and setting new directions. But that's not the whole story. Development is a process that requires you to self-consciously examine and reexamine your assumptions. Ideas of which you are unaware may be holding you prisoner. This is especially true if you are caught up in the whirl of changing conditions and environments.

How can we be blinded by our own unchanging assumptions? There is an ancient story of three blind men, each touching a different part of an elephant. The man who touches the ear says the elephant is rough to touch but very supple. The man who touches the leg says the elephant is sturdy and solid like a pillar. The man who touches the trunk says the elephant is flexible and strong. The lesson from this story is that limited experience, like touching only part of the elephant, provides only a limited picture. The important thing is to be aware of our assumptions, not take them for granted, and to be willing to change or even abandon them as we grow with our business. Accept change as a challenge, not a death sentence. Remember, a bend in the road is not the end of the road, unless you fail to make the turn.

Conclusion

In the history of mankind, major shifts have brought about different ways of *being* and *doing*. One such major shift took place when people went from hunting and gathering societies to organized agricultural societies and formed nations. With the advent of city-states, innovations like pottery, the smelting of tools, and the domestication and usage of animal power improved the means of production. Organic and natural myths from the hunting and gathering societies based on being in the natural environment were transformed to reflect the new statehood environment that comprised large society, manmade institutions, and nature: the new belief dealt with proper civic order and one's relationship to statehood. Another major shift came with the rise of science and industrialization that allowed us to be disassociated from nature while still part of a society. In a number of Western countries, the new belief was transformed to define the relationship between statehood and the individual and the individual's civic right to live as one chooses. With industrialization, machine power replaced animal power. Physical work was still important but the age-old craftsman replaced his mastery of tools with the mastery of machines to suit the assembly lines of mass production.

Historians will be the judge, but it appears that we are now undergoing another transition—a transition to mastery of work that, for the first time, places a premium on mental rather than physical work. This new environment requires a different management approach because we are no longer managing tools. We are managing human development. This is not just a way of *doing business*, it is a way of *being in business*.

5

The Collective "We" in Japan

Collectivism is to Japan what individualism is to America. These differences in cultural values shape the way people within each society think and act. From the planting society came harmony, collectivism, and integration. The Japanese put a high value on qualities such as conciliation, accord, accommodation, moderation, conformity, softness, and order.[1] From the hunting society came individualism, distinctiveness, and separateness. North Americans put a high value on qualities such as achievement, activity, progress, efficiency, and practicality.

Culture acts like an invisible hand that provides order, direction, and guidance in our everyday lives.[2] In most day-to-day situations, cultural assumptions allow us to operate with proficiency. There are, however, many circumstances where we need to question our assumptions because they can become a liability, especially when we interact with different cultures. Even within our own cultural environments, our assumptions can confine us to a restricted range of behavior and understanding. This is especially true with changing circumstances and the evolution of different attitudes. Assumptions that limit our understanding and accentuate only certain aspects of our being prevent us from achieving our full potential. When we take certain values for granted, they detract from our other needs. For example, in the West, individualism means it is acceptable to make unilateral decisions; pushed to its extreme, however, individualism detracts from the advantages we can gain from participation and integration. Comparison helps us put in perspective our own value system, that invisible hand that provides order and direction. But before we make a comparison, we need to examine some elements of the Japanese value system.

Culture, with its greater emphasis on certain values, shapes executive roles. For example, making decisions and coordinating are two equally important functions that must be undertaken in any corporation. How we do this reflects what we value. In corporate North America, being an executive is synonymous with taking action and making decisions. In corporate Japan, as one rises to the executive level, executive responsibilities become those of maintaining harmonious coordination within the company and good relationships outside the company.[3]

Before I discuss the differences between Japanese and North American cultures, let me say there is an overwhelming number of similarities between nations.[4] Raising children, laughing with friends, and discussing business issues are common to all people. Culture shapes the human values and behavior preferred by a given society. The full range of values and behavior exists within all societies, and in part that is why we as Westerners can understand the value in harmony. Societies differ because each one puts more emphasis on certain values and behaviors than others.

Assumptions that shape our cultural values are not always easy to discern, but examining them is a worthwhile endeavor. By making comparisons with other cultures such as Japan, North Americans can put into perspective and understand some of our basic assumptions and make visible that invisible hand. Not developing this perspective can be costly. Before discussing Japanese values and making a comparison between Japanese and North American cultures, let's look at the cost of assumptions within the business context.

Cultural Assumptions and What They Cost

For most Americans, getting down to business and putting forward an offer represents an honest way of opening a discussion. But in some cross-cultural situations, this straightforwardness receives the cold shoulder and loses the cooperation needed for a strong business relationship. The North American way of pushing a proposal forward is often perceived in Eastern cultures as aggressive and overconfident.[5] In those cultures, calling someone by his or her first name, being informal, or making a proposal before proper introductions have been made can be perceived as arrogant and insensitive. Cultural blindness translates into lost business in the billions of dollars, simply because we fail to question our cultural assumptions and actions.

In America, cultural differences are often treated as irrelevant. According to Bonvillian and Nowlin, from 20 to 50 percent of American managers sent abroad by their companies return before completing their assignments. When this happens, the cost to the corporation ranges from $55,000 to $150,000 per manager.[6] According to a 1990 study, this returning manager failure rate costs corporate America billions of dollars each year.[7] Although many factors in these failures could be listed, frustration caused by managers not adequately understanding their host culture tops the list. Few corporations offer their managers cross-cultural training, workshops, or seminars.[8]

> *If you think education is expensive, try ignorance.*
> —Derek Bok, President, Harvard University

The high cost of managers not completing their overseas assignments is relatively easy to measure. This cost, however, is very small when compared to the number of foreign contracts lost because negotiations have failed due to cultural blindness and insensitivity. Failure to recognize and work with our own cultural assumptions and those of others may have cost corporate America billions and billions of dollars in lost foreign contracts.

Let me emphasize that losses stemming from incorrect assumptions or cultural blindness are not limited just to foreign business. Within a society, erroneous cultural assumptions also are responsible for losses in domestic productivity and are an important factor contributing to strained personal relationships. When you are abroad, your own assumptions become more obvious and you usually are aware of their cost when something goes awry. But within your own country, your assumptions may be specific to your subculture, and they are not so obvious. In your home culture, mistakes also may be very costly. For example, in an American corporation, the heroic, individualistic manager who takes total control of a situation and saves the day may feel good about himself as his culture has taught him to do, but his actions do very little to motivate frontline workers or foster teamwork and group participation. Many managers praise teamwork—but only if everything that is decided or done is what they want. Thus, the manager who fails to examine his or her cultural and subcultural assumptions may cost a company thousands or even millions of dollars in lost productivity.

The set of values we are raised with predisposes us to see things in certain ways, and this predisposition can be influential throughout our lives. As you read this chapter, try to be aware of your own values; then set them aside as much as is possible and get ready to learn about the fundamental assumptions of another culture. For the moment, as any good chef would recommend, let's take a bite of bread and clear the cultural palate as much as possible before sampling a different culture. I will begin with a brief tour of Japanese political history and then look at the Japanese culture and the concept of oneness.

A Brief Sketch of Japanese History

The first settlers who established the indigenous agrarian culture of Japan are said to have come from Central Asia. According to legend, the sun goddess Amaterasu sent her grandchild, Ningi, to rule earth.

One of Ningi's descendants, Jimmu Tenno, became the first emperor of Japan in 660 B.C.[9]

It was during the powerful Yamato kingdom that the emperor's claim to the throne was established for all time. (Later, Confucianism and Buddhism were introduced to Japan.) After 14 mythical predecessors and 110 human predecessors, the Japanese emperor is descended from an unbroken, deified lineage that still rules the imperial house today.[10] There has never been a revolt against the imperial house, in part because it serves as both a political and a religious authority that "reigns but does not govern."

From the earliest beginnings, the emperor's authority has been limited by powerful families, advisers, and bureaucracies. Between 837 and 1160 A.D., the Fujiwara family ruled Japan by controlling the emperor. A group of rural warriors called samurai, who felt they were not given enough power, then seized control of the government.

Kamakura Shogunate (1192–1333)

Minamoto Yoritomo established a military government at Kamakura. He took the title of shogun (meaning general or ruler) and assumed the privilege of giving it to his son. Without an army, the emperors became helpless. For the next seven centuries, until 1868, Japan was to be ruled by the shogunate. During the Kamakura period, European-style feudalism spread across the land. In the thirteenth century, the Mongols twice invaded Japan. On their third attempt, the Mongols were struck by a typhoon and were defeated by the skilled samurai. The Mongols lost all hopes of conquest. The Japanese called the typhoon winds *Kamikaze,* the winds of the gods. However, the Kamakura Shogunate was weakened by the Mongol invasion, leaving powerful warlords fighting each other.

Ashikaga Shogunate (1338–1567)

For the next two and half centuries, feudalism steadily extended across Japan. During the Ashikaga period, continuous warfare took place between powerful military lords called *daimyo.* The fighting reached its climax in the sixteenth century, and after many takeovers, the victorious house of Tokugawa founded the third and last military shogunate in Japan.

Tokugawa Shogunate of the Edo Period (1603–1868)

In the Tokugawa period, a new, centralized, and stratified feudal system provided military peace for 250 years. In order to protect themselves, the Tokugawa Shogunate introduced a policy of national isolation that kept out foreigners as well as new ideas that were considered a threat to the established order.

The feudalistic alliance of the Tokugawa period had four fixed classes of citizens: the samurai, the peasant, the artisan, and at the lower level of the social echelon, the merchant. There was very little mobility between classes and, consistent with the Confucian tradition, each class was assumed to provide a different but necessary function for society. Duty to the lord, the *daimyo,* was absolute and unconditional. Loyalty, inextricably bound with honor, self-sacrifice, and courage, occupied a central position in the culture.

The samurai held the dominant position in society and were expected to display the highest of human virtues: dedication to duty, to public interest, and to the state. During this period Yamamoto Tsunetomo, a Zen monk, lamented the bygone era of the true samurai and decried the lax attitude of the young and amiable samurai who sought to satisfy only their self-interests.[11] Yamamoto's book, *The Hagakure: A Code to the Way of the Samurai,* explained the philosophy of *Hagakure:* "when a samurai is confronted with two alternatives, life and death, one is to choose death without hesitation."[12] The code directed the samurai to disinterest himself in self-love, petty intellect, and self-interest in order to strive for his cause. Zen Buddhism taught the samurai to put aside temporal desire.

This was consistent with the *bushido* ethics, or "the way of the worrier," that fostered the willingness to fight to the death or to execute oneself for one's lord. The samurai had to "think of his lord with life and soul . . . with unflinching devotion" to defend his lord, be loyal and sincere, and have the courage to protect the honor of the fiefdom. Fundamentally, a good samurai was "to act in an inconspicuous way, think of one's lord in earnest, and be fond of one's service."[13] Ideally, the samurai was "a reverential man, stern and quiet," with self-composure and a firm mind.[14] In contrast, the merchants were perceived as greedy, with concerns only for private gain; they were regarded as intermediaries between artisans and distant consumers.

During the peaceful Tokugawa period, cities grew, trade increased, art flourished, and merchants amassed wealth. The merchant class ventured into a greater variety of economic activities as consumerism rose. With the increased use of money over the traditional barter system, prices fluctuated and rose. While the cost of goods went up, revenue for the samurai, a public servant, remained the same, putting him at an economic disadvantage. Many samurai saw the wealthy merchants as the ones responsible for stimulating consumerism, creating monopolistic conditions, and causing prices to rise. The urbanized merchants were perceived as acting for selfish interests in order to make huge profits.

Some predicted dire consequences if such an attitude spread to the samurai class. An adviser to Shogun Yoshimunu warned that the civil administration, occupied mainly by samurai, was being corrupted as some samurai began to value comfort more than duty. Private interest over public devotion was considered trivial, shameful, and incompatible with samurai duty.[15] But commercial activity persisted, and as the years passed, the samurai saw their position worsen. To add to the strain, in the mid-nineteenth century, foreign pressure was pushing Japan to break its policy of national isolationism and to open up to foreigners. Friction grew in the society, and the discontented samurai plotted against and overthrew the shogun. The last shogunate came to an end.

Meiji (1868 to present)

In 1868, under the Meiji restoration, the prototype of Japan's modern government was established to better handle foreign affairs. In 1889, the Meiji oligarchy instituted a constitution. Although the Meiji restoration altered the old political and social structure, fundamental traditional attitudes changed very little. While the new system gave ministers greater individual accountability, it only took a few years to see the prime minister's power reduced in the name of political equilibrium. The samurai who occupied many of the political and bureaucratic positions retained key posts in the government, unwilling to share power with the merchants, for whom they had little respect. Also during the early Meiji period, many descendants of the samurai class entered corporations, replacing the entrepreneurial class. It was only a matter of time before samurai values emphasizing loyalty, self-sacrifice, and duty infiltrated the corporate world.

Samurai Enter the Corporation

Early in the twentieth century, the profit-oriented, entrepreneurial merchant class was replaced by the samurai class. The samurai class gave business a military tone. From the sword to the pen, from the battlefield to the boardroom, the introduction of the military model to the corporate world came from businessmen who were descended from Tokugawa samurai. The new samurai ethic rejected the formerly negative image of the Tokugawa merchants as a class of ignorant, vulgar, grasping, and immoral citizens whose individual pursuits had been considered egotistical and their profits odious.[16] Although our Western tradition readily accepted individual pursuits and profit, the Japanese maintained their fundamental values of group solidarity to a master and the samurai virtues of dedication, loyalty, purity of spirit, and readiness for self-sacrifice. The idea of reciprocal obligation to one clan was deeply embedded in the Japanese feudal tradition.[17] Thus, a Japanese corporation's primary consideration became to fulfil its overall obligation and social responsibility to the nation and to its employees.

Japanese tend to think of the company as one big family. The Tokyo Chamber of Commerce describes human relations within corporations this way:

> In our country, relations between employees are just like those within a family. The young and the old help one

another and consult together in both good times and bad,
and they are enveloped in a mist of affectionate feeling.[18]

There is nothing feudalistic about Japanese corporate life. They recognize the need for profit to ensure an organization's survival. The difference is that corporations talk about profit potential in two significant ways: (1) as a way of maintaining permanent employment, and (2) as a means of fulfilling a company's duties as a responsible corporate citizen of Japan.[19] Business priorities in Japan put the accent on both the need for growth and market share because, according to Wolferen, this is a "nobler pursuit" than profit alone. To illustrate the point, we know that Japanese stockholders view their holdings more as savings plans, whereas North American stockholders view their holdings as ownership.[20]

Oneness in Japan

The concept of oneness is to the Eastern mind what duality is to the Western mind. Duality is expressed in many variations in the West, and likewise, there are great variations in the adaptation of the concept of oneness in the Eastern world. In Japan, the concept of oneness means an integrated approach. Because of the high emphasis on oneness, the Japanese place high value on: (1) *collectivism,* or the *we* of the group, (2) *reciprocal obligation* based on personal relationship, and (3) *harmony* with a demand for cohesiveness. Although I discuss each of those values separately, all are strongly interrelated.

Collectivism

From the hunting society, where risk-taking was important, came individualism, distinctiveness, and separateness. In individualistic countries, people relate to the "I" and are expected to act as individuals. From the planting society, where collaboration was important, came collectivism, unity, and integration. In collectivist countries, people relate to the "We" and are expected to act as part of a group. In the West, there is an expression that says "the squeaky wheel gets the grease." In Japan, there is an expression that says "The nail that protrudes will be hammered in." While individual impulses are to be subdued in Japan, they receive our attention in the West. In the West the center of responsibility is the individual, while in Japan, the center of responsibility is the group. In brief, while the West pays attention to the individual, the East pays attention to the relationship between individuals.

Shintoism, Buddhism, and Confucianism are the three major spiritual systems that have influenced Japan. The introduction of Confucianism in the fifth century and Buddhism in the sixth century influenced Japanese thinking, and in turn, both were shaped by established Shinto traditions and political reality. Although these spiritual systems differ, they share the concept that the individual is not at the center of human endeavors, but rather, individuals are part of the greater whole. Shintoism espouses that the spirit resides in everything, not only humans and their ancestors, but rocks, trees, and water. As such, Shintoism affords no particular status to people because we all share the same essence. Buddhist philosophy further advances the notion that the individual does not exist as a separate identity by conceptualizing the nonexistence of "I" or self.[21] In Confucianism, a person is perceived as an individual enmeshed in a web of social relationships motivated by duties toward others. The person is not perceived as a self-sufficient individual but as a member of society who has social obligations within that society. The essential thought in Confucianism is the imperative of social obligation based on proper social relationships among people. In combination, the three different philosophical systems provide strong justification for the importance of the group in defining one's identity.

> *By nature men are nearly alike. By practice they get to be wide apart.*
> —Confucius

Selecting for a Fit. In the business context, great care is taken to select those individuals suitable to the corporate culture. In Japan, the white-collar employee (known as the *sarariiman,* literally, "the salary man") has attended the proper schools and proved himself to be a proper fit with company principles and colleagues. When selecting new employees, employers take utmost care to weed out those who may be considered to have bad personal habits. Being individualistic, opinionated, aggressive, or nonconformist is frowned upon.[22] Investigating agencies, called *koshin jo,* specialize in checking individual backgrounds of prospective employees. Not only former employers, but teachers and neighbors can be interviewed for their assessment. When a recruit is hired, a mentor is also selected to monitor the new employee.[23] Great effort and many resources are devoted to ensure the newcomer receives proper training and experience. Fitting in with the group is very important, for the group represents one's identity. Total loyalty is expected before one becomes part of the corporate family.

Group Consensus in Decision Making. Despite the apparent vertical structure in Japanese corporations, decisions are made by the group. While there are differences of opinion among individuals in a corporation, the Japanese are adept at attuning their personal convictions to the ideology of the group. Elaborate systems have evolved to include everyone in decision-making whenever possible. The *nemawashi* and the *ringi* systems, which submit and circulate a plan to all members for review, ensure everyone's input.[24] Kindness requires that differences of opinion be open to other perspectives. Strong group loyalty and cohesiveness also put pressure on members to conform to and align with the group. Such a decision-making process requires much discussion, consultation, submission, and resubmission to reach a consensus. By Western standards, decisions come slowly. The advantage of this process is that, upon reaching consensus, all members give their full support to the decision. Failure to support it would mean a loss of face for the dissenter. In America, it is common for executives—if they enter the consulting process at all—to refer to only a few members in the organization before making a decision. That means decisions and proposals are made quickly. Resistance to the decision by those excluded from the consultative process means that implementation of a proposal can be slower.

North Americans should not underestimate the importance of group cohesiveness. If an American is unhappy with a decision, he or she thinks nothing of asking a person with higher authority to overrule it. Not so with the Japanese. Working as a group, the Japanese are very sensitive to ensure that nobody loses face. A reversal of the decision by the boss would bring a loss of face, and if one member loses face, every member of the group is implicated. Decisions are reversed, but caution is exercised and time is taken to involve all members, including those who made the initial decision. The threat of losing face, combined with the lengthy and inclusive nature of all decision-making, ensures and maintains group solidarity.

Fitting In. In Japan, as in many Asian countries where group cohesiveness and identity are very important, a rich repertoire of behavior has been developed to help prevent the individual from losing face and suffering public embarrassment. Eastern cultures have developed elaborate cultural cues and responses that allow everyone to integrate with the group. For example, the Japanese use a more passive language to submit their ideas. Suggestions, open-ended questions, and generalized phrases allow the speaker to sense the mood of the listener, understand the situation, discern other positions, and adjust accordingly. Publicly challenging, disparaging people, or putting others on the spot is considered rude and vulgar; embarrassment can destroy good relationships and jeopardize cohesiveness and group self-identity. To avoid ostracizing the individual from the group, all efforts to maintain harmonious and good relationships are justified. When differences of opinion arise, confrontational situations or conflicts are discussed in confidence to allow the individual the chance to realign with the group.[25]

Group identity and group harmony are easier to maintain when one's role, relationship to the group, and sense of obligation are properly understood. Historically, the Japanese have experienced and accepted vertically structured relationships within the family, among neighbors or the clan, and in sociopolitical structures. Age, rank, and seniority are respected and recognized through the proper use of language and behavior. This courtesy extends between subordinate and boss and, depending on their age or gender, among colleagues. The Japanese take their roles seriously and trust that others will do the same; breach of trust disrupts group cohesiveness.

Different roles also imply different obligations. Reciprocal obligations between employee and company, between superior and subordinate, and between different functions are based on personal obligation, and these, to the Western mind, seem to override cold, hard logic.

When doing business in Japan, don't underestimate how important it is for the group to champion a common front. Be sensitive to where and when to discuss certain issues. The Japanese, like the Americans, have the same interest in resolving conflicts, but they do it in a different way. Remember that, in their culture, conflicts are discussed privately where differences can be resolved. This allows everyone to have a say yet maintain the integrity of the group. If you open what you believe to be an honest discussion without the proper protocol, your arguments will be shrugged off and you will simply lose their business.

Reciprocal Obligation

The feudalistic structural system combined with the Confucian ethical code evolved into a strong tradition of reciprocal obligation. The samurai concept of incurring obligation is called *on;* the expectation of performing one's duties over and above one's personal needs is called *gimi.*[26] Neither is questioned.

Though the Japanese might not use this same analogy, today's Japanese management style can be described as paternalistic, and managers may be semitotalitarian or even severely totalitarian, with the top executive resembling a modern feudal lord, with all the traditional and prerogative entitlements.[27] Corporate training emphasizes dedication, perseverance, self-sacrifice, and the ability to endure hardship.[28] Obligation in Japan, however, is a two-way street. Trust is based on the mutual expectation that both parties will fulfill their obligations. Reciprocal obligation is carried by all members of the group, from the boss to the subordinates and vice versa.

Management expects devotion, loyalty, and commitment from employees. In return, management is expected to show benevolence toward employees. For example, mutual obligation requires that management will do everything to retain an employee even in severe economic conditions. Most North American managers do not take lightly the process of trimming the organization by firing employees, but they emphasize different principles in employer-employee relationships. In corporate America, the high value attached to self-sufficiency, economic logic, and measurable efficiency makes it easier to justify letting people go. In Japan, these principles would be foreign because firing a person is like letting someone from the family go; in North America, the benevolence factor is missing. In brief, while the West negotiates a contract, the East negotiates a relationship.

Reciprocity in Japan extends beyond obligation within the company. Most Americans would consider it a breach of etiquette (or in some cases, a breach of law) for a supervisor to ask about personal affairs or health concerns. In Japan, employees expect a good supervisor to ask about their welfare. The paternalistic approach also implies that employees accept advice on their affairs. Like North Americans, many Japanese meet potential marriage partners through friends, but up to 20 percent of all marriages in Japan are engineered through a *nakodo,* either the man's or the woman's work supervisor who acts as a go-between. The *nakodo's* function is to arrange for a suitable meeting place, provide a proper introduction, and then leave the couple on their own.[29] Known as *omiai,* these meetings arranged by work supervisors likely seem strange to North Americans, who prefer to separate work from their personal lives, but they provide Japanese workers with one of many ways to meet marriage partners.

Loyalty. Japanese companies are run and thought of as a big family where filial piety, respect, and loyalty bind workers. Members of a company are bound by a complex web of obligations toward others. Each member is expected to be selfless, put aside individual impulses, and act as a unit for the mutual benefit of the company. In North America, it is common to find companies run by individuals with distinctive personalities who are revered for their opinions. In Japan, men and women in high positions are expected to maintain unassuming public postures, present themselves as humble, and belittle their achievements.[30] Their primary responsibility is to watch over harmony within the company and maintain personal contact with government, clients, and other companies.[31]

Harmony

In all societies, there are times of conflict between the individual and the group. In such situations, many North Americans would let it be known they are in disagreement and would act according to their personal beliefs. Paul Anka's song "My Way" and American films that romanticize the individual pay tribute to the concept of the person who, having done things his or her own way, becomes the hero: demon-slayer and truth-seeker all in one. In Japan, harmonious relations are considered fundamental and paramount to the foundation of their society. That does not mean that the Japanese like their neighbors more than Americans do or have fewer conflicts with their bosses than Americans experience. But because the Japanese concept of harmony demands cohesiveness and an alignment with the whole, a breach of etiquette or acting against the group expectation is usually considered pompous, arrogant, and disloyal.

Independence vs. Interdependence in Conflict Resolution. Recall how the hunting society favored individualism, a confrontational approach, and distinguishing self from others to produce an independent manner where one stands apart from the group. The planting society, on the other hand, favored a collective focus, a participatory approach, and cooperation with emphasis on integration, affinity, and harmony. This resulted in an interdependent approach where one stands with the group. The cultural implications for hunting societies versus planting societies are clear. Western independence places emphasis on "either/or" perspectives that favor distinct and exclusive categories, while Eastern interdependence favors a "what if" perspective that embraces integration and inclusiveness.

Consequently, Westerners, with their independent value system, prefer a more direct, confrontational approach to conflict where communication is explicit and peripheral to the mood.[32] In a business context, the independent worker can be described as exclusive, competitive, and moving according to a plan. Being aggressive is about taking charge.

By contrast, the Easterner's interdependent value system exemplified by the Japanese prefers a more indirect, nonconfrontational approach to conflict where communication is implicit and sensing or intuiting the atmosphere is important.[33] Interdependence in a business context usually means people behave in an inclusive manner, showing concern for relationships, and moving in accordance with mood. Being passive is about being in touch with your surroundings. In brief, the West talks, while the East listens.

To the Japanese, it is important to retain the appearance of harmony within their group when dealing with outsiders. In public, avoiding conflict to maintain harmony within the group takes priority over resolving conflict. Conflicts or differences of opinion in the group are discussed in private, unlike the public or open group discussions practiced in the North American method of resolving conflicts. As an analogy, negotiation with a Japanese business person is like the courtship between a prospective bride and groom in Japan, where each tries to come to know the other through soft and humble questions. This does not mean these people do not have a position. Japanese are quick to recognize who stands at an advantage or disadvantage and to act accordingly; however, their approach differs from that of the North American who regards negotiating more as a poker game with immediate offers and counteroffers put on the table.[34]

In North America, getting the contract justifies the means. Differences of opinion between people and strained relationships are issues to be addressed later. Americans perceive a person whose public behavior is at odds with his private behavior as hypocritical and devious. Conversely, to the Japanese, behavior should be consistent with the situation. In public, the Japanese need to retain good relationships and avoid losing face is more important than resolving momentary conflicts.

The Japanese like to make a distinction between a public and a private reality. There are two words that reflect these two realities: *tatemae* and *honne*. *Tatemae* represents the outward appearance, the public truth, or what should be. It involves acting according to what the group expects and by what conventional etiquette prescribes. *Tatemae* is the public face a person shows to others.[35] *Honne* represents the person's genuine feelings.[36] North Americans may think of *honne* as presenting their "true" or "real" self. Though the Japanese people experience conflicts and discontent like any other people, they believe there is a proper place and time to express their real opinions.

The cultural roots for this idea are deeply ingrained in Japanese thought. Zen makes a distinction between what is illusion and what is reality; similarly, the Japanese distinguish between public decorum and indiscretion. To Americans, acting one way and believing something else can be perceived as deceitful or hypocritical. But looking at it from a Japanese perspective, deception could equally be construed as pretending there is no difference between public and private reality. Americans do recognize the need for public decorum and the need to tow the company line to create the desirable impression, so *tatemae* should not be an entirely foreign concept. In keeping with the Japanese concept of harmony in its fullest sense, *tatemae* is, however, of greater significance in Japanese culture.

Alignment. Aligning behavior with one's surroundings to preserve harmony and strengthen the group is central to the Japanese ideal of harmony, or *wa.* For the benefit of the whole group, one is expected to refrain from displaying personal feelings. Japanese people are constantly aware of others and know precisely how much elbow room they have.[37] This means they are careful not to disturb the *wa* of society, and therefore, they put high values on human qualities such as accommodation, accord, conformity, compromise, conciliation, courtesy, moderation, order, softness, and unity.[38]

In Chapter 10, I discuss the three main components of emotional competence. Briefly, emotional competence requires:

1. The ability to comprehend your own feelings
2. The ability to manage your impulses accordingly
3. The ability to be aware of and assess other people's feelings (empathy)

While the American emphasis is on being in touch with oneself, the Japanese emphasis on the *wa* greatly fosters the ability to empathize and the ability to attune oneself to one's surroundings.

Sensing the Mood. The Japanese can feel awkward with foreigners because they find it hard to read foreigners' intentions. Japanese people take great pride in their ability to sense the mood. They believe that cooperation depends on reading other people and reacting to them, and thus they put more importance on feeling or sensing the mood than on reasoning. Managing by intuition (*kongen*) means honing the ability to tap into the essence that pervades the universe and to make good use of it. The Japanese pride themselves on their ability to anticipate the needs of others.[39] An employee who cannot do this is not considered management material. Managing by intuition, instinct, or inspiration does not mean the Japanese do not use logic but that they focus on gut feelings and intuition before spreadsheet analysis.

Contrasting the advertising campaigns done in Japan with those in North America illustrates the values of *tatemae* and *wa*. In America, most ads are direct and rely on the hard sell by concentrating on the product's benefits. It is common for advertisers to demonstrate the explicit advantages of products; to emphasize tangible incentives such as price reduction, special offers, and warranties; and to compare products. In Japan, however, such an approach fails because it is perceived as discourteous, egocentric, and arrogant. In their advertising messages, the Japanese prefer context over content. Effective advertising, in their view, promotes the familiarity and trustworthiness of the producer. The product is not the centerpiece of the promotion. Instead, the emphasis is on setting. Messages often are suggestive and left incomplete; soft music and gentle voices frequently convey a sensory experience. This is the aesthetic of *suki,* the importance of content.

Moving for a moment from the advertising world to the art world, we can find another example of the *wa*. Takashima Shuji, director of the National Museum of Western Art and professor emeritus at the University of Tokyo, offers some interesting comparisons in his discussion on the aesthetic of *suki* as it applies to the arts. He notes that, according to a recent poll at the Forty-Sixth International Venice Biennial Art Exhibition, out of fifty pavilions, the Japanese pavilion received the most favorable response from visitors.[40]

The pavilion and artwork very much reflected the Japanese concept of harmony. In the aesthetics of *suki,* the Japanese like to communicate a unifying quality of taste. As Shuji explained, *suki* results above all from a desire to create a harmonious whole from various objects of beauty without destroying the individuality of each work."[41] Unlike the American and French pavilions, which were dedicated to a dominant individual artist's exhibit, or the German pavilion, which was divided into three distinct exhibition spaces to accommodate three different individual artists' works, the Japanese exhibition represented the "combined efforts of several artists who attempted to harmonize with one another even while expressing their own vision."

Octavio Paz, a Mexican poet, summarized the Japanese approach very well. "The objective," Paz stated, "was not to inhibit individual spontaneity but, on the contrary, to open up a free space in which each talent could manifest itself without doing damage to others or to itself."[42] While each artistic work was accorded its own space in the Japanese exhibition, the exhibition sight lines allowed several works to be visible at once, while partially concealing and subtly interacting with each other.

Like all art exhibits, the Japanese exhibition received praise as well as criticism, but most noticeable were the harsh comments from the distinguished Swiss curator, Harold Szeemann, who wrote that the exhibit "was not art" and that "if the exhibition does not make its point first and foremost through the works of art" it has little merit. The American critic Sam Hunter said, "Unfortunately, no synergistic effect accrues from the combined individuality of the five artists."[43] Such comments reflect a Western penchant for clear and tangible themes, and may indicate a difficulty in seeing things from a different cultural perspective.

The Cost of Oneness

To reiterate, Japanese companies are like big families in comparison to their American counterparts, and they take a paternalistic approach toward their workers. Reciprocal obligation implies mutual obligation between employer and worker. Each trusts the other to honor expected commitments. Loyalty to authority and acceptance of hierarchy is balanced with equalizing elements such as delegation to frontline and bottom-up decision making. In Japan, group commitment means that individual wages are based on group performance, not individual initiative. Rewards are given to the group in return for collective effort. Conformity to expectations reinforces harmonious relations and augments the sense of cohesion and belonging to a distinct group. But pushed to the extreme, collectivism, personal obligation, and harmony create excessive patronage, detract from system-based accountability, and stifle creativity.

Economic Success and Failure

From the 1960s to 1991, the Japanese economy grew an average of 5.0 percent annually.[44] In the eighties, the Japanese dominated the market in consumer electronics, semiconductors, and as we well know, the automobile industry. But the bubble burst in the early nineties, and with decline in the economy, many Japanese became disillusioned. Land values fell drastically and the average economic growth fell to 1.4 percent between 1992 and 1996.[45] In the last ten years, the number of psychiatric clinics offering help for the burned-out *sarariiman* has increased tenfold.

How can we account for this economic turnaround? We know that Japanese labor flexibility, the work force's commitment to hard work, and a management style favoring collective bottom-up decision making and integrated responses are largely responsible for Japan's business and economic success. Their integrated approaches give them a tremendous advantage in complex and knowledge-based industries. The Japanese gave us total quality control, lean production, and the efficiency of cross-functional product development.

Japan's high productivity in export industries such as autos, electronics, and telecommunications made it one of the top global competitors. However, we should not overlook Japan's domestic business, which accounts for approximately 80 percent of the Japanese economy.[46] Unlike their export industries, productivity within the domestic sector is low. Like a double-edged sword, the same factors responsible for their success can contribute to lower productivity. There are costs associated with the concept of oneness.

Reciprocal Obligation in Distribution

The Japanese distribution system is more like a social network than a business system.[47] The cumbersome multilayered distribution network not only makes it very difficult to sell cheaper foreign products in Japan but adds substantial costs to Japan's own manufactured products. A multidistribution system also exists in America, but the difference lies in the number of middlemen comprising the Japanese system and the fact that buying and selling along the distribution line is based on personal relations. Transactions are based on more than price considerations—they take place between buyers and sellers who have established good relations over the years. Additionally, retirement in Japan comes at the early age of 55, which means it is not uncommon for a person to serve as a middleman between, for example, one's former manufacturing firm and contacts established over years of dealing with various wholesalers and retailers. Consequently, on a per capita basis, the Japanese have twice the number of retailers and wholesalers as the Americans. Japanese customer expectations and personalized service all contribute to the costly distribution system. But in the end, the great number of layers means the retail price in Japan is three times the factory price compared to 1.7 times the factory price in the United States.[48]

The Japanese are aware of the cost burdens in their distribution system. Although some manufacturers would like to cut off some middlemen, they find themselves bound by strong personal relations and the traditional sense of reciprocal obligation that overrides the business requirements for expediency.[49] When a person thinks of the corporate group as a large family, it is not easy to disengage.

North Americans also tolerate some additional cost because of personal ties, but they are accustomed to dealing at arm's length and are more likely to point out the inefficiency of personal ties and eliminate nonproductive members from the system. For Americans, business is business, not a social obligation. For Japanese, these

seem to be cold, calculated, objective measures that should not prevail over personal ties.[50]

In-House Obligations: The Cost of Harmony and Integration

Shintaro Hori contends that white-collar inefficiency is a problem all
over the world, but particularly so for Japanese companies. Japan
pays a high price to tolerate mediocre domestic companies. Hori
argues that the added cost of poor white-collar productivity contributes significantly to this situation.[51]

By 1993, companies had taken only a piecemeal approach to
trimming their white-collar overhead costs. They were reluctant, in
part, because of cultural values that promoted reciprocal loyalty
between employer and worker. Hori contends that many white-collar
jobs are redundant. From a business perspective, the retention of
workers who provide no competitive value either in the short-term
or the long-term adds substantial cost to the Japanese consumer.[52]

The Japanese are not known to take an adversarial stand against
other groups. Their emphasis on harmony and a shared sense of purpose is reflected in their preference for conciliation over litigation or
confrontation. They believe that public bashing and litigation creates
distinct winners and losers and that the consequences of confrontation can disturb the stability offered by obligational relationships.
Being adversarial does not fit with their concept of harmony.

Typically, Japanese businesses function with integrated, semi-
autonomous and semidependent groups who share power through
cooperation. Japan is governed by this set of relationships that recognize interrelated forces without a strong center.[53] The Japanese are
not in the business of pointing out discrepancies, but rather, business
is based on finding points of commonalty. In North America, suc-
ceeding as an executive is synonymous with individual leadership
skills and autonomous decision-making. In Japan, as people rise to
the executive level, their responsibilities become those of a coordi-
nator. Executives are expected to watch over the harmony within the
company and to establish and retain good relationships outside the
company.

In Japan, it is difficult to place sole jurisdiction or accountability with one person. Accustomed to making group decisions, the Japanese executive avoids taking personal responsibility and making unilateral decisions. No single person is in charge because the Japanese prefer an approach that is inclusive and integrated. This also means that pointing the finger Western-style is difficult because of diffuse responsibility. From a Western perspective, this line of command lacks clear accountability.

The Japanese integrated approach facilitates the exchange of information that is so valuable in complex and highly knowledge-based industries. Although it is common to have a system that disciplines people, people should also have the means to discipline the system. In the Japanese political system, there is no well-founded administrative method to adjudicate conflict between different interest groups, no system to put into question institutional processes.[54] In politics and in industry, integration means that changes, even when recognized as evident, are difficult and slow. When pushed to its extreme, integration can be rigid and forbidding.

The Commercial Cost of Oneness: A Case in Point

Cross-cultural studies on American and Japanese service industries such as airlines, retailers, banks, and restaurants put the difference in the productivity gap as high as 40 percent in favor of the United States.[55] Going to the movies in Tokyo on average costs twice as much as in New York.[56] In 1992, an average 89-square-meter house in Japan cost $372,600 compared to $121,000 for an average 153-square-meter house in the United States.[57] On a per square meter basis, a house in Japan costs five times more than in the United States. It is cheaper for a Tokyo family to fly across the Pacific to Canada and travel to Banff or Whistler for a one-week ski holiday than to ski in Hokkaido, Japan.

Low productivity in domestic industries adds a tremendous cost to Japanese domestic consumer goods. To be sure, the extra cost is in part created by unique consumer tastes, demands for quality, service, currency exchanges, and safety standards. But the myriad of business regulations and the demand for integration within the Japanese context add their own costs. As in other countries, excess government controls in some sectors provide little benefit to the mainstream Japanese person. For example, government controls over farm subsidies, together with the Nokyo federation of agricultural cooperatives, means a Japanese family pays five times more for rice than a family in Singapore, where rice is imported.[58]

Economic Shift

Since the economic bubble burst, some Japanese companies have broken with tradition and have instituted elements of American-style performance management. For example, Japan Airline Company has decided to cut its number of full-time positions and take on more part-timers. This move is already creating greater wage differences between high and low performers and undermines a cherished value, seniority. Whereas individuals traditionally were paid based on the group's performance, they now are paid for individual productivity. It is too early to determine the effect of moving from evaluating group merit toward a more individualized contractual system or to know to what extent it will be applied in the future, but as Shintaro Hori states, "Success in the twenty-first century will require Japan to harness its traditional strengths in order to develop new ways to pack value into every white-collar activity just as manufacturers have found ways to make every step of the production process meaningful. This will not be a painless process, and it can be expected to take years to refine. But it is the only path that can lead to global competitiveness."[59]

Japanese people take great pride in a task well-performed. From Japanese garden displays to the tea ceremony, they practice what needs to be done until it is perfect. Proper form also demands behaving correctly rather than succumbing to individual impulses. Correcting one's imperfections, making continual improvements (kaizen), and learning from elders are all strong traditions in Japan. In such a society, conformity makes daily activity easier and more predictable. The disadvantage of conformity, however, is the loss of versatility and individual initiative. Conformity creates an environment where people are afraid to make mistakes. In keeping with *kaizen,* Japanese are great at improving existing manufacturing efficiencies, and this must be continued. But to avoid embarrassment, Japanese management takes a wait-and-see approach toward novel solutions. Conformity leads to copying new products and avoiding major breakthroughs.

Cultural Shifts in Traditional Business

The *shinjinrui* are the younger generation of Japanese workers, a new breed who, unlike the *sarariiman,* disdain blind loyalty to the company and the self-denying work ethic.[60] Referred to by some as the Nintendo Kids, the younger generation's relationship to traditional authority is changing. Computerized interactive games have given younger people the belief they can shape things according to their personal needs. Interactive games teach them that they can define, evaluate, and shape any situation for themselves.[61] When using an interactive game, young people know everything can be explored, reprogrammed, and fixed according to their personal needs. The Internet also means the younger generation can solicit alternate sources of information apart from traditional ones.

Recent surveys have found that a large number of young employees would be willing to switch to another company that offered better working conditions.[62] To these employees, a job that provides personal satisfaction is more important than a commitment to a lifetime employer. Some of these young employees even talk of going home at five o'clock in the afternoon. This represents a substantial change from the past when anyone who would change companies would have been considered a traitor.[63]

To some established corporate men, the *shinjinrui* represent a threat to the Japanese way of life because their new approach threatens the sense of belonging and working hard for the collective good. To compound establishment fears, cartoon magazines such as the popular *Shonen Jump* encourage readers not to be distracted from small pleasures by such things as family, school, or community, claiming instead that it is best to go one's own way.[64] This situation reminds me of the sixties in North America. Then, long-haired, "do-your-own-thing" flower power once represented a similar threat. Big business perceived the new generation with its freedom-loving lifestyle as unable to adapt to the corporate demand for dedicated work. Today, working longer and harder hours than their predecessors, these corporate hippies talk about the need for team effort and networking.[65]

Shonen Jump respects many of the traditional Japanese values, and to be sure, the Nintendo kids retain many of the thoughtful courtesies so particular to group harmony.[66] According to Eto Shinkichi, respecting collectivism, recognizing hierarchy, and following the bottom-up method of decision-making are still part of Japanese life.[67] But according to Tsushima Michihito, so is the development of a greater sense of autonomy, self-discovery, and self-fulfillment.[68] The new generation of young Japanese seems to have retained the majority of its core values and to be only adding a slight variation to their repertoire of traditional values. The higher degree of individualization, although disconcerting to many elders, may well ease new demands for functional distinction brought on by changes in globalization, social complexity, and economic conditions. While the new generation seek a higher degree of autonomy, they also maintain their ability to work as a group, their values based on harmony, and their strong sense of obligation. With this perspective, they are likely to represent a formidable competitive force in the marketplace. Japan must not adopt the "either/or" from the West, but rather retain the "what/if" concept while integrating the advantages offered from both the notions of duality and oneness.

6

Western Me,
Eastern We

Chapter 5 provided a brief summary of the formation of the Japanese character. In this chapter I will continue that discussion by comparing Japanese and North American cultural foundations and discussing the implications of these fundamental ideologies as they apply in today's business environment. Briefly, we will review some key differences between these two cultures to illustrate Eastern and Western principles.

Individualism and distinction are to North America what collectivism and harmony are to Japan. From the ancient hunting society came *duality,* which in the West finds expression in distinguishing yourself from others, heroism, and being different. This finds expression in an independent and confrontational approach where you can stand apart. From the planting society came *oneness,* which in the Far East puts emphasis on integration, affinity, and being in accord with your surroundings. Being in accord with your surroundings finds expression in an interdependent and cooperative approach where one is allied with the group.

Contrasting Western independence and Eastern interdependence, we have seen how the West puts emphasis on an "either/or" perspective that favors distinct and exclusive categories, while the East embraces a "what if" approach that emphasizes integration and inclusiveness. Where North Americans will put a high value on individualism, independence, self-direction, and economic efficiency, the Japanese concept of wa (harmony) means that they put a high value on human qualities such as accommodation, accord, conformity, compromise, conciliation, courtesy, moderation, order, and softness.[1] It bestows a high value on collectivism, interdependence, self-restraint, solidarity, and loyalty.

In a business context, the independent approach champions a working environment that is exclusive, where people are competitive, and seek to take charge. Taking charge means knowing what you want and moving with a plan. The result is a direct, aggressive, and confrontational style. Communication in meetings is explicit, puts focus on the content, and is peripheral to the setting. Business is done at arm's length with distinct responsibility defined for each individual. Defending one's self interest is acceptable.

By contrast, interdependence in a business context characterizes the working environment as inclusive, where people show concern for relationships and value being passive. Being passive means being in touch with your surroundings and moving with the situation. This approach results in an indirect, passive, and nonconfrontational style. Communication in meetings is implicit, puts focus on the context, and value is placed on sensing the atmosphere. Business is based on personal relationships with responsibilities shared among those within the group. One's action is governed by aligning one's interest with the collective interest.

Business Goals and Their Relation to Values

Like other social institutions, business survives if it contributes to the society's needs. The general purpose for business is converting resources into a desired output. One would expect business objectives and modes of operation to be based on business logic, which theoretically should be the same everywhere. But we know that this is not the case. Business and management principles are largely influenced by cultural values. For example, a common business objective is maximizing the return on investment. In North America that translates to maximizing profits, while in Japan it translates to maximizing market share. Therefore, opening a business negotiation by presenting facts and figures showing how to maximize profit may be accepted practice in North American boardrooms, but it may not be the best way to start a business discussion in Japan.

The concepts of private ownership, profit, and market share, acceptable business objectives in both Japan and North America, are valued for different reasons in each culture. First, I will examine how European ideologies developed during the industrial age and were adopted in America. Then I will show how these ideas differ from the Samurai ideologies that evolved in Japan. That is, by comparing business objectives in these cultures, I will illustrate the strength of each ideology and its effect on business practice.

Western Industrial Ideology vs. Tokugawa Samurai Ideology

Progressive humanism is a highly valued concept in America. With advancements in science and technology came the notion that, through understanding, you could control change and make things better. The pursuit of profit is consistent with the fundamental values of political freedom, individual interest, and private gain. The justification for the pursuit of individual self-interest is grounded in the philosophy of seventeenth- and eighteenth-century thinkers such as John Locke (1632–1704), David Ricardo (1772–1823), Adam Smith (1723–90), and Herbert Spencer (1820–1903). Smith, a British economist and moral philosopher, claimed in his influential work *The Wealth of Nations* that self-seeking men, when "led by an invisible hand . . . without knowing it, without intending it, advance the interest of the society." Individuals, he said, in the pursuit of self-interest, will do what is good for others in order to maximize their personal gain. In that sense profit and private ownership were not only justified but desirable because they also served society's interests.

These ideas gained greater emphasis in America than in Europe, because in part many North Americans sought to escape established European institutions. Change came to be seen not only as possible but as desirable, and social progress became synonymous with material progress. Taking charge and achieving visible and measurable goals has become, for most North Americans, the primary source of an individual's self-identity, and many have come to relate their identity primarily to the work they do. The market, after all, provides a fair playing ground for the private entrepreneur to compete based on individual ability.

By contrast, Japanese history gave rise to a different sense of the individual. Samurai ethics, you will recall, rejected the unfavorable image of the Tokugawa merchants whose individualistic pursuits and profit seeking activities were considered egotistical. Moreover, generating profits was inconsistent with the samurai virtues of dedication and readiness for sacrifice. Today, the big Japanese corporations tend to think of the company as one big family. While recognizing the need for profit as a means to ensure an organization's survival, they also regard profit as a means to maintain permanent employment and to fulfill their obligations as responsible corporate citizens. Business priorities in Japan emphasize the need for growth, for maintaining position within the hierarchy, and for increasing market share. In 1988, a survey indicated that 87 percent of management in Japanese companies favored aggressive growth and market dominance as their top goals compared to 20 percent in the United States.[2]

Logically, one can justify both goals—maximizing profit or maximizing market share. Profit ensures the resources for an organization to survive, while maximum market share provides product exposure and recognition required for sales. Though business requires both profit and market share, the justification for the actions taken to reach these goals is shaped by cultural value systems.

Business Operations and Their Relation to Values

Although practice within a culture can be different from cultural ideals, a culture's ideologies provide the overall direction for action. Just as there are Japanese who are motivated by profit alone, there are many Americans who are motivated by factors other than profit.

Although the Japanese are known for their collective approach, there are many Americans who work well in groups. But let's look at the rules rather than the exceptions, and through comparing both cultures, explore the advantages and limitations of fundamental ideologies in Japan and North America. Individualism, for example, favors creativity, accountability, and action, but keeps many people from participating in pivotal roles. The Japanese notion of collectivism promotes corporate knowledge and being in tune with the market and business environment but can impose stifling conformity and shy people away from creative solutions.

The Self

North Americans admire individual accomplishment, and in general terms the cultural hero is a self-made, self-reliant person who accepts risks, takes charge, gets the job done, makes things happen—now. Measurable achievement is what counts. Americans' preference for individualism, independent problem-solvers, and assertiveness stresses success through self-reliance. Social rank or title counts for little unless it is gained through individual effort; reverence for age or family background pales in comparison to individual accomplishment. Deference to others is perceived as a sign of weakness.

Personal Reward

Consistent with the values of individualism, North Americans routinely reward individuals for good performance. In Japan, however, it is the group that is rewarded, not the individual. This is an important idea to remember, for as an American, you may routinely direct praise to workers for individual effort. But to single out a Japanese colleague or worker for specific praise could put that person at odds with fellow workers, be embarrassing for everyone, or even jeopardize a career. In Japan, individual reward challenges group solidarity, and rewards are given for collective effort.

In a collective society, personal appraisal puts emphasis on such things as cooperative attitude and knowledge of the collective ideology, as well as on the individual's ability to work with the group. Today, we hear many American corporations talk about the need for cooperation, but most management styles are designed to recognize only individual effort and measurable performance. Collaboration Western-style is more about the coordination of activities needed to reflect the leader's individual self-assertion. Yes, Americans do form and work in groups, but these groups in America are more like mergers that can be dismantled and reformed. They are about enlightened self-interest. Collaboration Eastern-style is about individuals contributing a part toward the whole and serves as a reflection of the group's identity. It is more like a family.

To individualistic North Americans, it is easy to underestimate the importance of group cohesiveness. Their "let's-get-down-to-issues" attitude can appear overly aggressive and self-interested to Japanese businesses where open meetings are reserved for formality and for acknowledging points of agreement. The North American–style discussion of differences would embarrass the Japanese because it is perceived as interfering with the group cohesion. If group discussion in a Japanese office gets heated, the discussion will be ended abruptly to avoid offending individuals. Self-interests and individuality are subjugated to strong group affiliations and a sense of corporate identity that must be preserved.

Obligation

In all cultures, the sense of obligation is the glue that binds people together, and as such, it has a large influence on corporate structures and modes of operation.[3] In the East, obligation has been largely influenced by Confucianism, while in the West it has been influenced by Christian principles. Comparing the idea of obligation in these two cultures will illustrate the manifestation of these ideologies in the business context.

The Confucian Imperative

Social obligation is the Confucian imperative, and ethical principles define the proper nature of social relationships among people.

Generally, the five central human relationships are those between ruler-minister, father-son, husband-wife, elder-younger brother, and friend-friend.[4] Confucianism attaches different levels of moral oblig-ation to these different relationships, as obligations are graded in importance and assigned varying ranges of intensity and value. Confucianism is expressed differently among the Asian cultures. Making a comparison between the Chinese and Japanese sense of social obligation will highlight some of the dynamics for doing busi-ness Eastern-style.

Chinese Loyalty

In China, the moral obligation between father and son has para-mount importance. The idea of *Jia*—duty to the family and respect to the parents—subordinates all other duties. The moral obligation of *Xiao*—the duties exchanged between the father, family lineage, and the son—established the moral imperative of filial piety.[5] In places such as China, Hong Kong, or Taiwan, loyalty is, first and foremost, to the family.

In feudal times, many Chinese families owned their own land and paid heavy taxes to the state. In return, the state reciprocated very little. With few formal laws, old Chinese society depended on the favors of the local authority, which was subject to change at any time. Land shortages and dense populations in the major centers also meant a high level of competition among families. With little ex-change, Chinese families became very self-sufficient.[6] Family and personal relationships were one, if not the only, means to ensure a certain level of trust and continuity. Trust, respect, and loyalty are absolute for the family. Obligation to friends and acquaintances were possible to the extent that there was mutual dependence on each party. And to others, courtesy should always be extended.[7] The exchange of resources was provided through a series of networks based on personal relationships. The reliance solely on family means that to date the great majority of businesses in Hong Kong and Tai-wan are family-owned.[8] Little to no trust is given to members out-side the family. That means delegation, Japanese- or American-style, is difficult. The Chinese management style resembles a hub-and-spoke reporting system.[9] The main mode of influence is based on the personality of the key member at the hub, most often the eldest male in the family.

Nepotism

To the Chinese, as in many non-Western societies, hiring relatives or close friends is a normal business practice that ensures trust, responsible action, and teamwork. Eschewing what they describe as nepotism, Americans shun hiring on the basis of familial relationships and seek those who are best qualified. Résumés are scanned for tangibles: education, experience, and work-related accomplishments—sales volumes, cost-reduction achievements, or number of employees supervised—those measurable indicators of job worthiness. In China, primary considerations for employment are compatibility with coworkers, trustworthiness, and loyalty to the group. When dealing in Latin America, Near Eastern countries, or China, a rush to judgment on hiring practices that seem to you to be clear cases of nepotism could cost you a deal. Likewise, foreign firms dealing with North American businesses should not be offended if a company refuses to hire relatives or friends.

Japanese Loyalty

Chinese Confucianism, transported to Japan, was altered to suit the feudal political realities of the Tokugawa era. There, Confucianism also made social obligation the imperative, but loyalty was centered on the human affairs of the group, with final authority residing in the feudal lord. In the absence of an alternate authority, this militaristic ruling class shaped its own ethical code, and filial piety, although important, occupied a lower position than duty and solidarity to the lord and the clan. In modern times, that loyalty has been transferred to the corporate work group. Reciprocal obligation defining the Self is a deeply ingrained feature of Japanese collectivist society. The Japanese, therefore, find it difficult to take individualistic or unilateral actions, because doing so would compromise the group's integrity and their sense of reciprocal obligation.[10]

American Loyalty

In comparison to the Eastern ideology of *oneness,* Western *duality* and Christian ideology legitimized individuality, self-reliance, and action based on one's conscience and principles. With the evolution of the mechanical order, the individual came to be seen as a self-sufficient person, naturally imbued with rights and powers. Unlike Japan, power in Ancient Europe was shared between the state and the Christian Church. People could use principles from either authority to advance their own position. When the church lost its power, the scientific method came to provide an alternative means of forming principles. As a result, Europeans have always been able to point to principles from one authority or another to advance their position. With time, acting according to principles of one's choice became not only acceptable but a sign of one's ability and self-reliance.

What are the implications for the business world in understanding the concepts of obligation in Eastern and Western cultures? In North America, practices that are considered bad or good are judged against abstract principles or rules of law. In Japan, thought and action that support personal relationships are considered good, while those that disrupt personal relations are considered bad.[11] For example, in the name of efficiency, American corporations can legally justify laying off employees. In Japan, laying off employees is considered bad for relationships—after all, you don't fire a member of the family.[12] If efficiency is critical for a Japanese company to achieve success, other avenues than worker layoffs will be explored. To the Japanese, the American approach to firing people is coldly objective and inhuman.[13]

Business as Personal Relationship

When doing business in North America, one expects direct and assertive discussions. After a brief but firm handshake and a few minutes of discussing the weather, Americans expect to get down to business: problems are analyzed, alternatives presented, and conclusions reached quickly. Doing business at arm's length is not only acceptable but considered good business. In this context, you can expect facts and figures, assertive language, and on the spot decisions. Generally, we reveal little about our personal lives and keep business separate from our private life. This is not a hard-and-fast rule. When doing business, having a personal relationship with the person you are dealing with is nice—but not necessary. The irony is that often Americans do business first, then get to know you.

By contrast, before doing business, the Japanese first like to establish personal relationships, believing that it is important to develop trust, loyalty, and confidence before any commitment is made. In Japan—as in most countries—a quick handshake is not sufficient. You first need to build rapport and obtain a high a level of trust before you can engage in business discussions. The Japanese want to know that you are respectable, responsible, and trustworthy. Moreover, doing business brusquely is considered rude because the indication is that you are not satisfied with the way things are proceeding, and perhaps more importantly, that you have more concern for the contract than for the person.

Litigated Obligation vs. Personal Obligation

When dealing with Japanese, you can expect questions that will seem personal and irrelevant to business. In Japan, it is normal to ask about the well-being of one's family and to expect questions about your age, how long you have been with the company, if you have had a promotion in recent years, how much salary you make, or even how you feel about Japan. To the Japanese, it is a way of getting to know you better. They look for cues that indicate sincerity, stability, integrity, and goodwill. If you are an American doing business in Japan, talking business will do little good until the Japanese get to know you better. As a rule, the Japanese want to know you better before they do business. You should reciprocate in this process: show an interest in your contact, his family, his country, and his company. Relationships based on mutual trust and reciprocity take precedence over potential profit, ensure harmony, and avoid litigation. Obligations in Japan are based on personal relationships—

not rules, not laws, not arm's-length dealings. Such things, the Japanese believe, destroy harmonious relations. On a daily basis, business activities in Japan revolve around interpersonal consideration rather than cold, rational facts and figures.

While it is true that Americans also give some consideration to interpersonal relationships in business matters, the Japanese dislike the North American legalistic approach to business contracts. Contracts are considered mechanical and restrictive, and the Japanese do not like to sign detailed documents that they feel serve to constrict the parties in the event of changing circumstances. The Japanese prefer flexible or vague commitments that they can alter to change with circumstances. In case of disagreements, Japanese prefer conciliation over litigation, and they do not like to resort to litigation to resolve problems. By developing strong interpersonal relationships and mutual obligations, their view is that both parties will work to resolve conflicts when they arise. This requires trust that can only be built when people know each other.

Relatively speaking, it is not so much that the Japanese differ from other nations in terms of how they deal with outsiders; rather, and consistent with the mechanical order, it is the Americans who differ in their ability to deal with outsiders at arm's length and who put facts and figures ahead of relationships. In America when things go wrong with a contract we litigate. In the West rights are to be protected, and litigation puts everyone on an equal footing to settle disputes. With approximately 16,000 attorneys, Japan has one attorney for every 7,800 Japanese. By contrast, with 700,000 attorneys, the U.S. has one attorney for every 360 Americans.

The small percentage of Japanese attorneys is in part related to the small number of applicants who are accepted and allowed to graduate from law school. But there is a much larger ideology at work here. According to the Japanese, litigation creates winners and losers, which is antithetical to the maintenance of harmony. In the West we look at our legal system as a means to resolve conflicts and prevent abuse by those in power. There is, however, an inverse relationship between rules and trust. Past a certain point, rules become restrictive, bureaucratic, and costly and bring about social dysfunction.[14] This is not to negate the value of law, but rules should be kept in balance. In Japan, an individual's holding power and governing by rules is frowned upon; consequently, power, as well as accountability, is diffused. This serves to prevent abuse, but at the same time, diffusion through valuing harmony makes it difficult to respond to specific problems and likewise needs to be kept in balance.

Egalitarianism vs. Hierarchy

North Americans minimize the relevance of hierarchy and stress the notion of equality: egalitarianism is a fundamental assumption in this culture. When making business presentations, people do their best to be informal and natural. Casual is as American as Levi's jeans. Americans have little variation in the way they address people of different cultural or socioeconomic status. We are very friendly and, in part, that is our way of being open, which contrasts with our direct statements and affirmative actions. After the initial contact we tend to call people by their first name or sometimes even a nickname.

The problem is that in many countries informality can be perceived as intrusive and pushy. Although well-meaning, Americans need to remember that in most other countries, egalitarianism is considered a sign of disrespect, arrogance, and ignorance of the proper order. Just as Americans accept distinctions among individuals, Japanese accept and respect hierarchy and distinction among different groups. In their view, harmony requires that a proper order be maintained between the different groups through the appropriate use of language and behavior within various hierarchies.

Communication: The Japanese and the North American Models

In communicating, Americans are more likely to bring in a variety of viewpoints, explore differences of perspective, provide arguments, clarify positions, and seek solutions. By contrast, the Japanese are more likely to explore areas of consensus, avoid conflicts, and seek to cultivate emotional ties. Stereotypically, some Japanese conceive North Americans as friendly, confident, and frank but also arrogant, critical, and dogmatic. The Japanese stereotype in American minds is of thoughtful, diligent, and courteous, but also deceitful, evasive, and cautious people.

Failing to recognize the different underlying cultural assumptions regarding communication can lead to frustration when cultures meet. Firm and direct statements by North Americans do not necessarily mean a dogmatic view, and when dealing with them, one should not interpret assertive statements as final, but rather as opening lines—their way of opening a discussion. Likewise, the Japanese habit of inserting periods of silence should not necessarily be interpreted as evasiveness or being noncommittal but rather as a way to reflect on the discussion. For the Japanese, time is required to sense the atmosphere and to develop awareness of the person's disposition; this is crucial for understanding and judging the level of commitment. Both means of communication have their advantages at different places and times. Those advantages are lost, however, when you limit yourself to one mode of communication.

Our mode of communication reflects many aspects of our cultural values. North Americans' inclination for clarity and delineation offers some advantages. Clarification allows for scrutiny of systems, definition of organizational disciplines, and a focus on individual accountability. However, taken to excessive levels, the inclination for delineation can repress participation and create a debilitating sense of isolation. Collaboration Eastern-style is about individuals contributing a part toward the whole, so a communication style based on sensing points of agreement and cultivating emotional ties is important. Pushed to its extreme, this communication model can turn on itself and bring stifling conformity.

Values and Philosophy

The American who desires to be "different" is conforming to American values. Individualism means each person is distinct. The Japanese who agree publicly with the group are conforming with Japanese values. Collectivism means each person is connected. We recognize something as being distant because we have things that are near us. We recognize something as being full because some-times it is empty. We recognize differences because we have some-thing in common. A society's culture determines where on a continuum certain values are emphasized and others are subordi-nated. For example, Americans value individualism, but still recog-nize the need to be team players—one trait may have a greater cultural priority. An awareness of other cultures' assumptions, com-bined with our awareness of our own culture's paradigms, helps us recognize the basis for our preferred behaviors. Such knowledge can alleviate frustration in dealing cross-culturally with others, as well as open avenues to different aspects of our being.

On a philosophical level the Japanese do not see the world as being made up of unrelated fixed substances. In a short essay, Professor Ito Shuntaro describes how the Japanese "view the world not as consisting of unchange-able substances but as a *flow or process* of constant change."[15] In other words, the world con-sists of *process* where relation-

How can you separate the dance from the dancer?

ships among things are preeminent over their actual substances. In such a world view, change and development are assumed to be interrelated and dependent on each other. For centuries the Western world made clear distinctions between cause and effect, matter and energy, subject and object. Starting with Kant's philosophy, how-ever, and later with Einstein's theory of relativity, many of today's Western scientists are no longer married to ideas of causality and recognize the effects of interaction. Generally, we can still say that in the West, we pay attention to the independence of substances per se. In the East, the emphasis is on the relationship between substances.

At a philosophical level, this Eastern world view is not about a dominant force describing all relationships but about interdepen-dence and interaction of all factors. One substance is not about being the first, bigger, smaller, or stronger or the cause of another. The emphasis is on the interaction between the two. In Japanese philoso-phy this dynamic is represented by *ki*—those interactive dynamic forces causing endless creation, change, and development.[16] This philosophy is consistent with the old Chinese concept of yin (feminine) and yang (masculine) that recognizes interdependence between opposites. Yin and yang, like the whole and the parts, can be recognized as different but related and interacting.

Fifth-century Chinese philosopher Mo Zi said, "the universe moves and changes with time. Hence, everything is in a constant state of continuous motion, change, and development."[17] This ancient philosophy has had an important impact on our modern world. Consistent with the notion of the ki, Japanese Nobel prize–winning physicist Hideki Yukawa (1907–1981) established the means of exchange between the proton and the neutron in the atomic nucleus. True to Japanese philosophical values, Yukawa rejected the concept of the proton and the neutron as unchangeable substances, and focused instead on the interchange between protons and the neutrons.

How do these fundamental assumptions from the East and the West—as expressed in cultural values and principles—affect today's business world? Let's use an example of the ki philosophy as it applies to a marketing survey of what people eat for breakfast. You, the marketer represent the subject, who questions a sample of people, who represent the object. Simply put, when you (the subject) ask people (the object) what they eat for breakfast, many will say, "Fruits, yogurt, and high-fiber cereal with milk." However, the reality is that many people have bacon and eggs with buttered toast and jam. On certain issues, people respond according to what they think the questioner wants to hear or according to their perception of what is a right answer. That is, your presence (you, the subject) influences the response of the person surveyed (the object). Sending a questionnaire that people complete in the privacy of their home would elicit a different response, but again this shows that the response is influenced by the type and form of interaction between the subject and the object. A personal survey, for example, will give you a higher number of people saying yes to eating yogurt than would a survey done by questionnaire. From a business point of view, it is important to understand the influence of the interaction—the ki of this situation—before you jump into the yogurt business.

Equally, the Western-style separation of subject and object, cause and effect, provides a useful philosophy to explain a great number of phenomena. For example, retail outlets of expensive and luxury goods such as furniture will tell you that their sales go down during a recession. Here cause and effect means that a downturn in the economy has caused furniture sales to decline. One retail outlet has little influence on the economy. Therefore, it is fair to say that (A) the economy has caused (B) your sales to go down. However, the ki principle would caution you and bring to mind the notion of interdependence: your sales might be down because of other factors such as a special promotion by your competition, change in fashion, or indifferent customer service.

An awareness of your influence on the object puts you in a better position to interpret the situation. As you exercise an influence on the object, it in turn, exercises an influence on you. An awareness of the situation, the environment, your belief system, and the object's influence on you, the subject, puts you in a better position to observe and enhance the value of your interpretation. Likewise, an awareness of the means by which you get the data and evaluate the information helps you understand your beliefs about your conclusions.

Business practitioners are well aware of both principles, but as Westerners we still prefer to make clear delineations, treating cause and effect, subject and object, as separate. (Notice in my Western preference for separation, I presented the theory, then an example.)

Universal vs. Relative

In the same manner as we make clear separations between cause and effect, subject and object, we often tend to associate our principles as having universal application, independent of time and place. Here, I relate the notion of the universal vs. the relative to the belief people have of the conclusions they get from the way they gather, organize, and process information. Culture has a large influence on how you gather information.

In the West the educational system emphasizes problem solving based on the scientific approach and abstract thinking. When faced with a problem, you are expected to find the root of the problem, determine the pattern that evolves from the problem, and define the rules or the laws that give rise to these patterns. You are expected to support your principles or conclusions with facts, not feelings.

North Americans believe the laws or principles that govern any given phenomenon have universal application. After all, Newton's law of gravity can determine what you weigh no matter where you are on earth or, for that matter, what you would weigh if you were on the Moon or Mars. Within our sphere of understanding, and allowing that such a law may be twisted by a black hole, the law of gravity has universal application. For many Westerners, social principles have been associated with the same level of validity and universality as found in natural science. But such a belief is likely more in keeping with our mechanical view that prefers clear and predictable outcomes.

> The purpose of a fish trap is to catch fish, and when the fish are caught, the trap is forgotten. The purpose of words is to convey ideas, and when the ideas are grasped, the words are forgotten.
> —Chuang-Tzu

Although we may agree on the value of social principles such as equality and freedom, interpretation of these values may vary tremendously depending on one's beliefs. Thus we must acknowledge that in part, feeling, not fact, forms the basis of our principles.

For example, politicians are quick to appoint to the Supreme Court judges whom they know to have similar inclinations to their own. This political expediency helps to ensure that principles, points of law, or constitutional rights be interpreted the same as by the lawmakers and the citizens who elect them. Presented with the same mass of data and figures, judges with different inclinations derive different interpretations. Judges are used here as examples because, more than most (and this is not said in a cynical way), they are well-versed and disciplined in the practice of objectivity and consistency. Yet, looking at the same principle as enunciated in the Constitution, judges, special interest groups, or citizens, whether liberal or conservative, can derive diametrically opposed conclusions.

For example, in the name of human rights, you can choose the relevant principle that fits your values to either justify or abolish abortion. Likewise, in the world of business, the principles of free-market economy and competitiveness can be used both to justify or limit corporate mergers. In the West, we have a tendency to believe that our principles have universal application and that, following a rational discussion, we'll all come up with the same conclusion. But social principles are not like scientific laws. Just because you point to a principle, that doesn't mean we all will reach the same conclusion. Principles are based on values and subjective opinions.

This is not a criticism. Far from it. It has often been said that variety is the spice of life. But social principles should not be confused or equated with the same level of validity and universality as the laws of gravity. Nor does this negate the value of principles. Principles can provide a common base for discussion and useful reference points for discourse, but your value system and feelings will influence your logical conclusion. You may claim a principle as universal and have the facts to support your contention, but don't expect the same universal conclusion from others.

It is equally conceivable to think in terms of the ki principle that puts the accent on being attuned to your environment and changing circumstances. It focuses on time-related issues; by that I mean if the circumstances change, the conclusion is different. Westerners may find this frustrating. Some Western writers have compared the Japanese to chameleons changing color with shifts in the environment. For the Western mind, for example, changing the director of a company does not justify changing the terms of the contract—to the Japanese mind it does. There are advantages in both value systems.

Decisions can be based on information that originates from a variety of sources: fact, gut feeling, political ideology, or articles of faith. As Westerners practically wedded to the cultural ideal of objectivity, we believe that we prefer decisions based on facts, though it does not follow that objective reality is solely represented by facts and figures. John Wheeler, a respected quantum philosopher, once said: "it seems that reality is defined by the question we put to it." In doing research, the sample you choose, the order and context of the questions, their contents and choice of words, suggest the answers and have a tremendous influence on them. Many Westerners become suspicious when dealing with other information sources such as intuition or inference because they threaten our notions of the objective and unbiased view. But then we are forced to remember that feelings are often based on observations and experiences that are more realistic than any isolated empirical data. Political decisions or articles of faith may reflect a perceived reality that can inform business opportunities. An awareness of your preferred information sources, balanced with other elements can enrich your decision-making process, as each source serves to feed and discipline the others.

Oneness and Duality

Both the concept of Oneness and the concept of Duality, when applied to industry, have produced tremendous successes and impressive advances. It is not unusual to find in the West some proponents who would wholeheartedly drop the mechanical or Duality concept in favor of oneness. How can we make a decision to adopt one or the other? Our culture provides us with the groundwork from which to start. The introduction of new concepts needs to be done with pragmatism and within the framework of one's culture. We need perspective as we learn to recognize the benefits offered by each of these different paradigms. Then we can realize that enjoying benefits from either concept does not mean dropping our culturally familiar, native concept or having to compromise one over the other.

In the business context, the oneness approach does not mean you have to negate the need for specialization or accountability fostered by duality. Dropping one paradigm to wholeheartedly swing to another will close the full spectrum of advantages offered by each perspective. Fortunately, the modern world offers the advantage of being in touch with other nations and, if we so choose, benefiting from each other's experience.

In all societies, change needs to be culturally contextualized. Change or transformation does not mean negating the fundamentals of what it is to be an American, Japanese, or an Arab, but rather, change means incorporating and assimilating new ideas within your value system. Different perspectives not only can provide you with greater insight and awareness of other ways of doing things, but they can illuminate your own cultural values and their influence on why you think a certain way.

Both dualism and oneness can be understood as representing different aspects of our psychological makeup. Dualism, pushed to its extreme, causes problems for North Americans, especially at the psychological level, creating consequences for individuals such as social isolation marked by an acute sense of alienation. At a corporate level, it makes you look inside at the system for answers rather than outside at reality. We can see how moderation in the concept produces a balanced dualism that is not about separation but about participation and integration. In Japan, when oneness is pushed to its extreme, some individuals suffer from *taijin kyofusho,* a social phobia where individuals have an intense fear of being offensive to others. At a corporate level it fosters patronage and inhibits people from taking action that would lead to greater efficiency, even when it is recognized as needed. Moderation in the concept of oneness results in a level of participation that recognizes differentiation as well as the need for distinction.

A Pilot Story: Communicating in Two Cultures

The airline industry has an enviable record when it comes to safety. Despite their good record, however, crashes do occur, and when that happens a thorough investigation is undertaken to determine the cause of the accident. Later the information is dispersed to various agencies who use it as a learning tool. Deborah Tannen, a respected specialist in communications, related the story of a conversation between the copilot and the pilot of an Air Florida plane before it crashed in the Potomac River in Washington, D.C.[18] The day of the crash was stormy and icy. The copilot, who had more experience than the pilot with icing problems, repeatedly called the pilot's attention to the ice buildup on the plane. The pilot shoved aside the warning, proceeded, and a few minutes later the plane crashed into the river. The black box recording made it fairly obvious that the copilot had expressed himself indirectly and in an unassuming fashion.[19]

In America, the obvious solution was to train copilots to become more assertive. Witness the great number of courses or seminars with titles such as Assertiveness Training, Self-Esteem, and Managing Others. How many seminars that deal with empathy and listening skills have you taken or heard of? Have you also noted that when listening skills are taught, it is done as a means to better understanding so that you can influence others?

As a direct result of this incident, some airlines now offer training to their copilots to express themselves in a more assertive way. But when Deborah Tannen presented this solution to a communications graduate seminar, a Japanese student pointed out that it would be just as effective to train pilots to pick up on subtle or nonassertive communication. Clearly, in this tragic case, had the pilot listened, or the copilot expressed himself in a more assertive way, the crash likely would have been avoided. Had either the concept of duality or the concept of oneness—or both—been emphasized, the outcome may have been very different.

In different nations both duality and oneness have produced impressive successes. Both modes of thinking also have their costs when taken to extremes. The point is not to argue which is the better system or to claim that we should compromise one with the other. Our culture provides the starting point from which we can adapt other views. Many corporations have enjoyed substantial returns from adapting the elements of the oneness approach within North American culture. But this has to be done with pragmatism and within a cultural context. In Chapters 7 through 9, I discuss what can be gained from the notion of Oneness in the corporate world. Finally, in Chapter 10, I will relate that to the person. Each system of thought accents, as well as negates, a different part of who we are. But as the pilot story indicates, both asserting oneself and listening offer great advantages.

7

Retooling the Corporation

There are two sides to every business equation: revenue and cost. And any business that focuses on one at the expense of the other will pay a price.[1] Good business consciously balances the interrelationship among customers, employees, and shareholders. Customers seek goods to fill their needs. Employees are inspired by an organization that fosters their development. Shareholders expect a reasonable return on their investment. To survive, an organization and its strategy have to motivate employees to meet customer needs at a reasonable price.

The optimal strategy is the one that allows your corporate approach to match market needs. To successfully develop such a strategy, companies must balance the advantages offered by both Western and Eastern approaches. Consider how the Eastern notion of oneness promotes collectivism, attunement, and harmony and encourages the sense of participation. The Western notion of duality promotes individualism, action, and distinction, which lead to entrepreneurialism and innovation. In organizations, our Western inclination for mechanical order promotes accountability. At its extreme, it gives rise to rigid rules and systems that favor abstract cold logic and discourage intuition, creativity, and judgment. As you become more aware of the Eastern preference for attunement, you may see the need to integrate various business functions and to encourage participation among your colleagues and workers. By adopting an organizational strategy that combines oneness with duality, corporations around the world will be better equipped to adapt to the reality of the information age.

Western and Eastern corporations take different business approaches. Consistent with our system approach, American business is based on contractual obligations and deals with other companies at arm's length. On the other hand, Japanese business is based on personal relationships and deals with other companies through cross-shared holdings called Keiretsu. To reiterate, Americans negotiate a contract, while Japanese negotiate relationships. Consistent with individualism, American accountability is defined and concentrated. Consistent with collectivism, Japanese accountability is diffused and shared. Americans reward individuals, while Japanese reward the group. In America, we value being different and look for major breakthroughs. Consistent with moving with the flow, the Japanese look for continual improvement (*kaizen*). Americans play poker, while the Japanese play chess.

Although there are differences between American and Japanese organizations, they do share a great number of similarities. To be successful, all organizations need a sound strategy. In business, the elements of a corporate strategy can be grouped into three major components:

- Understanding the market needs and the business situation
- Molding a corporate approach: a sound knowledge of the company's strengths and limitations
- Providing leadership; managing resources properly

Strategy is about creating a fit between your corporate strengths and market demand. You must learn to understand your market demand and differentiate yourself from your competitors. Although these three components are treated separately, all three are interrelated. To develop a successful strategy, an organization must integrate functions, activities, and interactions to fit the business situation.[2]

In this chapter, I will look at two areas: understanding the market and molding a corporate approach. In Chapter 8, I will look at leadership and the management of resources.

Understanding the Market

Paul Herbig in his book *Marketing Japanese Style* contends that two prevailing views distinguish Western and Eastern marketing principles. Simply put:

> The East listens.
> The West talks.

Listening

There are a number of reasons why new products fail. Poor timing, competitor strength, technical problems, lack of financing, higher costs than anticipated, poor logistics. But, the number one reason is the company's inability to determine the needs of the market. A number of surveys indicate that more than 80 percent of new products will fail unless they are unique, consistent with market demand. Customers will only buy from you if you give them what they want. To understand what they want, you need to listen.

If you recall from Chapter 1, emotional intelligence is about being in touch with yourself as well as others. Our individualistic inclination means that we tend to understand others or project what they need by looking at ourselves. In the West, we understand by looking into a mirror, while in the East, they understand by looking through a window. I believe these two different views are complementary to each other. To be successful you need to listen to understand what your customers want. But in today's competitive environment merely giving your customers what they want is not sufficient. Although we claim to listen, we often judge our customers' needs based on our own needs.

Don't take for granted that you are fully aware of what the customer wants. There may be gaps between what management perceives as important and what the customer perceives as important. Valarie A. Zeithaml lists numerous studies done at General Electric which show that, in evaluating appliances, a significant difference exists between management's and consumers' perceptions of quality.[3] The studies show that managers thought consumers would list workmanship, performance, and form as the critical factors in evaluating quality. However, when the consumers were asked what constituted quality, they listed appearance, cleanability, and durability.[4] Management's perceptions are understandable: without workmanship you don't get performance, and without performance, your business will cease to exist. But, in today's market, consumers do not simply expect performance, they take it for granted.

GE was able to respond because they knew what was needed. Without neglecting performance, GE engineered features affecting appearance, cleanability, and durability. The point is, when you are familiar with something, it is easy to assume you know what others want. Only by asking can you be sure your strategy is aligned in the right direction. In thinking about your customer's needs, it is important not to look in a mirror. Giving your customer complete satisfaction means converting your technical expertise to interpersonal expertise and meeting your customer's needs and expectations.

Listening is a great first step, but you also need to distinguish yourself.

Talking

Japanese corporations pride themselves on their down-to-earth competitiveness based on operational excellence and customer knowledge. Many Japanese companies provide more or less similar products and compete mainly on quality, service, and reliability. Where operational excellence is important, such as in the car industry, the Japanese have an advantage. These qualities are important, but in today's competitive environment, quality and reliability are taken for granted. Where unique products are required, such as in the software or pharmaceutical industries, not standing out puts you at a disadvantage. When you buy a watch, you take for granted that it will keep the time accurately for years to come. The unwillingness of the

Japanese to stand out means they miss the growing market that looks for product uniqueness. In such a market you are left to compete on service and price. Competing on operational excellence squeezes your sales margin because you compete mainly on price alone.

Understanding Your Market: Sensing and Attunement

Eastern cultures value a person's ability to sense the moods of others. Empathy (the ability to understand others and to identify oneself with others) gives us a great advantage when we are called upon to take action in certain situations. The ability to move with a situation can make the difference between success and failure. In a competitive environment, your ability to sense customer desires and attune your marketing strategy to market conditions will likewise make the difference between success and failure. Although we all say customer service is our number-one priority, our Western inclination diminishes our ability to empathize with and read the needs of others, and it makes us look at ourselves for the answers rather than at customers.

To succeed at marketing, however, you must learn to listen with the intent to understand beyond your own viewpoint. The marketing strategies reviewed here may not be new to you, but your ability to use them effectively and to respond to changing market situations can be greatly enhanced if you develop your ability to get in touch with others and—consistent with the ki principle—move as circumstances dictate.

You Can't Be All Things to All People

It is also common to hear that to be competitive you need to provide value-added benefits. Although you may agree with this statement, you must remember that value-added benefits are defined by the customer. *Value-added* means very different things to different people. For example, a techno-friend of mine values owning the latest technology. He was one of the first to buy a watch to which he could transfer his daily schedule from his computer. He bought the watch even though he had just changed jobs, was moving, and money was tight. For him, the value added was the means not only to keep abreast of the latest digital technology but to show his own personal style, his own signature. While people such as my friend will go to any lengths to get the latest technology, other people hold price point as paramount. To these consumers, a watch is a watch and they buy only what's on sale—which, of course, isn't usually the latest piece of technical wizardry. Still other consumers are loyal to specific brands. Even if their preferred brands are hard to find, these people will travel from store to store searching out their favorite items, and they tend not to quit until they get exactly what they want.

Competitiveness in the marketplace demands that you focus your company's strengths and that you align those strengths with specific market needs. Too often, we hear that quality is all you need for success. But today, quality is only the price of market entry, not a guarantee of a competitive edge.

As an organization, you need to decide where you can best compete by deciding where you excel and by offering that excellence to the customer group you can best serve. Some customers are only concerned about getting a standard product at the best price; other groups want to be first to have the latest technical innovation. For others, what counts is full service or a product designed specifically to suit their particular needs. Some only want something that is different from other products. You need to be selective and provide value-added benefits only to selected customers.[5] You can't be all things to all people. So your job is to determine which of your strengths best serves which group of customers. That's where you focus. And remember, if you don't take care of the customer, somebody else will.

Customer Satisfaction

There is a direct correlation between the level of customer satisfaction and the degree of loyalty customers feel toward your organization. A study done by Thomas O. Jones and Earl W. Sasser, Jr., at Xerox demonstrated that customers who claimed to be "totally satisfied" were six times more likely to repurchase Xerox products than customers who claimed to be only "satisfied."[6] Comparable studies across a number of industries led to similar conclusions. Only totally satisfied customers are truly loyal. These findings indicate customers who are merely "satisfied" are not completely committed, and neutral or dissatisfied customers are a sure loss.

Obviously, monitoring customer satisfaction is very important. This becomes more significant when you consider a satisfied customer will tell five friends about your products and services; a dissatisfied customer will tell ten. There is considerable variation in these numbers. We know it is six times easier to retain an existing customer than to find a new one. Your best strategy to remain competitive and gain market share is to give the customers what they want. But how do you do that? Simply put, you do it by gathering information, by listening to your customers, and by giving them what they ask for. In the year 2000 with the fall of the dot.com, Siebel systems sales grew by 100 percent. In an interview by Bronwyn Fryer, Siebel cited their "absolute commitment to 100% customer satisfaction." This is not lip service: Siebel first talks to its customers, finds out what they want, and then designs products and services that meet its customers' needs.[7] Listening to the customer also means listening to suppliers, wholesalers, retailers, and even your friendly banker, all of whom are involved with your product.

Information from your customer can come from market research surveys, 800-number telephone service, company records, and employees. We know listening can make or break a business; here is an example from the travel industry. In the airline industry safety and security are paramount. Many airlines provide similar schedules of arrival and departure times, prices, and type of aircraft. In this cutthroat mass-market, Sir Colin Marshall, chairman of British Airways, said his company's aim was "to ensure that British Airways is the customer's first choice through the delivery of an unbeatable travel experience."[8] This was made possible, he said, "by creating an organization that excels in listening to its most valuable customers and by recognizing that the people on the front-line are the ones who ultimately create value since they are the ones who determine the kinds of experiences that the company generates for its customers."[9]

In many situations, simple modifications, often at little cost, can put you in a very favorable competitive position. For example, on flights between Britain and Japan, British Airways was concerned about providing genuine Japanese food. The airline listened carefully to the responses from Japanese passengers. Their polite comments were, "For Westerners, you're doing quite well."[10] British Airways knew enough about Eastern conventions to know something wasn't quite right. It turned out that while BA had mastered *cooking* Japanese food, they did not realize the importance of the shape, size, and color of the food, nor did they understand the subtle nuances of arranging food on a tray. So they made simple modifications in the presentation of the food and provided their customers with more of what they were looking for. British Airways was able to provide a value-added service because they were listening to their customers.

The effect of value-added benefits is critical and imperative. Many people simply want to be heard, to feel you are taking their concerns into account. So be sure to give your frontline people some training in listening. And give them training in conflict resolution and some authority to resolve conflicts when they arise. If you resolve a complaint on the spot, *most* customers will do business with you again. If it takes more than five days, 40 to 50 percent of your customers will defect.[11] The contribution frontline people can make in this area cannot be overstated. A positive attitude and the ability to resolve a problem immediately require your organization to do two things: foster employee commitment and give employees the tools to solve the problems.

Marketing: Not Sufficient

You have built a multimillion dollar hotel and provide your customers with the best possible amenities. A guest enters the lobby after a big day. He arrives at reception to find nobody pays any attention to him. What are the chances you are going to keep this customer?

Close to 68 percent of customers who switch to the competition do so because they were treated with indifference.[12] The best market plan won't work unless you have the commitment of the employees, and to be committed, employees need to feel they can make a difference. Losing 68 percent of your customers because they are treated with indifference is a marketing issue that can only be resolved through integrating your corporate approach and leadership style.

Molding a Corporate Approach

Your corporate approach relates to your reporting structure, the level of delegation, the number and size of departments, the degree of centralization and decentralization, and information flow. It includes the systems that govern employee hiring, incentives, and discipline, and the procedures, rules, and regulations that direct your operation. Your corporate approach is determined by your corporate structure, which governs how people relate to each other inside and outside the organization, and how they do business.

Two prevailing management principles differentiate the ways the West and the East implement a corporate approach. Simply put:

> The West negotiates a contract.
> The East negotiates a relationship.

In Chapter 5, I discussed some of the disadvantages of business based on personal obligation. For example, in the name of efficiency, Japanese managers find it very difficult to let employees go. The end result is that the Japanese distribution system is very costly. Likewise corporate structure based mainly on contractual obligations gives rise to a mechanical system approach and has its cost. I would like to review some of the disadvantages and then discuss how we can integrate the advantages offered by both contractual and personal obligations.

In the driver's seat, the traditional manager sets the direction where responsibilities and levels of authority within different functional departments are clearly defined and assigned according to position. Negotiating a contract fits well with the scientific approach, which is based on the principles of division of functions, assignment of measurable tasks, and predictable results. Such a system favors standards, rules, and procedures that determine how a problem will be divided into tasks that are then assigned to different functional departments. At its extreme it allows our corporate approach to be governed by the demands of the corporate system rather than market demand and the business situation. This gives rise to a mechanical system approach that has little bearing on business reality. There is nothing wrong with systems. They provide discipline, direction, and focus. These qualities need to be retained, but pushed to their extreme, systems have two critical disadvantages: (1) they frame the answer, and (2) they sap productivity.

Framed Answers

All companies are faced with these challenges: identifying their strengths and fitting them to the market demand, integrating different functional areas, and giving employees a sense of participation. Although we may accept these challenges, our penchant for a mechanical order inclines us to systematically examine the inner workings of our organizations in search of clear, concrete, and measurable directions. "In fact," according to Peter Drucker, "approximately 90% or more of the information any organization collects is about inside events."[13] That is, more time is spent on satisfying the mechanics of the organization than on understanding the situation facing the organization.

Many people have heard the story of the drunk looking under the streetlight for his lost key. A police officer passing by asks him, "What are you looking for?" The man tells him, and then, trying to be helpful, the officer asks, "Where do you believe you lost your key?" The man says, "At the front door of my house." The officer patiently says, "Ha. Well, why are you looking on the street under the streetlight?" Indignantly, the drunk replies, "Because there's a light and I can see better over here than in front of my house!"

Clear objectives, like light, serve an important function by allowing a business to go forward. But you must go forward in the right direction. For example, fixing the mechanics of the organizational system may serve to alleviate employee doubts, but it has nothing to do with meeting the needs of new markets, new products, new programs, and customer service. Controlling costs is very important, but undue attention to costs has more to do with our need for the visible, the measurable, and the clear-cut than it has to do with business reality. In a dynamic environment, you need to sense and read the demands placed on your organization; that is, you must look *outside* your organization. Once you have aligned your company with market demand, *then* look inside to harmonize your operation with business reality. This is how a balanced corporate strategy meets challenges.

The structure and its systems are not the problem. Structured organizations and systems provide useful frames of reference, focus, and the discipline to get the job done. The problem comes when the structure dictates what people do instead of allowing the people to dictate the structure. An optimum structure provides the mechanics that allow employees to solve the problem. It transfers ownership to employees and puts solving the problem above complying with the system.

American-Style Keiretsu: Negotiating a Relationship

Starting with an example of transfer of ownership, let's explore some structural issues. Bound by cross-shareholding, the Japanese *keiretsu* system represents an effective network of corporate organizations that share information and buy from each other. Negotiating a relationship means that Japanese business interactions between companies, functional departments, and customers are based on personal relationships rather than on contracts. The following example of an American-style *keiretsu* system combines the Eastern advantages of integration and participation with the Western advantage of promoting accountability.

By incorporating elements of Japanese business style, Chrysler increased its profit per vehicle from $250 in the 1980s to a record $2,110 in 1994. As stated by Jeffrey Dyer in *Harvard Business Review*, "borrowing from the Japanese practices, U.S. manufacturing has cut production and component costs dramatically in the last decade by overhauling their suppliers' base."[14]

To do this, Chrysler broke away from the standard industry practice of awarding contracts based on the lowest measurable bid. Prior to the 1990s, Chrysler engineers designed components and suppliers built them. Detailed contracts specified Chrysler's requirements, and suppliers were chosen based on who came in with the lowest bid for the production of parts and components. Competition in the mid-1980s forced Chrysler to seek new ways to improve production.

Chrysler then looked at Honda Motor Company's supplier relations. Based on the study, Chrysler changed some of its practices. Instead of renewing a supplier's contract every two years, Chrysler now gives business to the supplier for the life of the model with the possibility of extending the contract beyond its original term. Instead of relying solely on its own engineers, Chrysler involves suppliers' input at the design stage of the car. With sharing of information, distrust between manufacturing and suppliers gave way to cooperation. It became the responsibility of *both* the manufacturer and the suppliers to find ways to reduce costs. The results have been impressive. The time needed to develop a new vehicle dropped from 234 weeks to 160 weeks, and the cost fell substantially.[15]

How did Chrysler bring about this remarkable result? They knew that in Japan many of the suppliers' executives had formerly worked for auto makers. Through their keiretsu network, Toyota and Nissan owned from 20 to 50 percent of the equity of their largest suppliers. Chrysler adapted those practices that were suitable within the American context. Chrysler did not exchange executives, nor did it buy equity in its suppliers; in fact, Chrysler retained the American practice of dealing with suppliers at arm's length. However, it did adopt a modified Japanese relationship approach between supplier and manufacturer. Like the Japanese, Chrysler involved the suppliers. It realized the advantages of an integral approach, but in retaining an arm's-length relationship with suppliers, Chrysler found it easier to drop underperformers when necessary.

Adapting the integral approach offered great advantages. Traditionally, suppliers were not willing to self-criticize. In the new approach, both supplier and manufacturer looked at what needed to be done to assure their business relationship. Furthermore, as Dyer said, "Beyond the incentive of improving their own profitability and increasing their business with Chrysler, suppliers appreciated being listened to for a change. Under the traditional system, suppliers were rarely asked for their ideas or suggestions for improvement; they were simply given a discrete task and asked to perform that task for a price."[16]

Negotiating a relationship is a great start but by itself cannot guarantee success. Allocating capital expenditure, marketing the right product at the right time and the right place, cost efficiency, and adapting to changing technology are all important. The integration of working knowledge from all business units is needed for corporate success.

Working Knowledge

In 1950, about one-third of the work force was involved in knowledge work. In the 1990s, close to four-fifths of the work force in developed countries are involved with knowledge work, with close to 28 percent requiring a high level of knowledge.[17] Knowledge work depends on the application and productive use of information. Peter Drucker points out that "In knowledge work, . . . the task is not given, it has to be determined"; there are no answers, only better choices.[18] According to Peter M. Senge, better choices come from pooled knowledge found in learning organizations.[19]

The division of tasks, clear accountability, and the mechanics of the bid system provide clarity but should not determine the end result. Systems favor explicit knowledge that comes from technical reports, financial statements, and research. Sole reliance on explicit knowledge diminishes the gain that comes from implicit knowledge. Implicit knowledge comes from informal association, participation, and working together. It is the type of knowledge that resides in experience and judgment and can be released only through personal exchange and relationship. Effective working knowledge comes when you combine implicit and explicit knowledge.

Working knowledge requires that all group members have

needed information, be able to influence the decision, and receive feedback both on the process and the outcome of the project. The soundness of the decision depends on the ability to weigh the validity of the relevant information from different members of the group. Although data relate more directly to explicit knowledge, the ability to weigh their relevance depends more on the implicit knowledge that comes from relationships and from working experience. Let me illustrate. You are planning a holiday with your spouse. If you have been together for a number of years, you likely know each other's likes and dislikes, and you are more effective in your planning. If your spouse has a strong preference for sun holidays (implicit knowledge), you know pretty well what the reaction will be if you bring information home on a ski holiday (explicit knowledge). Likewise in business decisions, along with the information presented, the personalities involved, your role, your position in the organization, the nature of the project, time constraints, and the social setting all influence the quality of the decision. Although some information can be judged on objective criteria, sound judgment is required to evaluate the relevance of the information that comes from familiarity, experience, and relationships.

In the industrial age, capital and technology were the key factors of production. Then, the aim was to maximize returns on investments in physical assets. A command and control structure put senior managers in the best position to make decisions about product choice and production usage. On the assembly line, one could evaluate how much work was done by watching workers' moving arms.

Things have changed. Today's capital and technology are no longer the key factors of production. They have become mere tools of production. Knowledge work is now the key factor in modes of production. Evaluating this work is difficult since it has no moving arms. You depend on your employees' commitment to giving you their best. Fostering employee trust, delegating power to employees, and, in short, ensuring employee dedication will give you access to working knowledge. Knowledge constitutes a real factor in attaining a competitive advantage, and it cannot be managed like capital, information, or machinery. This calls for a new way of doing things, a new way of molding your corporation to align with your business situation.

Spending 90 percent of your time looking inside the organization system frames the answers to questions that have little bearing on business reality. Mechanical systems create bureaucracies that erode entrepreneurship and subordinate the individual to the system. As they stifle flexibility and innovation, bureaucracies create resistance to change because they prevail upon their people to look inside the organization rather than outside to the market. This is like driving a car looking only at the instruments rather than watching the road. As General Electric's chairman and CEO, Jack Welch, puts it, "a [bureaucratic organization] is an organization with its face toward the CEO and its ass toward the customer." Equally important, overly relying on systems favors cold abstract logic above human relationships. This makes people feel vulnerable, gives rise to cynicism, and saps productivity.

> Today's superior organizations have two assets: customers and employees.

Sapped Productivity

Negotiating contracts and dealing at arm's length with concern for the bottom line brings accountability, discipline, and focus, but where systems dominate human relationships, it creates a sense of helplessness and loss of commitment. Francis Fukuyama, in his book entitled *Trust*, quotes a study showing that in 1993, only 37 percent of Americans felt that they could trust "most people," down from 58 percent in 1960.[20] Relocation due to industrial restructuring based on the cold logic of economic efficiency, spiraling litigation, expanding state interference in every sphere of our personal lives, and an increased sense of social isolation, all reflect and contribute to an increased level of cynicism and distrust. For many, restructuring means firing. For corporations, distrust and cynicism will continue to erode loyalty, commitment, and innovation. The result is that employees feel disconnected and have no trust. According to *Business Week,*

"The danger for corporate America is that the disconnected may sap productivity . . . [because employees are] . . . less willing to put in the extra effort needed to keep customers happy say execs and experts."[21] Mechanical restructuring based on cold logic can produce compliance, but to gain a competitive edge you need commitment.

As mentioned, 68 percent of the customers you lose will leave you because they feel they have been treated with indifference. When employees feel they do not count, they are more likely to treat others with indifference. Whether it be frontline employees dealing with customers or those involved in design and production as discussed in the Chrysler example, a corporation can gain productivity when employees feel they can make a difference. To move from compliance to commitment, you need a corporate structure that combines the discipline and consistency of systems with the sense of participation afforded by relationships.

Your corporate structure needs to transfer ownership of work to those who are best suited to solve problems as they occur. Success in the information age will go to the organization with the ability to be flexible, responsive, and effective. The organization's new role is to support rather than to subvert and to develop rather than to control. The question may well be asked, What is that corporate structure?

Corporate Structure: What It Should Do

To extinguish a wood fire, it is most effective to use water. If you are faced with a gasoline fire, it is more effective to use foam because water may spread the flames and not accomplish the task. Likewise, organizations need to use effective corporate approaches to match market trends and douse the flames of competitors' actions. Our Western inclination for either/or solutions prompts us to look for one right answer, one corporate strategy, one management style, one approach that fits all situations. However, the ki principle I discussed previously asks us to adapt our style according to the situation and then be ready to adapt all over again.

A study by Charles M. Farkas and Suzy Wetlaufer found five

major leadership approaches that could be adopted to meet the needs of an organization responding to a given business situation.[22] The approach you choose, which in turn influences your corporate structure, depends on type of customer, market trends, competitor capabilities, industry regulations, advances in technology, and complexity in distribution and manufacturing systems including company core values and the character of employees' personalities. In a dynamic environment where innovation means survival, some executives see their role as promoting change and championing renewal. They favor an environment that embraces ambiguity and uncertainty, and they push aside control systems such as formal written reports, complex procedural rules, and infinitely detailed plans. These executives promote frequent and open communication with customers, suppliers, employees, and shareholders. Such executives favor hiring nonconformist employees who value independence, take initiative, and are willing to take risks. These organizations favor breakthrough products rather than product extension or modification. If you are in the software business or the fashion world, you probably use an approach that favors change.

When I fly, however, I'm not interested in having the pilots use the change approach. Who wants them trying new takeoff or landing procedures with a plane full of passengers? I want my doctor to use the latest technology and medicine. But I also want to know that it has been tested, retested, and approved. Some organizations are bound by legislation, and some, by the nature of their business, are subject to legal liabilities. In many companies, such as those in the pharmaceutical, finance, or airline industries, a highly structured system may be favored. Although the invention of a new drug or a new service requires an innovative environment where decisions have an enormous consequence, a step-by-step process is needed to ensure that no detail be overlooked. This requires a different corporate structure. Likewise, companies that employ a large number of professionals or those that provide on-the-spot customer service need a different corporate approach and structure.

Obviously, there are overlaps among all these approaches. But for the most part, matching your corporate strengths and limitations with market opportunities and threats means moving with the situation and not being stuck with a rigid mechanical order. The point is not to look for a structure that is a one-size-fits-all mold. What is important is to look for what your corporate structure should provide.

Business Logic, Human Disposition

Should a company be centralized or decentralized? Should it be large or small? How many divisions should it have? For example, through decentralization, large corporations can delegate decision-making to frontline workers, who are in the best position to know about and respond to customer preferences, competitors' actions, and local market trends. Decentralization gives a regional office accountability, flexibility, quick reaction time, and the ability to adapt goods and services to customer specifications.[23]

On the other hand, activities such as providing information services or conducting research and development work lend themselves to centralization. Centralization provides economies of scale, consistency, concentration of talents and expertise, and ease of exchange. For example, centralizing on-line financial information ensures that everyone (especially field personnel who may not be in the office often) has consistent information on topics such as terms of transactions, trading rules, yields, and tax considerations.

As you can see, there are a number of good business principles that you could advance to support centralization, decentralization, or a combination of both. However, business logic works best when it incorporates our human disposition. Human beings organize socially. People seek to form personal alliances within a group of others with whom they identify. From an evolutionary point of view, it seems we have been wired to prefer group sizes of about 150 members.[24] This favors a number of smaller divisions with which people can identify, interact, and gain meaning balanced with the need for integration, collaboration, and networking.

Within a group, the desire to obtain status in an organizational setting is part of human nature. Although the West rewards individual effort, we also put importance on egalitarian values. We must recognize and harmonize our human nature with our social values. An organization in which management treats everyone the same may fit our egalitarian values. But there is such a thing as people working harder because they have the opportunity to rise above someone else. Effective management will need to balance the advantages offered by an egalitarian approach with the need of some individuals to gain status. Business logic that dictates centralization, unit size, job description, and responsibilities needs to be harmonized with our human disposition and social values.

Autonomy and Discipline

At their extreme, rules, regulations, and standardization stifle productivity. In the name of innovation and productivity, many companies have given individuals full autonomy and thrown out the rules and regs. But starting with a blank sheet can be as counterproductive as having too much standardization. At Toyota, they have a number of standards, provide close supervision, and have a well-understood procedure that governs car design and production.[25] Standards that are produced by those responsible for their application are useful to define current capabilities and best practices. Standards used as checklists guide design, add predictability, and increase efficiency. At Toyota, standards, like well-understood procedures, are used mainly as milestones to ensure progress and facilitate learning. Corporate structure should provide a balance between control and our need for autonomy. Close supervision that provides for adjustments, promotes coordination, facilitates learning, and provides encouragement helps the corporation, the group, and the person all to reach their goals.

Creating Interdependence

Developing a strategy involves integrating functions, activities, and interactions to fit your business situation.[26] In today's competitive global environment, having a unique functional capability is not enough to give you a long-term competitive edge. The competition can duplicate an excellent sales force or the best R&D department. Your corporate strength depends on integrating various functions within the company and attuning them to market demands. One factor alone will not give you competitive strength; it is the integration of many factors within your approach that will make your company competitive. Inventing a new miracle drug is great, but you won't achieve top sales unless you have the distribution network.

Although we recognize integration's importance in theory, how can we accomplish it in practice? In many companies, the people in purchasing tend to favor current suppliers who have been reliable over the years. The appeal may be reliability and lower cost. The technologists, on the other hand, like to experiment and look for new capabilities and, thus, are open to new suppliers.[27] To reconcile these polar opposites, managers for the two different functions could report to the same executive, who, when presented with the alternatives' pros and cons, is in a better position to make a decision. It would then be that executive's role to recognize and to balance the competing perspectives. If it is not practical for the managers to report to the same executive, each could be given cross-functional or dual responsibility in which their departments depend on one another for certain services. The dual responsibility would force them to recognize their interdependence and foster cooperation between the dual functions.[28] Sprint, which is a $20 billion telecommunications corporation, bases no more than 65 percent of its individual division presidents' bonuses on their divisions' performance. The remaining 35 to 50 percent depends on the performance of other divisions.[29] These examples illustrate a system approach to resolving the needs for integration and synergy. As you can appreciate, negotiating a relationship that promotes cooperation could produce comparable results.

For integration to take place, it is important for people to see the whole—how everything fits together. However, expertise and functional departments are still needed. Improvement in cross-functional integration must not take place at the expense of in-depth technical and functional knowledge. Whether you are designing a car, looking for a new drug, or encoding new software, you need high-level technical expertise and functional departments. Your structure should encourage the flow of relevant information among different experts and departments while still maintaining functional specialization.

Your corporate structure must combine the advantages of business logic with human predisposition, the advantages of individual autonomy with system discipline. Standards, like systems, provide discipline, but when you look at your structure, you need to ask, "Are these systems needed? If not, why do they persist?" To evaluate your system you need to ask, "Is what we do useful to the customer, or is it done simply because the system requires it?"

Should you negotiate a contract? Should you negotiate a relationship? Contracts, standardization, rules, and procedures provide consistency, while relationships provide flexibility. Relationships stress long-term organizational bonding, partnership, and commitment and do not depend on fixed corporate structure settings. The optimum structure allows employees to solve customer problems. It integrates the different functional expertise to fit your situation and provides the tools, the budget, and the information to empower employees to leverage their skills and their knowledge. Rules and standardization favored by a contractual approach can provide useful guidelines and a wealth of knowledge. Process comes from shared understanding, demand, proximity, and relationships. Corporate structure should vary according to the situation by incorporating the advantages of contractual and relationship approaches while recognizing the need for business logic and discipline as well as our human disposition and need for autonomy.

Successful companies have learned to link the customer to the organization's capabilities. Market demand tells you what your customers are willing to pay for. Your corporate structure and resources tell you what you are good at. But when all is said and done, work gets done by people. The willingness of employees to commit is greatly influenced by your corporate core values, that is, what you stand for.

Pushing responsibilities to frontline workers constitutes one of the critical factors of success. This means workers must be given the mandate to make decisions needed to solve problems or take advantage of opportunities. There is an interrelationship between what the market is willing to pay for, what you are good at, and what you stand for. And what you stand for will have a great deal of influence on employee willingness to take on responsibilities. Call it reengi-neering, instituting entrepreneurialship, or total quality management, empowering your employees toward a common purpose has a great effect on their commitment to the organization.

Empowerment

The degree to which employees should be empowered depends to some extent on your corporate approach as well as on the willing-ness of management to transfer ownership and of employees to accept responsibilities. Empowerment means employees have the authority to change what they are responsible for.

Although both management and employees accept empower-ment in theory, it is different in practice. "Empowerment" where management institutes processes that employees must adhere to without deviation or where employees quickly run to management for help is not really about empowerment. In Chapter 8, I will discuss in more detail some of the stumbling blocks to empowerment. Suffice it to say here, some managers are often reluctant to let go of authority. A number of man-agers would find it difficult to adopt another mode of man-agement other than command-and-control. Likewise a number of employees are ready to endorse empowerment as long as they are not accountable. We need to accept that a great number of employees are risk-averse and prefer the certainty and comfort of well-defined tasks. There is nothing wrong with that, and it is especially suitable for a cor-porate approach and functions that require routine work. Your cor-porate structure needs to give leaders the ability to take into consideration different employee and management dispositions. Empowerment does bring a greater level of commitment, but it is

Two stone cutters were asked what they were doing. The first said, "I'm cutting this stone into blocks."

The second replied, "I'm on a team that's building a cathedral."

unrealistic to expect that all employees and management will be willing to fully participate.

Overall, your ability to empower will greatly influence the level of innovation and productivity. A great number of employees prefer to be movers rather than passive observers. These employees want full responsibility to shape their work objectives, define the tasks, and specify how they can be achieved. It is also fair to say that all humans seek meaningful work, recognition, and acknowledgment for their contribution. Managers, like employees, seek respect and need to be given space in a supportive environment where they can interact and create in a meaningful way.

Establishing Order and Purpose

Peter Drucker has said, "Society, community, family *are*; organizations *do*."[30] Their purpose is to produce benefits consistent with society's needs and customers' expectations. A group of individuals capable of self-organization and cooperation can create greater economic wealth than an individual acting alone. Working as a group toward a common goal can create a deep sense of purpose and satisfaction. To attain that common goal requires the establishment of order and control to ensure all activities contribute to it.

Control has often been associated with power, and power is often related to corruption. But as Roger Dawson states in his discussion on power, "It really isn't power that corrupts, is it? It's the abuse of power. You wouldn't say that water is bad because occasionally we have floods and people get killed."[31] Any form of power, whether it be legitimate power, reward power, coercive power, reverent power, charismatic power, expertise power, situational power, or informational power, can be abused when taken to the extreme. That is the difference between abusive power and constructive authority. Here I consider three forms of authority that particularly suit my Western/Eastern discussion. These models are commonly referred to as the carrot-and-stick model, the pyramid-chain-of-command model, and the shared-values model.

Carrot-and-Stick Model

The carrot-and-stick approach is used to reward or discipline employees for expected behavior and performance. Rewards such as commissions and bonuses can serve as a powerful motivator to bring about desired response and sustain changes in a new direction. But employees, like customers, have different needs, and they are motivated by and respond differently to rewards. Providing material rewards for measurable performance fits very well with the Western view and, for some employees, becomes a tangible measure of their success and may be sufficient in itself. To participate in a team's accomplishment, to receive recognition for a job well done, or to associate with fellow workers are just some of the other rewards that workers view as more-than-fair compensation.

While many organizations use positive motivators, the stick approach is also prevalent in organizations of all types. There are a number of situations where discipline needs to be exercised, but when it is required, the application of discipline should not jeopardize the integrity of the person. The exercise of authority through intimidation, threats, and sometimes even physical force brings results in the short term, but in the long term it usually has negative effects such as fear, cynicism, retaliation, and anger. Fear undermines cooperation, destroys creativity, and burns out the best of employees. Reengineering with fear will change employees' expectations that the workplace can be a rewarding and stimulating environment, and it will promote instead defensive action, confrontation, and the loss of hope.[32] Cynicism and distrust will ultimately lower corporate performance.

Rewards by themselves can create dependency on explicit expectations. Where every action is well-defined and related to a reward, employees can feel manipulated. Equally, employees can use that situation to manipulate results to conform with expectations. While material rewards serve as a motivator, alone they are not sufficient to keep people's energy and enthusiasm fully charged. For most employees, the chance to contribute directly to the decision-making process is not only rewarding but also encourages commitment. As stated by Richard Freeman, "firms that give workers financial incentives but do not empower them to make decisions are unlikely to benefit from their incentive regime." Employee involvement improves productivity more than incentive pay alone.[33] The chance for employees to act as partners and take part in decision making is largely influenced by the corporate reporting system and shared vision model.

Pyramid-Chain-of-Command Model

The chain-of-command model is outlined by an organizational chart that defines the framework of responsibilities, authorities, and duties. The organization's chart is accompanied by a set of explicit rules and procedures that govern roles and relationships according to position in the organization.

This model is effective in highly regulated industries, stable business environments, and in areas where there can be no error between design and application. In highly regulated industries such as banking or pharmaceuticals, the pyramid model can effectively ensure no details are overlooked and no errors are made. Some people work best in well-defined roles. For them, this approach is an efficient means of production as long as rules and procedures work for the employees, and the employees don't work for the rules and procedures. Where market consistency is important and for employees who prefer well-defined roles, the pyramid or, if you like, the bureaucratic approach brings accountability, efficiency, and a greater level of predictability.

Taken to the extreme, rules and procedures give rise to mechanical bureaucracy where everyone is boxed into a fixed role. Negotiating a contract brings conformity, and conformity has its price. The box approach can be stifling; it can discourage initiative and dampen creativity. When the box approach becomes rigid, employees spend most of their time feeding and satisfying the requirements of the system, working for its rules and procedures. The result severely limits the organization's flexibility to adapt to changing conditions, and performance output is hampered and curtailed.

Expected collaboration and well-understood social differentials in relationships can also bring conformity. As a hierarchical society the Japanese are well aware of every individual's position, status, and expected role. Although business based on relationships fosters healthy exchange of information and flexibility, looking for appeasement can impede the exchange of relevant information. At its extreme, concessions to preserve a public image bring conformity and curtail the benefits of working knowledge or the Japanese consensus ringi system. As an egalitarian society, Americans are more likely to downplay the power differential demanded by social and corporate pyramids. But whether you are boxed in by mechanical rules or by well-delineated differential relationships, it brings about rigidity and conformity and hampers the advantage of working knowledge.

To be effective, the pyramid approach needs to combine the reliability of structure with the flexibility of relation. In balance, the pyramid approach brings the advantages of accountability, consistency, clarity, and predictability. Although the three modes of authority are treated separately, they are interrelated. If you combine the pyramid approach with the shared-values model, you will reap the benefits of both.

Shared-Values Model

Lately, corporate vision and core values have taken the spotlight. Working toward a common goal gives people a sense of belonging and of identity. In many situations, it's not what the vision *is* but what the vision *does*.[34] For example, Ford's vision to build affordable public transportation for the general population and the Japanese pursuit of "zero defects" in their manufacturing changed whole ways of doing things. As has often been said, people like to feel part of something bigger than themselves, and a shared vision that fits a larger purpose elicits a sense of unity and the greatest form of commitment. A sense of making a difference in the world and feeling pride in what they do excites people.

Vision does not of itself guarantee performance. In recent years, many executives have undertaken the task of formulating a corporate vision in the hope of increasing corporate performance. The results have been disappointing. A study by the Jensen Group found that of the companies surveyed 70 percent had revised their corporate mission to bring about change, but only 9 percent felt the revised mission had helped them to achieve their goals.[35] How can we account for this failure?

Many companies recognize that the quality of input and performance is greater if they treat their employees as business partners. For many managers, this has become quite evident, and they take great care to communicate their intentions. But although more than 60 percent of managers believe they treat their employees as business partners, only 27 percent of employees believe they are treated as business partners.[36] In part, too many corporate visions represent one person's goals imposed on the rest of the organization.[37] These personal goals are represented and portrayed as visions. While these imposed visions can produce results, you should not confuse them with shared visions. An all-imposing vision that brings collective sanctions on members to conform can become intimidating and, like a heavy dose of rules and regulations, stifle initiative. An imposed vision provides order and direction but not necessarily enthusiasm or commitment.

Visions work best when they are shared. A shared vision, while it should allow for deviation, comes from common values that take into consideration everyone's input. The big picture is painted with little strokes.[38] A shared vision is based on educated insights into trends in technology, shifts in customer needs, and changes in regulations that demand input from a great number of employees.

A shared vision is discovered rather than invented, and it evolves over time.[39] The primary role of executives is to capture and capitalize on the foresight of employees throughout the organization. Shared visions are created by leaders who are not afraid to walk around and participate and who are able to articulate the emerging corporate knowledge.

Shared vision provides the direction and order that pulls people toward a common goal and focuses the operation on satisfying customers' expectations. The vision, which also influences the mission statement and core values statement, is like the hub of the wheel that keeps everyone moving toward the same goal. The vision tells people why they are working and paints the big picture of what they want to achieve; the mission statement tells them what they do and how, for whom, and where they do it. The core values provide the ideological and binding principles that guide companies through their business strategy and operational practices, although these strategies and practices are adapted to changing business situations. The vision should define the script well enough to coordinate and integrate activities for action when unexpected events occur, and it should be flexible enough to permit improvisations.

Developing a shared vision is easier said than done, and it requires leadership. I will discuss leadership in Chapter 8, but suffice it to say that although a shared vision reflects a commonly held belief, it is the role of the leader to inspire and articulate such purpose and meaning. A shared vision creates a sense of identity and loyalty where everyone feels responsible for the success of the company.[40]

> *Softness and hardness are opposites. So are oneness and separateness. These opposites generate, define, and enhance each other.*
> —*The Tao of Zen*

Both North Americans and Japanese, through their reward and disciplinary systems, have had a dose of the carrot-and-stick approach. In keeping with our inclination to negotiate a contract, Americans put greater emphasis on the organizational chart and rely on legality, rules, and procedural systems. By softening the imposition of rules demanded by the pyramid approach, you can retain the advantage of clear accountability and add the advantages of more flexibility, of having the ability to adapt and attune the organization to the situation, and of bringing about greater commitment and dedication that comes from a shared value system.

Our Western inclination for mechanical order, for cause and effect, makes us look for the one right answer, the one right structure, the one right process, the one right rule. The mechanical order makes us look for clear and explicit information to negotiate our contractual obligations. Negotiating a relationship puts more weight on judgment, intuition, and experience. It relies more on implicit information with emphasis on the circumstances surrounding the present situation. In combination, contracts and relationships give us the advantages that come from accountability and flexibility, logic and intuition. Combined, they give us working knowledge.

Mass Craftsmanship Production

The modern organization needs the capacity to combine the efficiency offered by mass production with the preindustrial effectiveness of individualized craftsmanship; hence, the term *mass craftsmanship production.* Unlike traditional division of tasks, mass craftsmanship gives the person the tools needed to perform all the required work when and where it is needed. It combines the different functions into an integrated whole and gives those responsible for the job the tools to solve the problem.

In this system, marketing, manufacturing, and finance may be separate from the organization's point of view but not from the customer's. The customer judges the service as a whole and does not score each department separately. All employees, therefore, must work on the premise that they work for the customer, so the organizational structure must support a process allowing all employees to solve problems. This makes employees feel they are part of the organization by giving them a sense of ownership and significance. In such a process, the customer wins, the employee wins, and the organization benefits through greater customer loyalty and gains in productivity.

But what are the payoffs of getting everyone on board? John Browne, the chief executive who engineered the revival of British Petroleum, believes that all companies in the global information age face a common challenge: using knowledge more effectively than their competitors do. With research and development costs three times higher than those of its major competitors, BP was having a hard time making money.[41] In 1995, BP spent an average of 100 days drilling deep water wells; by 1997, they had cut that time to 42 days. Today, BP's research and development costs are among the lowest in the industry. How did they do it?

In an interview with Steven E. Prokesch, Browne lists four key elements that give a company a competitive edge. The company should create distinct "assets and market share, technologies, organization, and relationships." Your corporate culture, management, and areas of specialization give you your unique assets and market share. You need distinct and leading-edge technology to give you "an advantage in competing for customers and partners." A distinct organization is one where "its people are highly motivated, understand exactly what they have to do to help create great value, can see the results of their actions, and have a sense of ownership."[42] Distinct relationships develop by working with partners such as suppliers, contractors, the community, other businesses, and the customer.

For Browne, "The top management team must stimulate the organization, not control it." Individuals need to feel "they [can] control the destiny of our businesses." This can be done by having "those closest to BP's assets and customers . . . run their business." A company organization should be divided so it gives people "pride of ownership." People need "to see the impact of their actions on the business' performance."[43] Because of John Browne's insistence on breakthrough thinking, BP was able to reduce the development cost of the Andrew field from $674 million to $444 million. In breaking from their traditional way of doing business, a cross-disciplinary team from BP working in partnership with contractors drove the design and management of the project. This breakthrough thinking allowed everyone to have input and to share the benefits. In the end, the transfer of ownership to the front lines brought great benefits for all involved.

The Optimum Structure

The optimum structure is the one that best complements your business approach and is most consistent with the market demand. Many arguments exist for and against creating interdependence, reengineering for a process-oriented organization, decentralizing and centralizing, and determining whether to emphasize rules or results, but the system that works best is the organizational structure that creates interdependence and transfers ownership to employees to allow those close to problems to solve them. Your system needs to transfer ownership to the frontline people, who are responsible for customers, capital, and technology. Your system, including structure, objectives, policies, and standards, must provide discipline and focus, and it must foster participation.

Looking for one structure that fits all is consistent with the mechanical view of rules and procedures, but it does not necessarily fit the situation. Undue attention to the structure should not deflect attention away from the most important and critical factor—the people who make it happen. There is no one structure that fits all. Your system must promote integration and participation, and it will have to mold itself to suit the different talents, corporate culture, and personalities of your business environment.

Transferring ownership to frontline employees requires a structural change as well as a change in process. The greater challenge, however, is putting into question and perhaps even attempting to change people's assumptions and attitudes. For managers, it means putting aside their egos and letting go of authority. For department heads, it means greater collaboration and acceptance of their mutual dependence. Between suppliers and buyers, it means sharing information and negotiating relationships based on long-term reciprocity. And for employees it means greater dedication to learning and to taking initiative.

While many good books and publications point the way to implementing these new roles, you can appreciate that successfully overhauling a corporation's approach is easier said than done. Where does a company begin? What does this new style of management look like? What are the stumbling blocks? Let's move on to the next chapter and see what we can discover.

8

Leadership

When all is said and done, the understanding of market needs and the molding of a corporate approach is done by people. Call a market what you want, it is people and their needs that the corporation is there to satisfy. Call a corporate approach what you want, it is people who make the decisions and execute the plan. A leader's job is to create the environment that allows employees to make things happen.

Leaders should be able to shape the vision, set strategic direction, influence events, and inspire purpose. Your corporate environment, a good dose of personal competence, and the skill to mobilize resources all affect your ability to shape the vision, set direction, and influence events. Although these aspects are interrelated, the ability to inspire purpose is most illusive. Whether it be in the military, politics, nonprofit organizations or industry, great leaders have one thing in common: the ability to inspire, to create identity, and to give meaning. In every field of endeavor, terms such as *integrity, perseverance, self-discipline, energy, flexibility, confidence, sense of justice and fairness, assertiveness, empathy,* and *creativity* are used to describe leaders. Leaders must have the ability to pick up cues and the capacity to sense and understand the viewpoints of others. They need drive and must be able to monitor and control their behavior to fit the situation.[1]

Daniel Goleman in his discussion "What Makes a Leader?" contends that although technical skills, long-term vision, and IQ are important ingredients to performance, emotional intelligence is twice as important.[2] In Chapter 10, I will cover in greater detail the relevance of emotional intelligence and competence. For the present, as discussed in Chapter 1, it is emotional intelligence that gives us our ability for self-awareness, empathy, and self-regulation—that is, control of our impulses. Our value system greatly influences the way we lead, and by combining both Eastern and Western values, we will increase our ability to lead.

If you recall, in Chapter 1 I defined the role of the American executive as motivator, provider of direction, and maker of decisions. This is in keeping with our view of the distinct individual who knows who he or she is and takes charge. The role of the Japanese executive is to maintain harmony within and good relations outside the organization. This typifies the Japanese view of harmony and obligation toward others. Great leaders combine those two roles. Strategic direction is important, but for it to work, leaders need to foster strong connections and cultivate effective networks within and among different working units. To do this and gain commitment, you need the ability to articulate a vision reflecting a common purpose that leads to action. In the corporate sector, delegation means the leader provides the environment that allows employees to take part in achieving the common purpose.

> *In the West the focus is on the individual. In the East the focus is on the relationship between individuals.*

How do you create meaning? What are some of the problems, what are the challenges? Let's look at some of the challenges to leadership and the stumbling blocks that prevent us from putting the needed changes into practice. Taking a balanced approach, I will discuss what makes for good employees, as well as the characteristics of good leadership.

Challenges to Leadership

Our Western pursuit of heroic individualism and distinction has created an enviable class of entrepreneurship and innovation. However, in its extreme, our Western inclination to take control negates participation and group effort. Assuming total control where no one has input brings compliance, not commitment. People need to feel they count. In the extreme, individualism and a mechanistic approach isolate, discourage input, and make people feel indifferent. Some will further feel worthless and helpless. To create purpose and meaning, leaders must create the environment that makes people feel they count and that they can contribute by being part of the solution.

In the Western world, the institutionalization of a mechanical order in the corporation means that management values and pays attention to the tangible and the measurable. With the integration of the mechanical order, the focus is on logic, economic utility, and rules at the expense of loyalty, commitment, and relationships. A CEO's crunching ability to cut costs is important but has little to do with generating trust and inspiration. The prevalence of a mechanical view also means that intuition, judgment, and imagination often are treated as optional. Leadership requires the ability to sense the mood and identify others' personal and collective goals. Rules have their place, but where they dominate, they deprive people of the ability to establish purpose. Rules deprive leadership of flexibility and the advantages offered by creative and innovative solutions.

In a 1994 article in the *Harvard Business Review,* Gary Hamel and C. K. Prahalad contend, "Despite excuses about global competition and the impact of productivity-enhancing technology, most layoffs at large U.S. companies have been the fault of senior managers who fell asleep at the wheel and missed the turnoff for the future."[3] Jack Welch, CEO of General Electric said,

> If we are going to satisfy customers and win in the marketplace, American managers have got to simplify more, delegate more, and simply trust more. We need to drive self-confidence deep into the organization. A company can't distribute self-confidence, but it can foster it by

> removing layers and giving people a chance to win. We
> have to undo a 100-year-old concept of leadership and
> convince our managers their role is not to control people
> and stay "on top" of things, but rather to guide, to ener-
> gize, and to excite.[4]

Traditional hierarchies operate under the assumption that people at the top *think* and people at the bottom *act*. For most employees, traditional vertical hierarchies are ill-suited to satisfy needs such as self-respect and self-development. These vertical hierarchies are like a dogsled team. Only the front dog gets a glimpse of the scenery. If you are the lead dog in such a structure, expect little discussion when you seek input about the lay of the land. Leadership is about providing everyone with a view of the scenery. In today's knowledge-driven economy, developing an organization in which everyone can see the horizon reaps benefits both for the individual and for the organization.

This depends on handing over ownership, ownership that allows employees to think about what needs to be done and gives them the authority to take the needed action to solve the problem. As a leader you must be able to articulate a common vision and to provide the tools needed. But very importantly, you need to realize which factors may hamper your ability to do so.

Look Inside Before You Initiate

Much of the change corporations set in motion during reengineering efforts does not produce the desired results. While there are several factors responsible for this failure, perhaps the most important one is the failure of leaders and managers to look at themselves. Although management often is good at engineering change for others, most managers are not very good at engineering change for themselves.[5] But unless management is willing to adapt too, ceaseless talking about change and attempts to change employees produces very little.

> To change and to improve are two different things.
>
> —German Proverb

In an article in the *Harvard Business Review,* Thomas M. Hout and John C. Carter contend that only senior managers can finish what reengineering begins. The concept of the CEO as a hero and the manager as a baron is dead. Citing an example of a reengineering attempt gone awry, Hout and Carter write, "Improvement stopped because senior managers did not recognize the myriad of ways in which they were hindering the re-engineering effort. Put simply, they [managers] were good at championing change but poor at changing themselves."[6] Let's look at some of the stumbling blocks that need to be removed if efforts to bring about meaningful and productive change are to succeed.

Stumbling Blocks

In the 1980s, embracing new ideas and programs became a way for companies to signal they were progressive. Programs of all types, from "out-sourcing" to "benchmarking" were adopted, but in many cases, these programs realized disappointing results. Surveys indicate program adoption failure rates range between 70 and 80 percent.[7] Still, in 1993, U.S. companies forked out $17 billion to listen to consultants talk about the latest business programs and solutions.[8]

Why do some programs fail? People, not organizations, create stumbling blocks. Here are ten of them. How many of these stumbling blocks do you recognize in your organization?

The Flavor-of-the-Month Syndrome

Managers, like their teenage children, are not immune to the latest fads.[9] Almost daily, new off-the-shelf, one-minute answers are introduced and championed as revolutionary, guaranteed-breakthrough solutions. Change for change's sake can provoke fear, deflect management time from viable business activities, and destroy your organization's core competencies. This does not mean you should be rigid. Changes are often needed, and it is management's responsibility to pick and choose from those ideas. A manager's job is not to seek novelty; it is to make sure the company performs. You need to be able to separate the seed from the chaff as you pick ideas pertinent to your business reality. Quick fixes would be nice, but they don't exist.

Hook, Line, and Sinker

Fads aside, there are many excellent ideas and programs. However, management must first choose those that are applicable and then adapt the proposed programs to the context of the company. Remember, a business theory is a model to provide direction, not all-encompassing answers. An Indian dish spiced with strong curry and chili peppers would do well in India but may need to be adapted to suit the American palate.

Lack of Involvement

For a new program to succeed, senior management must set the example and be actively involved. You need to assign key managers to a winning team to spearhead the change, but the team will do little unless it is fully supported by senior management. Many executives prefer to focus on operations rather than deal with touchy issues that may arise with the introduction of new principles. Although on paper companies look like machines, they aren't—they are made up of people. Like biological organisms, companies react to stimuli.[10] Your organization succeeds when your employees listen to the customers. In the same way, a program is more likely to succeed when you listen to your employees. Employee reaction can be used to fine-tune and balance the program to fit the culture of the organization. Equally important, lack of involvement sends the signal that the proposed program is not of high priority. You lead by example. Success requires involvement at every level.

Hidden Assumptions

Sometimes what we say and what we do are two different things. People generally behave in a way to retain control because they want to increase their likelihood of winning and decrease their likelihood of losing.[11] One way to retain control is to disguise and hide assumptions and premises. Often, under these circumstances, over-rationalization takes over, and assumptions are kept hidden.

Such hidden agendas are elusive and dangerous. While many corporate decisions are governed by sound business logic, it just isn't true that *all* decisions are made rationally and in congruence with organizational objectives. When a change or a problem presents a threat to personal agendas or exposes weakness, defensive reasoning takes over. To protect themselves, people will produce elaborate rational or scientific arguments in support of their pet corrective action plan. Doing research to get the numbers you want is easy. Credible explanations can then be presented as being scientific in order to get the desired response. (See Appendix A, "Research: How to Get the Answers You Want"). This is not to belittle research, nor is the problem particular to the world of business. To evaluate any research, it is important to be aware of a sponsor's agenda, the researchers' expertise, and more importantly, the hidden assumptions.

We all have areas of uncertainty. Being in touch with your assumptions and emotions will provide a better basis of rationality and action. From an organizational point of view, once assumptions are taken for granted, learning stops.[12] An organization must allow people to take risks in an environment where they do not have to fear ridicule or embarrassment or even job loss when they question established practices.

One-Way Communication

Is communication a barrier or a learning tool? If worthwhile changes are to take place, you need to address several factors. Recognizing your reaction to change, training for new skills, setting standards of performance, and securing support from management are the minimum requirements. All of this demands intensive, frequent, and honest communication at all levels. Don't expect communication to solve everything. Communication is a tool, not a fix. It is the dialogue that leads to understanding and better solutions.

Communication is a two-way street. It involves receiving a message as well as sending it. It is about listening, the delivery side of communication—and most of us aren't very good at it. The Chinese have two words for listening. One is *wen,* which is composed of two symbols: door and ear. It implies you hear the information. The other is *ting,* which comprises the symbols for ear, king, ten, eye, one, and heart. It implies listening with the ears, the eyes, and with one heart as if the speaker is a king.[13] This is understanding on a deeper level. Listening facilitates the learning that provides the self-corrective process needed in a truly dynamic environment. But there are two distinct types of listening: listening with the intent to understand and listening with the intent to respond, and the two should not be confused.[14] Listening with the intent to understand an issue or another's point of view does not necessarily mean you will change your mind or your position.[15] It means listening to gather information about the other person, to understand his or her perspective, or as Covey would say, to understand "another person's frame of reference."[16]

The label *open communication* has been used by many as the solution to a plethora of problems. However, many of these so-called open communicators are Artful Dodgers. They are most interested in promoting their own agendas—without dialogue—and they do all the talking while the rest of us do all the listening. At the end of their monologues, we're all assured that "this is an open discussion" and that "questions are welcome." Questions are quickly followed with an explanation of what is being done and a polite thank you for your concerns. Furthermore, too often open communication is followed by no action, which is followed in turn by another monologue.

While it is important to be skillful in the delivery side of communication, don't be an Artful Dodger. Don't hide behind your delivery. Artful delivery is truly a skill, but it is only one side of the communication equation; used by itself, without listening, it can be a great barrier to good communication. Be alert to the label *open communication.* It can signal a new way to hide problems, entrench a position, or promote one's pet theory.

Communication is worth very little unless people perceive your sincerity. A number of studies have shown that in spoken communication, the actual verbal content of the message accounts for 7 percent of the impact, while the nonverbal content of the message, such as the speaker's tone of voice, projected confidence, and credibility, accounts for 93 percent of the impact. The nonverbal content of your message confirms, reinforces, or contradicts your verbal message. In other words, a number of researchers confirm what most people know: what you say is not so important as what you represent as a person. Well-prepared, rational, and eloquent statements about what you and the company stand for have little impact (or may even have the opposite of the intended impact) unless people trust you as a person. Communication can work for or against you. To be effective, communication has to be honest and clear and done with the intent to listen and to take corrective action.

Distrust

After management implements restructuring changes, employees trust management less. Contemporary North American corporate culture is characterized by layoffs, relocations, and plant transfers. This situation has left middle managers, specialists, white collar workers, and blue collar workers feeling alienated from their companies. While most employees will accept apparently worthwhile changes, a great number of employees believe management cheats, lies, and fails in leadership. In fact, surveys indicate 64 percent of workers do not trust management because they believe management lies.[17] But cynicism and distrust are not restricted to employees. Management's lack of trust in employees results in instituting top-heavy organizational structures and control systems. Too often, mistrust, more than business requirements, dictates the organizational activity and management style. The irony is that the more system you introduce, the more distrust you get, which again leads to the addition of still more system of control.

Trust is still very much part of Western values. Medieval Christian ethics such as compassion, obligation to others, loyalty, and a sense of duty have not entirely disappeared. But in a climate of escalating restructuring based on the prevalence of hard cold rules over human bonds, trust, loyalty, participation, and commitment may further erode unless we soften our penchant for the mechanical order.

The Need to Retain Control

Good managers are able to create a strong sense of pride in their people, and they have the ability to focus on the competencies of the people who work for them. The problem with the need to control is that, for many, it is a need for personal power and the manipulation of others. According to Robert Swiggett, CEO of Kollmorgen, "What drives most executives of traditional organizations is power, the desire to be in control. Most would rather give up anything than control."[18]

In his classic studies of large corporations, David McClelland, a distinguished research professor of psychology at Harvard, concludes "that the top managers of a company must possess a high need for power, that is, a concern for influencing people."[19] The need for power as a determinant in achieving a top management position was found to be a better predictor than the need for achievement or affiliation. However, McClelland observed that in good managers the need for power was not oriented toward personal aggrandizement but toward outcomes for the organization.[20] The better managers were described to have a high need for power balanced by a high ability to subordinate their own egos for the good of the organization.[21] Better managers were more mature and less egotistical, more positive about their self-image, less defensive, more willing to seek advice from experts, and more able to demonstrate a democratic coaching style.

Obviously, there is a difference between exercising influence to accomplish organizational goals and manipulating others to satisfy a person's need for power and aggrandizement. Exercising power to influence organizational goals works.

Throughout history, one of the best means to retain control has been through keeping others ignorant.[22] Too often, the manager's inner need for control keeps him or her from supplying information to employees. Do not underestimate the need to retain power. While most managers recognize the value of an informed employee and the relationship between the employee's knowledge level and the organization's effectiveness, proper information channels may not be in place. As you review your organization, consider how information is transferred to and from employees and how you might facilitate keeping your employees sufficiently informed.

Personal Disposition

Our upbringing has a large influence on the way we judge things and make decisions. Whether our parents encouraged competitiveness or cooperation, were authoritarian or permissive has a large influence on how we relate to others. As a manager, your personal motives more than your business logic may be reflected in your corporate structure and policies.

In Chapter 10, I discuss how the four major personality styles influence negotiation. While some people are impressed by pictures, others are impressed by data. Some want to review all the details while others only want the conclusion. What is important to remember is that the request for further market analysis or budgetary control may have more to do with personal disposition than corporate requirements.

We have a great capacity for adaptation, but don't underestimate the impact of your upbringing and the influence of your predisposition in overriding your awareness of your leadership style. Sometimes we cannot escape these early influences. There are times when you may have to consider working for an organization that operates in an environment more suited to your personality. An awareness of your personality type puts you in a

> *Choose a job you love, and you will never have to work a day in your life.*
>
> —*Confucius*

better position to choose a suitable organizational environment in which to work. As well, it allows you to recognize when the demands you impose on the company may have little to do with business reality.

Cultural Blocks

Cultural assumptions and their influences have been discussed under "Problems to Leadership" and throughout this book. The Western ideology of rugged individualism favors the confrontational approach—that is, the individual who takes charge, who knows the answers, who sets direction, who makes key decisions, and who motivates the troops. Taking charge and exercising control fits the hero image. Of course, your position is easy to justify because you can always point to a fundamental of Western culture: individual initiative. But there is no justification for taking charge to the point where no one else can take initiative; that hurts the organization. It does little to motivate others or to encourage informed options. In today's educated environment, people are skeptical and they are quick to distinguish between the essential and the irrelevant. Because we accept individualism in the West, we readily accept heroic pursuits. If we push these heroics to the extreme, though, we pay the price of excluding participation.

The Western mechanical order favors a structured bureaucracy that demands clear functions and delineated tasks. On an organizational level, we pay less attention to the interdependence of each department or to those outside the corporation such as suppliers, government agencies, and the surrounding community. At the individual level, this means a premium is placed on logic with little attention to intuition, disposition, judgment, and interpersonal relationships. The problem with this dominant cultural bias is that workers and the marketplace seldom behave in accordance with the mechanical rigidity of a bureaucracy. The cultural assumptions then become cultural blocks to change, innovation, shared vision, and the advantages offered by interdependence, participation, and cooperation. In short, an insensitivity to our cultural biases and an unwillingness to recognize cultural assumptions other than our own can leave us out of sync with effective corporate approaches and meeting market trends.

Relationship Pitfalls

Many of the attributes listed for good employees are also needed for leadership. In a study of emerging executives who failed to live up to their apparent potential, Morgan W. McCall, Jr., and Michael M. Lombardo identified a number of fatal flaws responsible for the shortfall and demise of those promising leaders.[23] Listed were:

- Insensitivity to others
- Arrogance

- Betrayal of trust
- Performance problems

Experience, understanding the industry, skills, and knowledge are essential elements of performance problems. But corporate performance by itself is not a guarantee of successful leadership. Failed leaders tend to lack integrity, to treat others like dirt, to shirk responsibility, to be know-it-alls, and to take offense when others make decisions or stand out. The majority of these flaws (and often most critical) relate to the candidates' lack of interpersonal skills. Eastern values such as collectivism, attunement, and accord make you focus on the relationship between individuals. Having confidence in your own skills is a good start, but to lead you will need to inspire others. And you cannot inspire others unless you are in tune with their needs.

Let me give an analogy for these pitfalls: using a crowded eight-lane highway requires excellent driving skills. But a good driver needs more than just good driving skills. If you want to make a left turn, it is important that you show your intention by signaling. Before you turn you also need to look to see if you are cutting off other vehicles. Good driving skills, showing your intentions, and looking out for others are all required to be a good driver.

These stumbling blocks can and must be recognized if leaders are to bring about meaningful and productive changes in our North American corporate culture. But as I said earlier, to launch a climate of positive change, employees and executives must recognize mutual responsibilities. Let's look at employees' responsibilities and then conclude with a formula for leadership.

Employees' Responsibilities

We know successful companies require a reasonable return on capital, attractive profits, solid cash flow, and lower operating costs. Surveys in Europe and North America have shown executives believe that the critical issues facing business are customer satisfaction, product and service quality, cost competitiveness, work force skills, and return on investment. All say they need dedicated employees with an organization that is flexible, lean, and innovative.

Dedication

Responsibility is a two-sided coin. Much has been said about management and leadership, but employees have responsibilities too. In a study at AT&T's prestigious Bell Laboratories, Robert Kelly and Janet Kaplan showed individual productivity depended "on the ability to channel one's expertise, creativity, and insight into work with other professionals."[24] The subjects of their study, the engineers at Bell, all had academic credentials and technical competence to do their jobs, but these abilities proved to be poor predictors of individual productivity. The following is an adaptation of nine factors that Kelly and Kaplan determined as contributing to individual performance:

1. Taking initiative—going above and beyond the requirements of the job
2. Creating access by networking with coworkers to exchange technical expertise
3. Taking responsibility to self-manage work
4. Working in teams to accomplish shared goals
5. Exercising leadership skills in building consensus
6. Contributing one's experience in helping leadership set directions
7. Listening to other perspectives and viewpoints as they relate to the organization's larger context
8. Displaying work (in writing and orally) with skill
9. Recognizing the required organizational savvy to navigate among competing interests

Of the nine points, star performers believe the key requirements are taking initiative, followed by networking and self-management. Overall, star performers believe in going above and beyond the call of duty and in taking action to benefit others and not just themselves. This is in contrast to middle performers, who believe skillfully displaying work skills and organizational savvy should be rated as the most important job requirements.

Surveys indicate that employers' views on the desirable attributes of employees have changed little over the years. The majority of employers surveyed list desirable attributes as:

1. Good communication skills
2. Positive attitude
3. Adaptability
4. High performance standards
5. Good work ethics
6. Acceptance of responsibility
7. Concern for quality and quantity
8. Honesty and reliability
9. Willingness to keep learning
10. Ability to analyze

Taking the initiative, creating a network, and accepting responsibilities for high performance require good communication skills, a positive attitude, and the ability to adapt to changing demands. Performance requires both competence and interpersonal skills and attention both to individual development and relationships between individuals.

Star performers are consistent with executive expectations for dedicated employees. Just as employers expect commitment, employees should be able to expect opportunities. Such reciprocal obligation requires a sense of belonging, shared vision, and a certain level of trust between the organization and the employees. You may expect commitment, flexibility, and hard work if in return you provide security, training, and benefits and integrate workers in decision making. Employees seek respect and want their opinions to count.

In addition to financial benefits, workers derive a sense of professional and intellectual satisfaction from work.[25] For many, work allows for development, personal growth, and a place to establish meaningful relationships. People seek significance and are very sensitive to others in their environment. A leaders' responsibility in an organization that seeks performance is to provide an environment from which people can draw a sense of significance.

Leadership

The needs to belong, to do well, and to be a part of something are a fundamental element of our humanity. Many people decry commitment and loyalty as a thing of the past, but the ingredients for commitment and loyalty are still highly valued. Loyalty, however, cannot be bought—it has to be earned. Leadership is not about privilege, position, or title; it is about responsibility. Leadership is a means to an end.[26] Leaders create shared vision that is able to unleash employees' entrepreneurial spirit and to give people a sense of significance.

Here I will talk mainly of leadership. But before doing so, we must recognize that leaders and managers have different roles and both are needed to run an organization. Leaders set strategy, while managers implement logistics. Prevalence of one style over another or the use of an inappropriate style in a given situation creates problems. As Peter Drucker says, "Management is doing things right; leadership is doing the right things." Management is more interested in rules, procedures, and efficiency. Many prefer the certainty of the spreadsheet and derive their authority from their position. Managers look at the details and are driven by internal conditions within the organization.[27] In comparison to management, leaders are more interested in the big picture and are driven by circumstances external to the organization. Although leaders and managers have different functions, both have to transfer ownership to employees, and it is leaders who need to set the stage.

The twentieth century created a number of amazing transformations that will forever change the way we live. To name but a few, we launched the airplane, split the atom, identified the structure of DNA, and invented the microchip. In a free market unrestrained by class and pedigree, individuals and corporations unleash an amazing number of initiatives and create unprecedented wealth, health, and education for the masses. From Henry Ford to Albert Einstein to Theodore Roosevelt, great titans, thinkers, and leaders appeared in all walks of life. The car allowed for the comfortable suburban escape, penicillin released people from the misery of infections, and the TV brought Broadway entertainment to your living room.

Like many titans of his time, Henry Ford was autocratic and kept absolute control of his organization. By today's standards, Ford is considered paternalistic for instituting policies to make sure his workers would not blow their money on vices such as booze and cigarettes. At the time, assembly workers required little training and education and were paid little. Ford was criticized for committing "an economic crime" by the *Wall Street Journal* for paying his workers double the average wage in the car industry. But increased productivity allowed Ford to do so. Ford violently opposed organized unions, but he wanted his workers to be able to afford a car, at a time when only the rich could afford one. In an article on industrial giants, *Time* magazine reported, "When Ford stumbled, says Lee Iacocca, it was because he wanted to do everything his way."[28] Ford was asked to diversify, but in keeping with his absolute autocratic style, only the black Model T was produced. By the time the new Model A appeared, GM had started to gain ground by introducing a variety of models and prices to suit all tastes.

Today's sophisticated market and industrial complexity demand a greater variety of leadership styles. Leaders must be flexible and adapt their style to fit the situation and corporate culture. This could range from being democratic to authoritative or from being affiliative to coaching.[29] Many of today's workers look toward their career for personal growth. To create meaning, successful leaders today need to get workers involved in the development of the corporation. Leadership styles need to fit the situation and will continue to evolve through the twenty-first century. Leaders may need to give up complete control in order to gain control over what counts: results.[30]

Leader: A Formula

Top management at 3M, a company well-respected for its innovation, sees its role not so much as directing and controlling, but more as developing employees' initiatives and supporting their ideas.

Leaders should be able to inspire purpose, shape the underlying structure, set strategic direction, and influence events. A leader's function is not to manage or control but to create a vision and implement the vision consistent with the set of core values governing all actions within the organization.

Vision

People are greatly motivated by a vision that intends to better an organization or society. Henry Ford's mission to build a car "so low in price that no man will be unable to own one" was revolutionary, innovative, and entrepreneurial at a time when industry believed that cars could be built only for the rich. People are greatly motivated by the social worth of a vision that provides a higher purpose.

A vision provides shared values, purpose, and identity to all members in the organization. To inspire, a vision should paint a mental image of a desirable future and guide the strategic direction. To some, a utopian vision may provide a deeper sense of purpose, and people will go to great lengths to justify their pursuit of that vision no matter how many resources or how much time it takes. In the corporate world, leaders need to act in the organization's long-term interest, but they also have to look at the consequences of both long-term and short-term decisions. While an idealist believes the short term doesn't count, the cynic believes the long term will not happen.[31] The corporate leader, as a pragmatic dreamer, has no such luxury.[32] A leader needs to be able to influence events and underlying structure. In the corporate world, a vision should provide a challenge toward a greater contribution while remaining realistic.

> Water may be soft, but it is the stream that shapes the valley.

Identity

To be a leader you must have the motivation to lead. Skills and competencies can be trained into a person, but the passion to run an organization cannot.[33] Still, wanting to run or control an organization for its own sake does not make you a leader. The need for power by itself or for personal aggrandizement does little to inspire others to commit to the organization's goals. Yes, you need to think of yourself as a leader. The need to influence others and run an organization serves as a great motivator to leadership, but others will be inspired when they see your action directed toward the collective good. Your leadership ability will depend directly on the extent to which you can subordinate your ego to the needs of the organization.

Monitoring

Leadership takes place when people are willing to follow. As McClelland contends, better leaders were found to be more mature and less egotistical, more positive about their self-image, less defensive, more willing to seek advice from experts. You will recall that insensitivity to others, arrogance, and betrayal of trust represent the major pitfalls to leadership: in other words, poor interpersonal skills. You are a leader because people recognize you as such. It means you have good understanding of your own needs, good control over your feelings, and the ability to empathize, and you are able to connect with people. Simply put, a leader needs emotional intelligence. To create a vision and inspire people to work toward a common goal requires you to be able to read what makes sense for others. It means you have the ability to create an environment in which people feel they can fulfill their full potential.

Self-Esteem

You may have a great plan, but do people believe you can carry it out? Leaders must project an image of credibility and worthiness; they must be persuasive and have a high level of self-confidence. If you lack self-confidence, people won't believe you have the capabilities and competencies to carry out the corporate mission. You may have those needed capabilities, but unless you project an image of credibility people will not trust that you can carry out the plan. Without trust, people feel vulnerable no matter how well articulated the vision is. The level of trust depends very much on the organization's track record of keeping commitments and the perception of the leader's integrity, honesty, competence, and sensitivity to others.

Delivery

Whether leadership is activist, religious, corporate, or political, what you say and how you say it are both important. In the debate of content over form, we may say "do not judge a book by its cover," but we also know that "a peacock is beautiful because of its feathers." It is your ability to communicate and choose the right words that elicits the desired response. Symbols, metaphors, stories, and rhetoric all serve to enhance your ability to get movement. In your delivery, body posture, eye contact, vocal variation, even the choice of pronouns such as *we* and *us* are important. This is not about charisma but rather about your ability to communicate what is significant to others.

Organizations are comprised of people, and people are quick to recognize whether leaders behave in a manner consistent with their personal interest or with the company's stated values and goals.[34] Projecting the right image, saying the right things can be powerful when doing so is consistent with your own values and behavior as well as with the corporate vision and mode of operation.

While the West focuses on the individual, the East focuses on the relationships among individuals. A leader needs to be honest about what he stands for, as well as respect what others stand for. A leader must respect individual aspirations as well as the social context needed for team performance. A leader with integrity is expected to be persistent while being patient, to be firm while being kind, and to entrust while being involved. This requires a strong personal sense of ethics characterized by honesty, fairness, and the ability to value others.

Effective leaders have strong connections with their fellow workers. They are capable of listening, assimilating input, and then articulating a common vision that resonates with a shared feeling. Leaders are risk-takers, but they are not reckless. They are determined and have confidence and self-discipline while they show flexibility and initiative. They have courage, and they have the ability to inspire and to maintain a shared sense of purpose, ownership, and values.

9

Sun Tzu

A Strategy Through Time

Throughout this book, I have drawn information from diverse sources: books on mythology, articles in the *Harvard Business Review,* quotations from ancient philosophers, and research on brain physiology. In this chapter, I discuss Sun Tzu, who wrote around 400 B.C. describing military tactics used during the period of the Warring State in China.[1] In his translation of *Sun Tzu: The Art of War,* Samuel Griffith notes that Sun Tzu believed "the only constant in war is constant change."[2] Whether we like it or not, the military, who have been charged with carrying political orders throughout time, have much to teach us about change and about strategy. Sun Tzu himself recommended that all alternatives be explored before the state engaged in war. But then, as now, countries often went to war without exploring all the alternatives. Since Sun Tzu's time, technology has changed, but many of the fundamentals of his strategy are still relevant. By recapping some of the major components as they apply to people, we can make a useful comparison between strategies for change in ancient times and strategies for today.

Modern Strategy

The optimal strategy in business is to define your unique position in the marketplace and then create a fit between your corporate strengths and market demand. To survive in today's competitive environment, an organizational strategy has to motivate its employees to meet customer needs at a reasonable price. Business needs to attune itself to the environment, integrate its activity, foster participation, and take action that is consistent with changing circumstances. Corporations need to adapt to changes in technologies and regulations, accommodate social shifts, differentiate themselves from their competitors, and satisfy customers' demands by providing value-added features with their services. A strategy must incorporate three major components:

1. An understanding of market needs and business situations
2. A sound knowledge of the company's advantages and limitations
3. The proper management of resources

A corporate strategy should find opportunities in the marketplace by being explorative. Any process that limits the scope of discovery hampers opportunities. Market discoveries can come from anywhere in the organization: a salesperson talking with customers, a researcher reading about the latest in plastic technology, or workers retooling a machine to facilitate its optimal operation. All can provide ideas about a new way of doing things.

We are accustomed to thinking of a CEO as the one responsible for strategy. In defense of CEOs one could say, "From the mountain top, one can see where the river is going." While the CEO may well have a broad perspective, we can complement that assertion with a statement by Chesterton: "One sees great things from the valley, only small things from the peak."[3] Corporate strategy should be democratic to offer everyone a chance to influence decisions. Executive responsibility is to foster a process that allows employees' insights to emerge.

The best strategies are those that are left broad enough to adapt to changing conditions. Precise articulation of a strategy with a fixed plan stifles initiative and the ability to respond according to circumstances. Changes in people's behavior, market demands, and competitor's reactions are complex and varied. Therefore, your strategy should not attempt to identify clear answers to new questions; rather it should provide guidance to accommodate the changes. Having a plan is fine, but a plan should be looked at as only a means of communicating your intentions. Thomas Watson, founder of IBM, predicted that the world demand for data-processing computers would be less than fifty machines.[4] Had Watson stuck to his plan, IBM would not exist. Changes in market conditions, competition, or any number of innovations can quickly change demand for your goods.

> The future is never clear; you pay a very high price in the stock market for a cheery consensus. Uncertainty actually is the friend of the buyer of long term values.
>
> —Warren Buffet

Your organizational structure and process must provide the discipline, focus, and flexibility to accommodate changing conditions. As a system, your organizational structure and process should be seen as a tool used by the people who perform the work. The Western mind may want a system that provides clear divisions and procedures, but strategy, like wisdom, requires tolerating a degree of uncertainty. The discipline provided by your system should not control but support and should allow you to be reflective, reflexive, and responsive.

Ancient Strategy

Some military organizations have kept good records and provide useful information about strategies that may have relevance for today's business world. A military campaign, like a corporate plan, depends on its people for implementation, and this seems to have changed very little through the ages. Let's look at some of Sun Tzu's work and compare it to our contemporary corporate strategies.

Understanding the Situation

Can you respond to the business situation and meet the market demand? We learn from the ancients that a strategic plan should be able to respond to circumstances in an infinite variety of ways. Sun Tzu writes, "As water shapes its flow in accordance with the ground one must respond in accordance with the situation."[5] Sun Tzu lists five fundamental factors to consider in appraising your relative strengths: the morale of the soldiers, the effects of the weather, the constraints and demands of the terrain, the quality of the command, and the logistics and value of the doctrine.[6]

Adjusting Sun Tzu's terms to today's context provides five fundamental factors that apply to contemporary organizations: the dedication of your employees, the effects of market conditions, the constraints and demands of business situations, the quality of management leadership, and the logistics and value of your strategy and planning. Then, as now, there are those factors you can influence and those you cannot. What you can and cannot control dictates your response.

The effect of the weather and the constraints of the terrain are those factors, Sun Tzu contends, over which the military has no control, and therefore, it has no choice but to adapt to them. For the modern corporate world, the effects of market conditions and the constraints and demands of business situations are beyond one's control. Like Sun Tzu's ancient armies, businesses must learn to adapt to an ever-changing economic climate and to the constraints of the business terrain as brought about by changes in competition, legislation, technology, and the economy.

"Now an army may be likened to water, for just as flowing water avoids the heights and hastens to the lowlands, so an army avoids strength and strikes weakness," writes Sun Tzu.[7] Competition requires adapting your corporate strengths to match and fill a void in the market. To do this, you must recognize your limitations and circumvent those market niches where you hold little advantage. According to Sun Tzu, a general takes "calculated risks but never needless ones."[8] This means you adapt to the situation, altering plans to meet changing circumstances. "Just as water adapts itself to the conformation of the ground," Sun Tzu reminds us, "so in war one must be flexible; he must often adapt his tactics to the enemy situation."[9] While customers are not the enemy, as customer tastes change, so must your operation adapt to meet new circumstances.

According to Sun Tzu, "In war, numbers alone confer no advantage."[10] He contends that morale, intellect, and circumstance are more important. Good planning, especially sound knowledge of the situation, is critical. Sun Tzu believed that "an army without secret agents is exactly like a man without eyes or ears."[11] Then, as now, organizations require information before they take action. To understand market needs and know where your greatest strengths are in relation to your competitor, you need ongoing information about market trends and shifts. Based on that information, your actions need to relate to the reality of the circumstances and not to mere wishful thinking.

Having an understanding of market needs and the business situation is critical to setting corporate directions. Customers are reasonable, but when choices are available, they expect complete satisfaction. Shifts in market demand depend on several factors: the type of product and service available, changes in customer needs, the level of competition, the maturity of the industry, changes in regulations, and advances in technology. A corporation needs to adapt to and comply with changing circumstances, and then to be successful, it must have information about market needs in order to provide that critical element of customer satisfaction.

Having a sound knowledge of the company's advantages and limitations puts you in the best position to provide value-added features to your client and gain a competitive edge in those areas where you can excel. Excelling in operational efficiency, product leadership, or customer service depends on whether you align your organizational advantage with the market needs. For the most part, however, matching your corporate strengths and limitations with market opportunities and threats means fine-tuning your corporate approach to fit market opportunities.

Understanding Yourself

Having the right general is a good start, but every army needs a vision. Sun Tzu tells us, "One who is confused in purpose cannot respond."[12] What are the core values of your corporation? What is its vision? Before you decide to engage in a strategy, you need to evaluate your organization's strengths and limitations. Sun Tzu said,

> Know the enemy and know yourself . . . [and] you will never be in peril. When you are ignorant of the enemy but know yourself, your chances of winning or losing are equal. If ignorant both of your enemy and of yourself, you are certain in every battle to be in peril.[13]

It is important to be honest in assessing your organization's capabilities and limitations, your competitors' advantages and weaknesses, as well as market opportunities and dangers. You have to match your organization's strengths against market opportunities, shy away from areas where you have limitations, and avoid market threats. One must "ponder," in the ancient general's words, "the dangers inherent in the advantages and the disadvantages inherent in the dangers."[14] On planning, Sun Tzu said:

> Planning is that by which harm is avoided and advantage gained.
>
> By taking into account the favorable future, [you] make plans feasible; by taking into account the unfavorable, [you] may resolve the difficulties.[15]

Your corporate strategy should allow responses to circumstances in a variety of ways and, moreover, allow expeditious action when the correct course presents itself.

To run an organization, you need resources and competent people to manage those resources. As the ancient Chinese saying goes, "A sovereign who obtains the right person prospers. One who fails to do so will be ruined."[16] But having the right person is not enough. That person must be delegated the responsibility *and* the authority to perform the job within his or her field of expertise. Head offices, like sovereigns, need to allow for local action. According to Sun Tzu, action needs to be governed in accordance with prevailing circumstance, for, as he writes, "The advance and the retirement of the army can be controlled by the general in accordance with the prevailing circumstances. No evil is greater than the commands of the sovereign from the court."[17] Similarly, Sun Tzu says, "When it is expedient in operation, the general need not be restricted by the command of the sovereign."[18] Bureaucracy binds people to rules and procedures, and governs their actions in accordance with a fixed pattern. A quote from this ancient general says it well: "To put a rein on your people is like tying up a hound and then asking him to catch an hare. . . . Those who do not use local guides are unable to obtain the advantages of the ground."[19]

Managing

Sun Tzu says that when there is discord in the army, it cannot take to the field. Conversely, when the enemy's army is in harmony,

> . . . you must avoid attacking. . . . [You should not attack the enemy when their] superiors love their subordinates, where [their] rewards and punishment are carefully considered, and where those who display merits are given suitable positions.[20]

As Sun Tzu contends, "little strength is needed when you give people responsibility that fits the situation and suits the person."[21] These words of wisdom come from a different time and a different place, but they have relevance for us today. While oneness and duality put different emphasis on certain values, both philosophies suggest that a system works best when it responds to the needs of the people and not when the people respond to the needs of the system.

At its extreme, the West's mechanization of organizations and its emphasis on legitimacy places hard rules and fixed procedures above the human need for participation. This situation has eroded workers' sense of solidarity and human bonding in favor of calculated and calculable mechanics. However, in recent years, the market has been supporting many of those companies that were the first to ask customers what they wanted and then worked toward providing an integrated approach toward supplying a complete service. The market has shown that it favors leadership that is willing to dilute its own authority in order to gain results.

When all is said and done, the proper management of resources comes down to evaluating your situation and taking an approach that fits your strengths. There are many possible approaches, but they all need to be fitted to specific situations. Generally speaking, a fluid structure allows the process to adapt to the customer's requirements. But whatever structure fits your organizational culture, industry, or market, the prevailing principle that should govern the process is the one that gives ownership to those responsible for solving the problems. Facilitating ownership means the work has to be structured in order to encourage greater employee involvement, participation, and decision-making. It means giving responsibilities to those responsible for the work, providing the tools to make it happen, and delegating the authority to solve the problems.

In the East, Confucian ethics can be summarized by the word *reciprocity*. In the West, Christian ethics can be summarized by the word *compassion*. These two common codes of ethical behavior have survived the test of time. A derivative of the Golden Rule can be transliterated as: Lead as you would be led. To quote Sun Tzu, "The General must be the first in the toils and fatigue of the army."[22] Lead by example, he argues, and people will respect you; they respond best to leaders demonstrating wisdom, sincerity, humanity, courage, and self-control. This dictum was true in Sun Tzu's time, and according to modern surveys, it is true today.

The new leadership role demands the ability to listen, to foster a shared vision, and to attune the organization to the situation. The new role demands that leaders act in the organization's long-term interests and manage the context so employees are allowed to participate and take personal responsibility for the work. This requires earning the trust and respect of people through acting with integrity, ethics, a sense of justice, and firmness tempered by kindness. The challenge requires that leaders be able to put the needs of others first, above their own personal considerations, and to commit to core values based on sound ethical principles.

10

Peace of Mind

The Western Me, with its accent on individualism, emphasizes distinctiveness and advances the understanding of oneself. The Eastern We, with its accent on collectivism, emphasizes harmony and advances sensitivity toward others. This book is not about giving up individuality, but it is about complementing distinctiveness with unity and participation. Western principles and our mechanical rules have served us well, but when expediency prevails over common sense and good judgment, rules can detract from the spontaneity of life.

Focuses on the Me or on the We are not opposite ways of living in the world but are part and parcel of the same thing. As such, they define, shape, and enhance each other. When in balance, Western and Eastern views should allow for individual autonomy as well as group participation. Combining notions from the Me and the We is not about giving up aspects of who we are, but rather, it is about awakening dormant parts of human nature. System logic provides discipline and should be retained. Instinct provides insight and should be fostered. In combination, they complement each other.

This chapter is divided into three main sections, Competence: Knowledge, Skills, Emotions; Me and We: A Relationship; and Detachment: The Spiritual Self.

Competence requires that you have a good dose of knowledge, skill, and emotional capability. These attributes are interrelated. All are important. In this book, however, I devote more time to the management of our emotions because we typically devote less time to this issue. Competence is not based on having one or two of these attributes but on having all three. Under the Me and We relationship, I discuss how the complementary relationship between the Civic and the Individual Self can serve to enhance both. Under Detachment, I discuss how the development and practice of values derived from the Spiritual Self can be used to provide clearer understanding and free us from our assumptions. To better understand our assumptions, let's look at some of our biological and cultural dispositions.

Competence: Knowledge, Skills, Emotions

Success in whatever task you undertake depends pretty much on the combination of knowing where you want to go, having reasonable talent, and cultivating the ability to keep going in the face of obstacles and defeats.[1] Knowledge tells you what to do and why. Skills enable you to do it. However, it is emotional intelligence that gives you the ability to regulate yourself, to respond appropriately, to persist during adversity, and to motivate yourself to accomplish a goal.[2] Knowledge, skill, and emotional intelligence are all essential. Choosing which is more important should not be your goal, but rather you should aim to combine all three factors.

Knowledge Development and the Mastery of Skills

To become an executive, a top athlete, or an accomplished musician, you need knowledge and skills. Learning what to do and how to do things is important. North America is blessed with good libraries, schools, universities, seminars, and training programs in all fields of endeavor. From the Internet to the library, information is available to suit everyone's preferred mode of learning. The accomplishment of a task requires mastery of skills. Playing the piano, playing hockey, and operating heavy equipment all require years of practice before a person gains a certain level of proficiency. From schools to on-site training, skills need to be continuously improved in order to adapt to changing demands. Knowledge and skills—both are essential. When we see our doctors we expect them to know about medicine. In addition to knowledge of biochemistry, physiology, immunology, and pathology, doctors require years of practical training before they become proficient in diagnosis and treatment. Likewise, in addition to industrial knowledge and years of practice, executives require a great deal of knowledge in marketing, production, and finance. Not only does it take years to gain the necessary knowledge and skill, but to be proficient you must keep up with the latest information on a continuous basis. Attention to knowledge and skill must be retained. But knowledge, like skill, has to be put into perspective.

> *I hear and I forget. I see and I remember. I do and I understand.*
> —Confucius

In the West, the prevalent view of mechanical order associates knowledge with cold logic and data. In business decisions, data from spreadsheet analyses, market research, and simulations are presented as facts. Business objectives are quantified and, ideally, reflect business principles, policies, and standards of operation. In its extreme, a mechanical view treats skills simply as a means to efficiency. Under this scenario labor efficiency is measured as the ratio of nominal output per labor hour to labor compensation per hour.

Quantification, clarity, and consistency based on principles, acceptable standards, or the law have served us well. They bring accountability, focus our efforts, inject discipline, and provide a means of comparison. This needs to be retained, but our demand for quantification needs to be balanced with intuition and insight.

The importance we put on mechanical quantification is seen not only in the corporation but likewise at the personal level. For example, gauges such as IQ tests and the SAT have been prominently used for decades to measure individual ability. But as Goleman contends, these tests by themselves are poor predictors of performance. "At best, IQ contributes about 20 percent to the factors that determine life success, which leaves 80 percent to other forces."[3]

Over the centuries, people have made the distinction between the heart and the head, between the emotional and the rational, between the mind and the body. But with the prevalence of the mechanical order, we failed to realize the degree to which rational thought is swayed by feelings and, at times, even overwhelmed by them totally. Despite the effect of emotions on our thought processes, tests that only assess a person's mathematical, spatial, or verbal ability came to be seen as a reliable measure of intelligence and were considered good predictors of a person's success.

Spreadsheet analysis, like credentials and test scores, suited the mechanical order and its demand for concrete, measurable, and observable outcomes. These concrete outcomes are appealing because numbers give a sense of precision and of certainty. But insistence on hard, cold logic makes us look for the right answer by following a set of rules and insisting on practicality. While logic certainly has its place, too much emphasis on this one method of problem solving deprives people of their intuition, judgment, and creativity.

Knowledge and skill are essential requirements to competence. But knowledge and skills are more than the sum total of what can be measured, observed, or defined. Much of our success is determined not by test scores, degrees, or diplomas, but by the interrelationship and interplay of knowledge, skills, and emotions. Hope, desire, fear, imagination, mood, body movement, all exercise a tremendous influence on our ability to persist, what we learn, and how we judge issues, solve problems,

Beware the man of one book.
—Ancient Roman Proverb

and make decisions. Intuition, judgment, and creativity, in addition to logic, are enhanced when you recognize the interplay between knowledge, skills, and emotion. In his book *The New Dynamics of Winning* Denis Waitley talks about requirements for outstanding accomplishments. Waitley contends that champions are willing to pay the price to enter the winning circle. We don't all want to become Olympic athletes, but observing what a top athlete does to accomplish something outstanding tells us something about competence. To achieve their goals, athletes are willing to delay gratification and, for years and years, keep on training. As you can appreciate, reaching any worthwhile goal requires persistence and a willingness to delay gratification. Both are part of emotional intelligence. But equally important, once you have developed the skills you need to reach a goal, you also have to believe you can make it. Waitley contends that once an athlete has attained a necessary skill and developed the requisite physical condition, 70 to 90 percent of the outcome of an athletic event is based on psychological factors—in other words, acquiring the skill to do something is not as important or as difficult as believing you can do it.[4] Competence, then, represents the interactive and cumulative effect of knowledge, skills, and emotion. It is not about having one or the other. Success demands all three. But because we devote so much of our time to knowledge and skills, I will here devote more time to emotional intelligence. Why is it so important?

Emotional Intelligence

Part of the reason for the importance of emotional intelligence comes from our ancient past. The human brain evolved during times when a person's ability to respond to an emergency could make the difference between life and death. For 99 percent of human existence, until the onset of agriculture, humans lived as hunter-gatherers.[5] Emotions such as anxiety, anger, or fear kept people on guard and had survival value. For example, the sight of a snake about to strike generated a fight-or-flight response in a human being, and how quickly the person responded made the difference between life and death. Research shows that strong, emotionally charged information goes straight to the emotional center (known as the limbic system) for quick action.[6] Call it instinct if you want—those with keen emotional radar survived. If our ancestors had to mull over the information received during a crisis, we wouldn't be around today to talk about it. Equally, acquiring a mate, dealing with rivals, and raising children were all problems whose comprehension and solutions involved emotions.[7] Anger, lust, fear, affection, sadness, jealousy, anger, and yes, learning—all contributed to a person's ability to respond to and resolve problems.

We have both negative and positive feelings: people have friendships and sometimes rivalries; we can feel grateful or at times feel jealous or resentful. In sport, we can enjoy the thrill of victory but also suffer the agony of defeat.[8] We are equally capable of pleasant feelings such as enjoyment, delight, satisfaction, acceptance, kindness, affinity, ecstasy, adoration, guilt, and remorse. Our biology seems to have imprinted in us the capacity to be cruel as well as the capacity to be kind. When secure, we are willing to take risks but we are also hardwired to avoid loss. There is much we can learn from the experience of our emotions.

A man flirting with a bigger man's wife might learn something about what not to do or when not to do it or a different way of doing it. If lust attracted the man, fear served to teach him a more rational way of how it should be done. But we need the ability to control our impulses, to discover a more reasonable way of doing what we want to do. Recent research by neuroscientists has revealed some of the neural circuitry responsible for emotional response as well as ample empirical evidence that links our emotions with our rational mind.[9]

Two Brains

Neuroscientists divide the brain into two parts:

- The limbic system, which is at the base of the brain
- The cortex, which forms the upper part of the brain

The limbic system is the storehouse of emotional memories. It provides the "flavor" of the emotions that correlate to our experiences.[10] Think of the limbic system as the storage site of our unconscious opinions.[11] The cortex is the part that mulls over information, makes comparisons, and allows time for strategic planning and organized action. It is what we call the "thinking part" of the brain, our mental capacity.

There are, however, very strong neurological links between the limbic system and the cortex. The interlink between the limbic system and the cortex allows signals that incite strong emotions to sabotage the cortex, impeding a person's ability to pay attention to the facts of a certain situation or make appropriate comparisons.[12] That is why, for example, when you give feedback about job performance the bad news speaks the loudest.

In most situations, the cortex shapes and governs our emotional reactions. After all, the bulk of the pathways or connections is in the cortex, not the limbic system. But it is also because of the interlink with the limbic that we have a rich storehouse of emotional memories that gives us our likes and dislikes. Without our emotional link, we would be totally impartial to a favorite place, a beautiful setting, or a loved one; our reason would be deprived of direction.[13] Our emotions give us direction and provide the impetus to organize and to fine-tune our rational thoughts. Instinct and logic feed and discipline each other. Intelligence is not about choosing between feeling or reason; it's about balancing them.

Emotional Competence

Emotions such as anger, happiness, fear, love, sadness, and surprise provide us with the impulse and the impetus to act.[14] How we express our emotions is largely influenced by culture. How we manage our impulses determines, in part, our competence. As Goleman says, "Those at the mercy of impulse—who lack self-control—suffer moral deficiency. The ability to control impulse is the base of will and character."[15] The ability to control impulses is not about eliminating impulses but rather about recognizing your emotions and managing their effects.

> Courage is resistance to fear, mastery of fear, not absence of fear.
> —Mark Twain

Goleman cites a wealth of examples and studies that show the importance of emotional competence. For example, one study found "that about 25 percent of children who were unpopular in elementary school had dropped out before completing high school, compared to a general rate of 8 percent."[16] Typically, outcast children are poor at reading emotions and tend to respond inappropriately to situations. Rejected, they display a greater propensity for hostility and are more likely to be anxious, awkward, or socially shy. Poor emotional intelligence not only hampers academic performance, but it can also result in a child's being pushed aside. "Impulsivity in ten-year-old boys is almost three times as powerful a predictor of their later delinquency as is their IQ."[17]

Whether they be of children or adults, studies show that emotions can sabotage our ability to use our knowledge and skills. Knowledge tells us what to do and why; skills tell us how to do it and when. Whether at home with your family or at work with your colleagues, "to the degree that [your] emotions get in the way of or enhance [your] ability to think and plan, to pursue training for a distant goal, to solve problems and the like, they define the limits of our capacity to use our innate mental abilities and so determine how we do in life."[18]

No psychological skill is more important than the ability to control our impulses; that is, the capacity to master our impulses and think before we act.[19] Studies on Olympic athletes, accomplished musicians, and other high achievers have shown that one of the key factors to success is their ability to self-motivate and to pursue, day in and day out, the series of relentless tasks required to do the job despite the temptation to do other things.[20] The ability to deny impulses in the pursuit of goals determines how well people use their skills and mental capabilities.[21]

As Goleman has observed, "two kinds of emotional proclivities lead children to end up as social outcasts. . . . One is the propensity to angry outbursts and to perceive hostility even where none is intended. The second is being timid, anxious, and socially shy. But over and above these temperamental factors, it is the children who are "off"—whose awkwardness repeatedly makes people uncomfortable who tend to be shunted aside."[22] This is typical not only of children but of adults who lack people skills. Recall from the section "Relationship Pitfalls" in Chapter 9 my discussion on the failed executive. The first three reasons for failure derived from an inability to relate to others, with performance problems falling into fourth place. The inability to pick up social cues hampers the ability to respond appropriately.

Three Factors to Emotional Competence

Being able to understand our own feelings, put aside our impulses, and empathize with others has both personal and social benefits. Emotional competence is about being strong in all three factors. As an analogy, if you give each factor a value between 1 and 10, with 10 as the maximum, $10 \times 10 \times 10$ will give you an emotional competence of 1,000. On the other hand $10 \times 10 \times 1$ will give you an emotional competence of only 100. As discussed in Chapter 1, emotional competence can be understood as the ability to:

- Comprehend your own feelings
- Control and manage your impulses
- Empathize; that is, to be aware of, identify, and assess other people's feelings[23]

Emotional competence requires you to control and manage your impulses so that you can acquire the necessary skills and knowledge to achieve your goals and attain a certain level of competence. Equally important, emotional competence requires that you have the ability to understand yourself and empathize with and relate to others. Empathy enables you to read others and adjust your response accordingly. The ability to guess what others are thinking allows you to build better social alliances and negotiate win-win outcomes. How comfortable you feel with others depends very much on your interpersonal effectiveness, the level of engagement and rapport you are able to build. Interpersonal effectiveness allows you to shift with the other person's moods. This skill depends on your ability to read emotional signals, and acting in a way that further shapes those feelings is at the core of fostering and developing successful relationships. Empathy plays a key role in your ability to manage people, gives you an advantage in selling, helps your romantic life, and is a life-saver in parenting.[24]

In addition to managing your impulses, emotional competence

requires that you have the ability to understand yourself and others. With our accent on individualism, we devote much time to exploring our individual distinctiveness. We pursue courses in self-esteem, taking charge, and assertiveness. These are fine activities, but achieving in these areas satisfies only one part of ourselves. As social beings, we get much of our meaning and sense of worth from social interaction. Why is this so important?

Humans as Social Beings. From ancient times, the family has served as a centerpiece in all human societies. As members of clans, human beings were never loners. As social beings, people have a profound need to belong. From an evolutionary point of view, our need for attachment has survival value. As Susan Johnson writes, "the need for physical closeness between mother and child serves evolutionary goals; in a dangerous world, a responsive care-giver ensures survival of the infant. Maintaining closeness is a bona fide survival need."[25] In early times, surrounded by predators, poisonous plants, and dangerous terrain, an infant needed to stay close to its caretaker for protection. This need for attachment ensured the infant remained close to its mother and, it seems, was essential for survival.

As children, our need for attachment ensures our survival. As a child grows out of infancy, new needs emerge. Around the age of eighteen months, a child separates from his or her caretaker to start exploring the surrounding world. This period of the child's development is referred to as the stage of "autonomy and independence."[26] Through exploration and experience, the child reared by responsive caretakers will gain the necessary skills and knowledge to survive as an adult. These dual needs for autonomy and attachment are essential for survival.[27]

It seems the conflicting needs for attachment and for autonomy are part of who and what we are, and together, they create the competence necessary for survival. In ancient times, for example, using tools to acquire food and build shelter demanded a certain level of personal proficiency. However, no matter how proficient an individual became at dealing with the elements of nature or fending off predators, working with a group provided the best chance to survive. As stated by Robert Wright, "Because social cooperation improves the chances of survival, natural selection imbued our minds with an infrastructure for friendship, including affection, gratitude and trust."[28] Today, things are much the same. Whether we are dealing with global warming or fending off the latest corporate takeover, we know that working as a group still gives us the best chance to survive.

Similarly, Wright tells us that "Our ancestors, it seems, competed for mates with guile and hard work. They competed for social status with combative wordplay and social politicking."[29] As people strive to find a sense of significance among others, there is a tension between the need to belong to a group on the one hand and the need to impress and distinguish oneself within that group on the other. Things have changed little, and hence the importance of projecting confidence. The mutual demands of cooperation and competition are still within us. The competence necessary for survival in our modern world still demands that individuals master the skills to complete certain necessary tasks and that they master the skills needed to integrate with a group and work together. This requires you to get in touch with yourself and learn to relate to others. This may well be what gives life its authenticity.

It seems our need for both autonomy and attachment is hardwired and provides survival value. The values of the Western Individual Self—individuality, independence, and distinctiveness—serve to enhance and accent our need for autonomy. On the other hand, the values of the Eastern Civic Self—collectivism, interdependence, and harmony—serve to enhance and accent our need for attachment. The evolution of different values in the Western and Eastern cultures has served to enhance different aspects of our being. But within us, we all have the need for both autonomy and attachment.

The Social Cost of Excess. While the Individual Self facilitates self-awareness, the Civic Self incites awareness of others. The values of the Spiritual Self in the West (self-restraint, diligence, compassion) and in the East (patience; humility; freedom from pretense, anger, and malice) serve to enhance our ability to manage our impulses. But each has its cost when taken to extremes.

Throughout this book, I have talked about the interrelationship among cultural values, institutions, and individuals. Cultural values largely determine what thoughts, feelings, and behavior people deny, extinguish, restrain, or accentuate. Cultural values shape the assumptions that guide our point of reference, which, in turn, affects our thinking: how we interact, what we do, and how we make judgments. For the most part, social values facilitate social exchange and function to give us our social graces and decorum. To be sure, there are social rules that have evolved to keep in check the rough side of human nature, but there are other social values that hinder our distinctiveness and our compassionate side.

Civic Self: A Distortion

Being part of a group provides an opportunity to form deep and rewarding relationships, a gratifying sense of belonging, and a sense of security. However, excessive demands on group cohesiveness can be stifling. They may even create emotional dependence on others.[30] Sole concern for the We can make you vulnerable to someone else's weaknesses, feelings, attitudes, and behaviors. Excessive dependency on the family or the group also makes you vulnerable to others' approval. It can bring about blind obedience and a state where you hide your grief, desire little, and feel afraid to explore your own potential. This vulnerability can

> "The easiest thing to be in the world is you. The most difficult thing to be is what other people want you to be. Don't let them put you in that position."
>
> —Leo Buscaglia, American educator and author

undermine your sense of self-worth. Excessive concern with family image or with a group's symbols and goals can sway you away from personal fulfillment.

Acceptance of hierarchy means humbling oneself to those above and patronizing those below. In balance this form of reciprocal obligation means respect is exchanged for protection. However, there are always those who are willing to take more than their fair share. The demand for obedience by a predominant member can lead to exploitation.

In Chapter 5, I talked about the cost of oneness at the corporate level. At a personal level, conformity to a group can undermine your own uniqueness and impair your ability to be happy. Harmony favors stability, security, and consensus. At its extreme, harmony demands mutual approval, with its sole preoccupation being the need to please, impress, and pacify. Endeavors, ideas, or even truth are rejected for fear of causing offense, and the pursuit of harmony becomes a substitute for inner peace that leads to self-denial.

Spiritual Self: A Distortion

One may ask, "Who are you?" The optimist would say, "Whatever I want to be"; with a twist, the realist would say, "Ha, exactly what I appear to be"; the religious believer might say, "A soul created by God"; while an Eastern believer would reply, "An illusion." After pondering the question, a philosopher might say, "My thought," while an artist would say, "My feelings."[31]

Spirituality is a complex subject with a rich variation of personal meaning. When I talk about spirituality here, I relate it mainly to the essential qualities that underline our values, principles, and relationships, which in turn influence how we see our obligations toward ourselves, others, our community, and surroundings.

Throughout this book, I have made reference to the mechanical order and how it influences our thinking, shapes our relationships, and forms our obligations. Insofar as the mechanical order exercises an influence on our obligations, it exercises an influence on our Spiritual Self. We may give to charity for reasons of compassion or to get a tax break, but the essential qualities of our obligations are different.

In the name of sacrifice, piety, and redemption, the rigidity of some religious practices has been abusive. But virtues such as kindness, fraternity, fairness, patience, and freedom from pretense, malice, and anger have much to offer the modern era. Such virtues not only require us to be aware of our egos and manage our impulses but also, as I will discuss later, can be enlightening. While being fluid, our Spiritual Self should provide discipline. It should be able to move with circumstance while it provides direction. To get the benefits of our Spiritual Self we must put the Individual Self and the mechanical order in perspective, while accepting its advantages.

Individual Self: A Distortion

Too much focus on individualism ignores an essential human need: the need to belong. The focus on individualism can dwarf our sense of unity and impair our ability to empathize with others. As a result, excess individualism serves to reduce our overall competence. Indifference toward others or the inability to read emotions has caused many bright intellectuals to founder and many great plans to fail. In the corporate sector, promising managers who are perceived as arrogant, obnoxious, contemptuous, or insensitive often fail because they cannot inspire or persuade others to get on board.[32] In Chapter 7, we saw how colleagues and managers at Bell Laboratory chose as star performers those engineers who had the ability to relate to others, help others, and create a network. A number of studies have shown that good relationships, whether in the family or in the community, depend on a good dose of emotional competence.

Individualism favors the man or the woman who takes charge. In excess, taking charge discourages participation, leaves little room for others to feel they count, and gives them a sense of worthlessness. Too much raw individualism hurts both yourself and others.

Mechanical Order. At an institutional level, a mechanical order favors systems and laws. Where it provides direction it is great, but as discussed earlier, where it dictates answers it creates a sense of helplessness and lost commitment, and contributes to an increased level of cynicism and distrust.

At a personal level, our Western mechanical view reduces the powerful influence emotion plays in our level of competence. A mechanical view favors system logic, but logic is like the tip of the iceberg, with emotion hidden below. The mechanical view elevates the importance of the measurable at the expense of instinct, creativity, and intuition.

A mechanical order provides discipline and transparency, but we want to make sure it leads in the right direction. Its rigidity limits the potential of our full capacities, takes away our ability to use judgment to fit the situation and the pleasure of moving with circumstances. The direction provided, whether it be by a mechanical order or social order, must be flexible enough to allow for imagination and hope.

In combination, raw individualism and a mechanistic approach have little to do with the ability to understand yourself, to regulate your mood, or to understand and motivate others. Emotional competence, then, helps you to discern and appropriately respond to moods and temperament. It helps you to understand yourself and other people in terms of what motivates them and how they work. Your ability to regulate your mood, commit, be assertive, and express appropriate feelings relates to emotional competence.

Extremes have a cost. In the West, our relentless pursuit of the Me and our preference for the mechanical order have created a sense of alienation and social isolation. Many people have lost their sense of purpose. Western culture pushes aside intuition, feelings, imagination, and insight. It replaces judgment and experience with rules and procedures. Pushed to its extreme, it undermines our ability to form sound relationships and to interact with others in a meaningful way. In addition, modern social transformation such as industrialization, suburbanization, and electronic leisure create an environment that disconnects people from each other, facilitating and amplifying an increased sense of social isolation. With isolation, our sense of unity is lost, which is not to be taken lightly given that social isolation doubles your chances of sickness or death.[33]

Our brains have been wired for reason *and* emotion. Each is influenced by the other. The mechanical culture's preference for reasoning may have subordinated the relevance of feeling, but in our brains, reason and emotion are still interconnected. What is needed is a recognition and balancing of both. When disciplined by reason, our emotions, even our passions, provide us with wisdom. Our competence depends on the mastery of knowledge, skills, and our emotions. They are not opposites but are complementary to each other.

Me and We: A Relationship

The desire to pursue individualism can be seen in the many self-help seminars, clinics, and books that concentrate on teaching people to take charge, to be assertive, and to get in touch with themselves. Despite the abundant help, however, surveys show that two-thirds of the North American population suffer from low self-esteem.[34] In the quest for independence, many people have lost the meaning that lies in a sense of unity. For many, striving for independence is a reaction, a running away from dependency.[35] The reality is that we live in an interdependent world.[36]

The notion that the concepts of oneness and duality are complementary has much to offer. Within each concept lies an emphasis on different parts of our needs. Being in tune with your inner self, the Individual Self, facilitates fulfilling your needs for autonomy and distinctiveness. In turn, being in tune with others, the Civic Self, allows for the expression of our need for attachment and participation. The Spiritual Self puts emphasis on values such as restraint, patience, concentration of effort, and freedom from anger, which have much to offer in managing our impulses and comprehending the impact of our own feelings. Your self-esteem depends very much on the combined and interactive effects of the Individual Self, the Civic Self, and the Spiritual Self.

Competence requires the combined and interactive effects of knowledge, skills, and emotional intelligence. The values espoused by the Individual Self, the Spiritual Self, and the Civic Self are complementary to each other. In combination, they contribute to our sense of self-esteem and build the confidence needed to pursue goals. Let's look at applying the combined advantages of the Me and the We.

Negotiating

The majority of issues on a day-to-day basis, doing business, discussing family concerns, undertaking a community project require that we communicate our intentions, negotiate openly and honestly, and cooperate with others. For example, winning an argument with a customer about the interpretation of a warranty clause does not make you a winner. You both lose. The customer goes home with a defective product. You lose a customer. Getting the upper hand creates resentment, fosters an adversarial approach, and eliminates the synergy that can be gained through cooperation. Alternatively, coming up with a win-win solution requires finding a solution that satisfies both the customer and your company. It requires discussion, negotiation, and cooperation. Many people are aware of the advantages and of the greater productivity that can be gained from cooperative relationships. But talking about cooperation, merely using the rhetoric, is different from doing it.

> Success is getting what you want. Happiness is wanting what you get.
> —Anonymous

Negotiation is not just part of business; it is part of our personal lives as well. For example, your son wants to borrow the car. Or you may be discussing a family vacation, looking for a new home, trying to decide which furniture to buy, or puzzling over what color to paint your living room. In each case, negotiation is required to arrive at a mutually satisfactory solution—the win-win solution. Let's look at the process involved in negotiating a fair exchange. There are three main principles in negotiating:

- *Identify what you want.* Develop a picture of it. Be precise but do not get stuck on one issue.
- *Determine what you believe the other party wants of you.* People don't want the same things, and what is important to you may not be so important to the other party.
- *Appraise the common ground between yourself and the other party.* Look for a win-win negotiation and do not try to get every dollar that you possibly can.

When negotiating, people use various tactics to present their side and gain their share. You may already take some of these tactics for granted, but let's briefly review several that successful business negotiators commonly use:

1. If you are selling, ask for more than the price that you are willing to accept. If you are buying, offer less than what you are willing to give. This allows you to determine the other party's value range, raise the perceived value of the offer, gain flexibility, and leave room for negotiating on issues other than price. For the same reason, do not jump at the first offer. If you are buying, show surprise at how high the price is. If you are selling, show surprise at how low the offer is.

2. Try to get the other side to submit his or her offer first. It tells you something about that person's position. Equally, do not be afraid to ask questions about what the other person expects and what he or she would like to see.

3. Avoid confrontation. Begin negotiating on common ground, create momentum, and leave touchy issues until later. Once the momentum is created, people are more likely to work at reaching a final solution. When presented with hostile statements, first acknowledge the concern and then present your point of view without telling the other person he or she is wrong.

4. When negotiating with more than one person, be aware of good guy/bad guy pressure tactics. We have seen these tactics in police movies where one officer will be rough with the suspect, and then while the first officer takes a coffee break, a second officer applies a softer approach.

5. Do not be afraid to say, "I have to consult with someone else before I make a decision." This allows you to consider alternatives, relieve the pressure, and come back with a counteroffer. As a buyer, play the reluctant buyer; as a seller, play the reluctant seller.

6. Concentrate on issues. While there will be people you prefer to deal with and people you will reject, do not be impressed or intimidated by a person's title, and do not let the other person's personality distract you from relevant issues. Be wary, too, of time pressure and offers of unrelated rewards such as "this trip to Hawaii is avail-

able only if you buy this condo now." Watch for people who try using power tactics. Statements such as "Experts say . . . " or questions such as "What would happen to your family if . . . " are designed to coerce the unwary.

7. Always be the one to write the contract. That way, you will have more control over what goes into it.

8. After the contract is signed many may come back and ask for small but additional services. When asked for a favor, always ask for a tradeoff.

9. Make it clear that you are willing to pull out if the offer does not create a win-win situation.[37]

Although these principles apply in most negotiations, the success of the negotiation depends largely on the quality of the interaction between the people negotiating. When you negotiate, personality styles exert a tremendous influence on the outcome. So it is important to understand how your personality influences what you do as well as how it influences others. Conversely, you need to understand how another person's personality style affects that person and how it affects you. Successful negotiators can adapt their tactics to different situations and to various personality types.

Personality Types

The following classification of personality types is a partial adaptation from Roger Dawson's book *Secrets of Power Negotiation*.[38] It reflects training courses and literature written by human resource consultants, and it is consistent with what I have observed, firsthand, in the work place. I have found it convenient to classify personality types into four major classes: the Driven, the Expressive, the Amiable, and the Analytical.

The Driven. The Driven is a pragmatic person who looks for useful information and gets down to business after a firm handshake. Drivens are formal, work on a time schedule, have their secretaries arrange appointments, are decisive, and base decisions on the bottom line. Drivens are self-confident, persistent, competitive, and forceful.

At the extreme, they can be insensitive, intimidating, and distrustful. They look at negotiation as a game to be won.

The Expressive. The Expressive is an extrovert: friendly, open, and enthusiastic. Expressives are impulsive and look for excitement and entertainment. They are persuasive, spontaneous, and are willing to take risks. They make decisions on the spot. At the extreme, they can be overly subjective and superficial. They like to inspire others and, in negotiation, are so enthusiastic they forget to listen and tend to ignore others' demands.

The Amiable. The Amiable wants to be helpful, likes to be around people, values amicable relationships, and hates and avoids pressure tactics. Amiables can be inquisitive and creative, but they can also overdo it by being nitpicking perfectionists. Amiables are modest and trusting, and they strive for consensus. They do not make decisions until they have established a good relationship with the other person.

The Analytical. Analyticals tend to be detached number-crunchers who produce charts and graphs for every conceivable situation. Many are professionals: accountants, engineers, architects. They are precise, punctual, and detail-oriented and do not make decisions until they have all the facts and figures. They can be conforming and objective but at the extreme, indecisive. In negotiations, Analyticals tend to ignore relationships, preferring instead to follow a rigid procedure and an established system of decision-making.

Each personality style has its advantages and limitations. Each is affected differently by the circumstances, situation, and timing of the negotiation. The point here is not to profess one personality style over the other but to show that successful negotiation depends on the recognition of the different personality. Drivens can make quick decisions with little information but can be overbearing and tend to create a win-lose atmosphere where everyone digs in their heels. Amiables understand others' points of view, and their demands tend to sway, depending on their feelings. Expressives are quick to make decisions, but in their quest to inspire, they do not necessarily take into consideration others' points of view. Analyticals stick to issues, but can be slow to decide and rigid, often demanding more data before they proceed to the next step.

A win-win situation demands negotiating an outcome where everyone feels like a winner. If you recognize your own personality style as well as the style of the person you are negotiating with, you are in a much better position to come to an agreement. If you are dealing with an Expressive, your presentation needs to be dynamic. Facts and figures will bore the Expressive but delight the Analytical. With the Amiable, small talk is great. But if you are dealing with a Driven, avoid small talk and get to the point. As I have said, Drivens see negotiation as a game to be won. So when dealing with a Driven, you need to ensure that the final agreement does not depend on only one issue. Try to discover the issue that is important to the Driven, then negotiate on the others. Pushing for a decision is fine with the Driven and the Expressive, but it is not effective with the Amiable or the Analytical.

If you offer something absolutely unique, have political power, or use your title—such as "the boss"—to get your way, you need very little understanding of others' dispositions. But on a daily basis, business deals in a competitive environment demand skills, knowledge, and an understanding of your disposition as well as of those you are dealing with. In addition to understanding negotiating principles and tactics to get a deal, you have to have something to offer. You do not compete at the Olympics just because you believe you can. You have to put in the time to get the needed skills. Likewise, to make your argument acceptable, you need to know your industry, where you stand in relation to your competitors, and what advantages you offer. Without something to offer, you have very little chance of negotiating any deal.

Knowledge and skill alone are not sufficient. As an Analytical, your disposition may be to present facts and figures that bore the Expressive. As an Expressive, if you fail to present data, you irritate the Analytical and don't get the deal. Recognition of your disposition helps you understand what you want to present, and recognition of others' dispositions means you can alter your presentation to suit your audience. As you can appreciate, this requires a good deal of emotional competence, which means not only controlling your impulses to monitor your behavior but understanding your feelings and having the ability to read others. It means cultivating the ability to understand the Me and relating to the We.

Cultural Values: The Invisible Influence

We understand the above model because we are familiar with the different personality styles. The example helps us to recognize the influence that each personality style brings into negotiation. You can appreciate that to arrive at a win-win situation we need to be able to understand our own personality style and to be able to read the styles of others. However, what is not so obvious is the influence of cultural values because they permeate our everyday lives.

The individualistic Western approach champions a system where there are clear winners and clear losers. For example, the legal system is based on an adversarial process where two extremes are presented: lawyers in a courtroom are expected to present one-sided arguments in favor of their clients. The function of cross-examination is to challenge the verity and logic of the

> *The fundamental delusion of humanity is to suppose that I am here and you are out there.*
>
> —Yasutani Roshi

premise offered by the opposing counsel and to nullify or discredit that position. The purpose of the process is to make apparent the compelling reality of who is guilty or not guilty. The adversarial approach can be seen in many other areas such as politics, corporate management, union negotiations, and academic debate.

On a daily basis, sports also remind us that there are winners and losers. Clearly, competitiveness has its place. Competition in sport, in the business world, or among different interest groups prevents complacency and serves to maintain excellence. Excessive or misplaced competitiveness, however, creates an adversarial atmosphere that is not conducive to cooperation.

In the West, we put great emphasis on confrontation and individualism. Individualism, Western-style, means you are your own person and do your own thing, which makes it acceptable to push your own agenda and to take immediate action. In the pursuit of doing your own thing, it is easy to find justification for your own inclinations. But no matter what your justification, in excess, this creates indifference. The mechanical order likes clear and delineated results, and it avoids the ambiguity that is needed to explore and accommodate interests. But discussion takes time. A win-win negotiation requires cooperation, which means that you must: (1) listen, (2) strive to understand the other perspective, (3) present your point of view, and (4) reconcile different interests. Interdependence is not about differentiation but about participation. Being strong "John-Wayne–style" means putting your own position forward, but putting your position forward does not mean being held by your position. Before you talk about cooperation, it is important that you acknowledge your disposition and how certain values favor and accentuate certain ways of doing things.

> *Whether you think you can or you think you can't, you're always right.*
> —Henry Ford

The pursuit of the Self cannot be done in isolation or at the expense of the We. Conceptually, Me and We are not opposite but, rather, complementary. They serve to define, shape, and enhance each other. The prevalence of the mechanical view also means that soft considerations such as imagination, intuition, quality of relationships, and feelings are pushed aside and treated as optional in favor of measurable achievement. Yet much of our sense of accomplishment and personal satisfaction comes from our interaction with others.

Rapprochement

Rapprochement is not about giving up individualism but about renewing a sense of unity. It is not about giving up rules but about challenging the rhetoric of principles that sever human bonds. Autonomy has its value. Individualism and the willingness to challenge have given America its competitive edge in innovation and entrepreneurial energy. Autonomy has unleashed an incredible amount of initiative and energy, and produced unprecedented high standards of living. Individualism fosters accountability, effort, and action. Pushed to its extreme, however, it has isolated people.

If North Americans would combine their emphasis on individuality with recognition that we are a part of a whole, the shift would enhance our ability for coordination and cultivate the personal gratification that results from affiliation and participation. Harmony does not eliminate distinctiveness. Harmony is not about being the same; it is about complementing. As we have said, in Japan the concept of oneness demands that human affairs, in the public realm, be conducted harmoniously. Japanese cultural emphasis on group identity demands that individual behavior reflect an awareness of others and sensitivity toward the group. Only when pushed to the extreme does harmony generate a conformity where everyone is expected to be the same. Such excess is not a moral issue, but rigid conformity to either the Western paradigm or the Eastern paradigm will negate a part of who you are. Each culture has overemphasized a different part of our humanity and capabilities.

Achieving a balance of individualism and group participation can enhance our lives, just as using moderate amounts of spice can enhance the flavor of food. For example, the Eastern accent on harmony may well favor the development of empathy and enhance your ability to sense a friend's mood, and your ability to tune into other people's feelings is greatly facilitated when you first are in tune with your own feelings. Harmonious relations do not necessarily have to suppress the Self. According to Zen, to exist you need to be separate, but at the same time there is no existence if you are only separate.[39]

> Oneness and separateness are opposite, but these opposites generate, define, and enhance each other.
> —Zen saying

Detachment: The Spiritual Self

Different parts of the world have placed different accents on different aspects of our being. In the West, the accent has been on the

Individual Self and one's unique characteristics. In the East, the accent has been on the Civic Self and on the ability to attune oneself with others and various situations. The Western tendency to encourage people to develop unique characteristics and the Eastern tendency to encourage people to develop the Civic Self both address important aspects of our being. Both are predicated on

He who knows others is wise. He who knows himself is enlightened.
—*Tao Te Ching*

the requirement to manage and to be in touch with our own egos. As human beings, we are conscious; we have the ability to manage our thoughts and behaviors in order to reach our full potential.

We may take comfort from the fact that we are not the first ones to be concerned with the development of our full potential. I draw the concept of detachment from Hinduism and Buddhism and modify its principles to fit the Western mentality. Hinduism, and later Buddhism, introduced the concept of detachment as a means to Nirvana. The Buddhist concept of detachment refers to the erosion of the ego so that you can join the World Soul. In this context, detachment relates to the dissolution of your ego, your desire, and your fear so you can become one with Being, one with the World Soul. In the Western context, the concept of detachment can be understood not as the dissolution of your ego but as a coming to terms with it.

In the West, a concept that tells us to erode the ego would need to be modified. It would have to be presented as a means of getting in touch with our feelings. An awareness of our feelings, of our fears, of our desires and what evokes them would then allow us to better manage them. Detachment can be understood as the management of your ego. The development and practice of qualities such as restraint, diligence, order (highly valued in Christianity), patience, and freedom from anger (highly valued in Buddhism) provide valuable ways toward the management of your ego. Management of your ego not only gives you greater emotional competence but clearer understanding that is free from an imposed system.

Applying Eastern Spiritual values like detachment to the Western personality needs to take into consideration Western values.

Detachment, in the Western sense, starts with the ability to distance yourself or detach yourself from imposed systems. It does not mean that you let go of desire but rather that you are aware of desire's influence although not attached to its conviction or imprisoned by its intensity. Detachment enables you to recognize the influence of your emotions, your needs, your impulses, and the assumptions behind your rationality. It allows you to gain greater separation between stimulus and response and to be open to all possibilities.[40] It is the ability to let go and to relinquish your attachment and to follow what is intrinsic to yourself.

> In the pursuit of learning, every day something is acquired. In the pursuit of wisdom, every day something is dropped.
> —Zen saying

We are all fashioned by cultural patterns that distance us from the whole of our selves. Our inner freedom to be spontaneous, to be ourselves, is often undermined by subversive elements of imposed systems.[41] A great freedom is to recognize when we gain the ability to distance ourselves from what is learned and are able to connect with our true self. Being distant or spontaneous does not mean being negligent or indifferent to others. It does not mean being casual about or indifferent to social norms, our responsibilities, or some form of system. It means that we follow what is intrinsic to ourselves and behave in accord with our inner natures.

> From the Ancient East: "Get rid of the self and act from the self."
> —Zen saying

> From the Modern West: "The true value of a human being can be found in the degree to which he has attained liberation from the self."
> —Albert Einstein

As an individual, you have to recognize that the full spectrum of your feelings is complex. Knowing yourself and understanding others allows you to unfold and flow with circumstance. Detachment recognizes the need to be one with oneself and one as part of a community. People derive a sense of significance from being themselves when interacting with others.

Peace of mind comes when we are in touch with our inner nature. Cultural values can enhance or diminish part of the Self by either suppressing or emphasizing the value of certain feelings. Our inner nature is subverted when our values divide and suppress part of our wholeness. Being in touch with our wholeness means we recognize the full complement of our facilities. We recognize the rational, intuition, emotion, imagination, aesthetics, the obscure, and our kinship with nature. We need a rapprochement that combines the values that have evolved from the Individual, the Civic, and the Spiritual Self.

Appendix A

Research: How To Get the Answers You Want

Even with the best of intentions, there are many areas where a research study can falter and give results that have no relation to reality. The order and context of the questions, their content, the choice of words, and what the question includes or omits can suggest, lead, and have a tremendous influence on how the questions will be answered.

C. William Emory cited an actual experiment to determine a favorite brand of ice cream using two different forms of questions.[1] In Form A, the researcher simply asked people to name a favorite brand of ice cream:

What is your favorite brand of ice cream?

_____

In Form B, the researcher stated that some people might or might not have a favorite brand of ice cream and then asked if the respondent did or did not have a favorite brand:

Some people have a favorite brand of ice cream while others do not have a favorite brand. In which group are you? (please check)

1. C. William Emory, *Business Research Methods* (Irwin, 1976), p. 211.

_____ I have a favorite brand of ice cream.
_____ I do not have a favorite brand of ice cream.
What is your favorite brand (if you have a favorite)?

Results

When using Form A, more than 77 percent of the respondents named a favorite brand of ice cream. Form A assumes and suggests that everyone has a favorite brand of ice cream and should report it. When using Form B, however, only 39 percent of the respondents named a favorite brand of ice cream. Form B assumes and suggests that people need not have a favorite brand of ice cream. These results could be presented as follows: one reliable research study states that more than 75 percent of people have a favorite brand of ice cream; meanwhile, another equally reliable research study states that less than 40 percent of people have a favorite brand of ice cream. There is a tremendous difference between the results of the two forms, and they give wholly different impressions.

This is not a slight against research. Competent researchers and the scientific community are well aware of the pitfalls and limitations inherent in the research process, and that is why they insist on the imperatives of verification by and open communication with other equally competent researchers. Research provides valuable information and, combined with good judgment, intuition, and experience, is essential before the launch of a major project. But in the name of research, statistical dogma can lead one down an erroneous path.

Statistical Dogma: Question for Results

Even with the best of intentions research can be misleading, but more often than we might like to believe, research is used to support someone's pet theory. Under the banner of research, individuals, interest groups, and organizations can use so-called scientific research to support predrawn conclusions or favorite beliefs. Simply put, what you want to see is what you will get, and if research can support your contention you can reinforce it with the artful use of language.

The Art of Presentation

Like the abuse or artful use of research, the abuse or artful use of language can create misimpressions and deceptions. This use is not limited to the West or to the present. Consider the following two metaphors used by ancient learned men to support arguments for different forms of government leadership:

> Mencius said: "People tend to goodness, as water tends downward."
> Shang Yang said: "People tend to self-interest, as water tends downward."

Mencius believed that government should lead by virtue, while Shang Yang believed government should be based on the sanction of penal laws, yet both believed that their form of government would bring the greatest peace and happiness to the people. Both contentions were explained using the same metaphor (as water tends downward), but the statements conveyed entirely different impressions.

Logic, research, statistics, and the right choice of words can all be used to support a pet theory or demand compliance to a pet political direction. I do not say this as criticism but rather as a caution that under the banner of Western research and spreadsheet financial analysis we omit the powerful tools of gut feeling, common sense, and sound judgment.

Notes

Chapter 1

1. Robert A. Segal, *Joseph Campbell: An Introduction* (New York: Penguin, A Mentor Book, rev. ed., 1990). Joseph Campbell relates dualism, which represents a cosmic division between the physical world and a nonphysical one, between human and God, between body and soul. Monism, on the other hand, prevails mainly in the East for Campbell. Buddhism, for example, does not teach the rejection of the body for the soul, but the experience of the soul in the body. In this book I use the term *duality* as it relates to the Self of the West and *oneness* as it relates to the Self of the East. See discussion in Segal, pp. 116–18.

2. Ibid. The terms *hunting society* and *planting society* have been used by Joseph Campbell. Segal states that "In later volumes of *Masks*, Campbell . . . parallels the beliefs of the West to those of hunters and the beliefs of the East to those of planters" (p. 77). Also see page 82, where Segal states, "In a separate essay [by Campbell] he most fully associates the outlook of the modern West with that of primitive hunters."

3. Ibid. Segal refers to "the Eastern belief in the oneness of all things and the Western belief in the uniqueness of all things" (see page 147). The West makes a separation between, let's say, God and man, and as such believes in the uniqueness of all things in terms of being different.

4. Joseph Campbell, *Primitive Mythology: The Masks of God* (New York: Penguin, 1991, first published in 1959), In comparing planting and hunting

societies, the concern of agricultural societies "has been of suppressing the manifestations of individualism" while the hunting societies "lay rather in the fostering than in the crushing out of impulse. . . . The accent of the planting rites is on the group; that of the hunters, rather, on the individual—though even here, of course, the group does not disappear" (pp. 240–41).

5. Peter M. Senge, *The Fifth Discipline: The Art and Practice of the Learning Organization* (New York: Doubleday Currency, 1990). Senge states, "Our traditional views of leaders—as special people who set direction, make the key decisions, and energize the troops—are deeply rooted in an individualistic and non-systemic world view. Especially in the West, leaders are heroes—great men (and occasionally women) who 'rise to the fore' in times of crises." In the learning organization, Senge calls for leaders to be "designers, stewards, and teachers" (p. 340).

6. Richard Tarnas, *The Passion of the Western Mind: Understanding the Ideas That Have Shaped Our World View* (New York: Ballantine Books, 1991). The term *mechanical* world view comes from Tarnas. He states: "Newton's achievement in effect established both the modern understanding of the physical universe—as mechanistic, mathematically ordered, concretely material, devoid of human or spiritual properties" (p. 280). Similarly, "For Descartes, mechanics was a species of a 'universal mathematics' by which the physical universe could be fully analyzed and effectively manipulated to serve the health and comfort of mankind" (p. 279).

7. Campbell, *Primitive Mythology*. Campbell says, "The planter's view is based on a sense of group participation" (p. 291). Similarly, "The accent of the planting rites is on the group" (p. 241). And finally, "In such a [planting] society there is little room for individual play. There is a rigid relationship not only of the individual to his fellow, but also of village life to the calendric cycle; for the planters are intensively aware of their dependency upon the gods of the elements" (p. 230).

8. Throughout this book, the comparison between Western Individualism and Eastern Collectivism reflects differences mainly between the United States and Japan. Although most Western countries are high on individualism, it must be recognized that Western countries like Greece, Portugal, and Venezuela are relatively high on collectivism. Likewise, Asian countries like Taiwan, Thailand, and the Philippines are higher on collectivism than is Japan. See Geert Hofstede, *Culture's Consequences: International Differences in Work-Related Values,* vol. 5, Cross-Culture Research and Methodology Series, abridged ed. (Thousand Oaks: Sage Publications, 1984), p. 158.

9. Harel van Wolferen, *The Enigma of Japanese Power* (Basingstoke: Papermac Macmillan, 1990). Wolferen states that "the *harmony* of Japanese *wa* is associated with a variety of universal human virtues or qualities such as conciliation, gentleness, accord, accommodation, mellowness, moderation, mollification, peace, pliancy, amiability, appeasement, conformity, softness, order, unison, compromise, and so on" (p. 314).

10. Boye Lafayette De Mente, *How to Do Business with the Japanese* (NTC Business Books, 2nd ed., 1994). A Japanese president has two primary responsibilities, according to De Mente: "to watch over the harmony and spirit in his company and to make and maintain the necessary personal connections with other companies, associates, government agencies, banks and important clients" (p. 84).

11. Campbell, *Primitive Mythology*. Campbell writes, "The accent of the planting rites is on the group; that of the hunters, rather, on the individual" (p. 241).

12. Daniel Goleman, *Emotional Intelligence* (New York: Bantam, 1995). Goleman cites a number of studies showing that "Dropping out of school is a particular risk for children who are social rejects. The dropout rate for children who are rejected by their peers is between two and eight times greater than for children who have friends" (p. 250).

13. Daniel Goleman, "What Makes a Leader: IQ and Technical Skills Are Important, but Emotional Intelligence Is the Sine Qua Non of Leadership," *Harvard Business Review*, November–December 1998. See p. 94 for quotes.

14. Goleman, *Emotional Intelligence*. Goleman states: "There are widespread exceptions to the rule that IQ predicts success—many (or more) exceptions than cases fit the rule. At best, IQ contributes about 20 percent to the factors that determine life success, which leaves 80 percent to other forces" (p. 34).

15. Senge, *The Fifth Discipline*, p. 169.

16. Goleman, *Emotional Intelligence*. Goleman takes from Salovey and divides emotional intelligence into five domains: (1) knowing one's emotions, that is, self-awareness; (2) managing emotions, that is, the ability to handle feelings; (3) motivating oneself, that is, the ability to delay gratification, stifle impulse, and keep on going; (4) recognizing emotions in others, that is, the ability for empathy; (5) handling relationships, that is, the ability for interpersonal effectiveness. See p. 43 for a detailed description of the five domains.

17. Ibid.

18. John Caspar, "The Smart Money," *Business in Vancouver* (1996). In talking about great customer service, Casper quotes Jane Handy, a public speaker who gives a number of reasons why customers leave and then says, "But worse, much worse, is this: 68 percent of customers who go elsewhere leave because of indifference. They just don't think that anyone really cares about them, and they go where they think they'll be better appreciated."

19. Peter F. Drucker, "Looking Ahead: Implications of the Present," *Harvard Business Review* (September–November 1997), p. 22.

20. In Chapter 4, I discuss the institutionalization of a mechanical view that relates why we in America like to believe that one rule, one law, one theory fits all. Research by Hofstede likewise warns against a management model that provides "one recipe" for all. What works well in one culture may not necessarily be transferred to another culture. In talking about management, Hofstede stresses that it cannot be "imported in package form." See Geert Hofstede, "Cultural Constraints in Management Theories," *Academy of Management Executives* 7, no. 1 (1993): pp. 81–94.

21. Valerie Lawton, "Canadian Workers Feeling Low," *Vancouver Sun,* May 30, 1998.

22. This example comes from Jeffrey H. Dyer, "How Chrysler Created an American Keiretsu," *Harvard Business Review* (July–August 1996), p. 42.

Chapter 2

1. Joseph Campbell, *Primitive Mythology: The Masks of God* (New York: Penguin, 1991, first published in 1959). In Chapter 2, Campbell discusses archetypal experiences that are common to all humans such as suffering, gravity, light and dark, male and female, birth, puberty, and old age.

2. Robert A. Segal, *Joseph Campbell: An Introduction* (New York: Penguin, Mentor, rev. ed., 1990). Segal writes: "In later volumes of [*Primitive Mythology*], Campbell goes further: he parallels the beliefs of the West to those of hunters and the beliefs of the East to those of planters" (p. 77). From a business point of view, I find it useful to think of hunting and planting societies as different types of economic systems. Campbell himself makes a link between the different economies—but for Campbell the difference in mythical beliefs between the hunting and the planting societies relates mainly to a difference in relationship between the individual

and the cosmos. As Segal states, "he [Campbell] roots the mythological differences in differing beliefs themselves: the Eastern belief in the oneness of all things and the Western belief in the uniqueness of all things" (p. 147).

3. The hunting and planting society divisions represent a simplification that combines a number of factors. In business, before you are ready to take on the operation of General Motors you have to learn a lot more than that the company's ledger has to balance assets against liabilities. But it helps nonetheless to know the two should be balanced.

4. Mythology is a fascinating field of study with many complexities. The overall generalization to follow about hunting and planting societies cannot be unequivocally applied. It is a matter of degree. I distinguish between hunting economies with their individual approach and planting economies with their collective approach. However, there are examples in hunting societies where collective and group effort was used. Likewise, there are also examples in planting societies where individual action was taken.

5. There is no firm date as to when myths change. But it is generally believed that with the advent of civilization and the introduction of organization and specialization, myths started to change. By 3500 B.C., with the formation of city-states, the organic myths lost their meaning. In *Primitive Mythology* Campbell discusses the fusion of the planting and the hunting myths as being superseded by the new cosmic order. He says, "A natural accord of earthly, heavenly and individual affairs is imagined; and the game is no longer that of the buffalo dance or metamorphosed seed but the pageant of the seven spheres—Mercury, Venus, Mars, Jupiter, Saturn, the moon, and the sun. These in their mathematics are the angelic messengers of the universal law. For there is one law, one king, one state, one universe" (p. 404). I believe that with the advent of civilization and especially later with the formation of the city-states, manmade order, civil institutions and a heavenly dimension were added to the ancient organic myth and, in time, replaced the earthly environment as a determinant of belief.

6. Karen Armstrong, *A History of God: The 4000-Year Quest of Judaism, Christianity and Islam* (New York: Ballantine, 1993): "First men had worshipped the forces of nature" (p. 344). In our modern age, our beliefs about nature and the relevance of its force come from science. As stated by Armstrong, "one of the reasons why religion seems irrelevant today is that many of us no longer have the sense that we are surrounded by the unseen. . . . Naturally [in ancient times] people wanted to get in touch with this reality and make it work for them, but they also simply wanted to admire it" (p. 4).

7. The bear story is an adaptation from Campbell, *Primitive Mythology.* See pp. 334–38.

8. Ibid., p. 339.

9. Ibid. As Campbell states: "The mystery of death, then, had been met and faced, both for the beast killed in the hunt and for man. And the answer found was one that has been giving comfort to those who wish comfort ever since, namely: 'Nothing dies; death and birth are but a threshold crossing, back and forth, as it were, through a veil'" (p. 342). The bear myth, like the buffalo, was one the many myths found in hunting societies. Likewise Campbell states: "The buffalo dance, properly performed, insures that the creatures slaughtered shall be giving only their bodies, not their essence, not their spirits. And so they will live again, or rather, live on; and will be there to return the following season" (p. 293).

10. Ibid., p. 241. Admittedly, hunting could have been done both in groups as well as individually. There are many exceptions to the rule, but Campbell's point is that in predominantly hunting societies individual impulses were not to be subdued.

11. Campbell, *Primitive Mythology.* Campbell states: "the men's role in the hunt had to be supported by the magic of their women. However, in the regions of the Great Hunt, . . . an essential unbroken masculine psychology prevailed, supported by tokens of prestige, skillful achievement, and the firm establishment of a courageous ego" (p. 389).

12. Bryan Sykes, *The Seven Daughters of Eve: The Science That Reveals Our Genetic Ancestry* (New York: Norton, 2001). According to mitochondrial DNA research, Sykes, a world renowned geneticist, claims that "It was the hunters of the Paleolithic that had created the main body of the modern European gene pool" (p. 194).

13. Segal, *Joseph Campbell.* Segal states: "For Campbell, the West preaches a division not only between humans and god but also within humans, between their bodies and their souls. That division, or dualism, is a microcosm of the cosmic division between the physical world and a nonphysical one. By contrast, says Campbell, the East preaches the identity of the body with the soul" (p. 116).

14. In *Joseph Campbell,* Segal comments on Campbell's book *Occidental,* in which Campbell makes a similar distinction between the Western and the Eastern values. Segal notes that "the commitment in the West to heroism; the indifferences to it in the East . . . the stress in the West [is] on

ambition and aggression; the stress in the East [is] on passivity and peace
. . . the stress in the West on distinctions and in the East on the rejection of
them" (see pp. 109–110).

15. Campbell, *Primitive Mythology*, p. 384. As you would expect, the infer-
ences made from such stories are based on the review of hundreds of comparable myths. Scholars theorize that the association of the Serpent with
woman and nature is due to the serpent's shedding of the skin, which, like
the moon's waning and waxing, represents the cycles of life. When a man
bled, it was usually from injury and pain. The menstrual cycle and the shedding of blood with no apparent injury gave women an aura of mystery—a
mystery in nature similar to the waning and waxing of the moon. Additionally, the power of gestation and giving birth gave the woman an aura
of sacredness. In ancient planting societies, veneration of the goddess
Mother the Creator was primary and dominant in a pantheon of supernatural
spirits and gods. To this day, Western culture still refers to "Mother Nature."

16. Ibid., p. 127.

17. Ibid., p. 291. Segal, *Joseph Campbell:* "Socially, hunters for Campbell
are individuals. They may hunt for the community, but they hunt on their
own and the community is often small. Planting, by contrast, is a commu-
nal activity, to which participants cede their individuality. Hunters hunt
when and where they please. Planters are bound by time and place" (p. 74).

18. Ibid., p. 240. In *Primitive Mythology,* Campbell says, "In such a
[planter] society there is little room for individual play. There is a rigid
relationship not only of the individual to his fellows, but also of the village
life to the calendric cycle; for the planters are intensely aware of their dependency upon the gods of the elements" (p. 230). He goes on to say, "The
accent of the planting rites is on the group; that of the hunters, rather, on the
individual" (p. 241). In quoting Campbell, Segal states that "hunters are
individualists and planters are subordinate to their communities" (p. 160).

19. Segal, *Joseph Campbell,* p. 85.

20. See note five.

21. Adapted from *Chronicle of the World* (London: Chronicle
Communications, 1989), p. 40.

22. Ibid. See p. 27, "Farming Villages Develop in Near East."

23. Armstrong, *A History of God.* Armstrong says, "the period 800–200 BCE

has been termed the Axial Age. In all the main regions of the civilized world, people created new ideologies that have continued to be crucial and formative. The new religious systems reflected the changed economic and social conditions" (p. 27).

Chapter 3

1. Karen Armstrong, *A History of God: The 4000-Year Quest of Judaism, Christianity and Islam* (New York: Ballantine, 1994). In talking about the unseen force Armstrong says, "Naturally [in ancient times] people wanted to get in touch with this reality and make it work for them, but they also simply wanted to admire it. When they personalized the unseen forces and made them gods, associated with the wind, sun, sea and stars but possessing human characteristics, they were expressing their sense of affinity with the unseen and with the world around them" (p. 4). Armstrong later writes, "They turn to the imaginary comforts of religion and philosophy in an attempt to establish some illusory sense of control" (p. 343).

2. Ibid. See note 23, chapter 2, above.

3. Ibid. "First men had worshipped the forces of nature" (p. 344). In our modern age, our beliefs about nature and the relevance of its force come from science. As noted by Armstrong, "one of the reasons why religion seems irrelevant today is that many of us no longer have the sense that we are surrounded by the unseen" (p. 4).

4. Douglas Todd, *Vancouver Sun* (Vancouver). Todd writes, "The old religious institutions are under fire." While interest in meaning and mystery is widespread, only about 25 percent of adults and 15 percent of teenagers say they place a high value on "religion" as such (according to the Canadian sociologist Reginald Bibby). In the 1960s, 80 percent of Canadian Catholics attended church every week, compared to 33 percent in the 1990s. However, more than 80 percent of Canadians believe in God's existence and "many Canadians are looking for different ways to find happiness, a moral code and a link with the divine."

See also Jim Sutherland, "The Poll Know Your Neighbours," *Vancouver Magazine,* December 1998, pp. 55–69. Sutherland states that 13 percent of Canadians describe themselves as having no religion. These numbers are significantly lower than Todd's. Sixty percent of Canadians consider religion as important.

5. Armstrong, *A History of God.* Armstrong writes, "As always, the new theology succeeded not because it could be demonstrated rationally but because it was effective in preventing despair and inspiring hope" (p. 61).

6. Joseph Gaer, *What the Great Religions Believe* (New York: Signet, 1963), p. 102.

7. Eliza Resford, *Great Religions of Our Time* (Qualicum Beach, B.C.: published by Eliza Resford and printed by Morriss Printing Company, 1986), p. 29.

8. Ibid. Resford writes, "Judaism is a religion of social Justice, not of personal salvation" (p. 30). See also Gaer, *What the Great Religions Believe.* Gaer states, "Above all, he is extolled as [a] God of Justice" (p. 109).

9. Armstrong, *A History of God.* Discussion in Chapters 1 and 2.

10. Gaer, *What the Great Religions Believe,* p. 145.

11. Ibid., p. 39.

12. Joseph Campbell, *Oriental Mythology: The Masks of God* (New York: Penguin Group, 1991, first published in 1962), p. 310.

13. Ibid.; from Gaer, p. 70. There are variations between authors as to what Confucius considers virtues. But the common virtues that keep recurring are kindness, decency, loyalty, respect, righteousness, courage, prudence, sincerity, diligence, propriety, and intelligence.

14. Ray Grigg, *The Tao of Zen* (Boston: Tuttle, 1994).

15. Ibid. Grigg quotes Victor H. Mair on the Tao Te Ching: "The Chinese classic emphasized political skills and social harmony in preference to the theistic orientation of the Indian scripture." As Grigg notes, "They [the Chinese] totally reshaped it [Buddhism] to fit the culture of China, remaking it from the transcendental and theological into the earthy and practical" (p. 7).

16. The values from hunting society may have well provided the seeds to individualism. But starting with the self-consciousness of the Renaissance, European curiosity about the New World, discoveries, rebellion against authority, and science, which I discuss in more detail in Chapter Four, added flavor to modern individualism.

Chapter 4

1. Peter F. Drucker, "The Theory of the Business," *Harvard Business Review* (September–October 1994), pp. 95–104. Drucker contends that

business has to revisit its assumptions and theories that govern an organization's behavior. As Drucker states, "Yet what to do is increasingly becoming the central challenge facing management. . . . in most cases, the right things are being done—but fruitlessly. What accounts for this apparent paradox? The assumptions on which the organization has been built and is being run no longer fit reality" (p. 95). Drucker goes on to say, "To establish, maintain, and restore a theory, however, does not require a Genghis Khan or a Leonardo da Vinci in the executive suite. It is not genius; it is hard work. It is not being clever; it's being conscientious. It is what CEOs are paid for" (p. 104).

2. Fernand Braudel, *A History of Civilizations* (New York: Penguin, 1993), p. 368. In discussing the founders of science, Braudel writes, "The major event, transcending all these efforts, was the establishment of a new model of the world: the abstract, geometricized universe of Descartes and, still more, of Newton, in which everything depended on one principle" (p. 368).

3. Richard Tarnas, *The Passion of the Western Mind: Understanding the Ideas That Have Shaped Our World View* (New York: Ballantine, 1991), p. 273.

4. Braudel, *A History of Civilizations*. Braudel contends that "Western Christianity was and remains the main constituent element in European thought—including rationalist thought, which although it attacked Christianity was also derivative from it. Throughout the history of the West, Christianity has been at the heart of the civilization it inspires" (p. 333).

5. Tarnas, *The Passion of the Western Mind*, p. 179.

6. Ibid., p. 288.

7. Ibid., p. 327.

8. Peter F. Drucker, *Post-Capitalist Society* (New York: Harper Business, 1993). In his discussion of capitalism and technology, Drucker discusses the transformation in the concept of knowledge between 1750 and 1900 (p. 19).

9. James J. Flink, *The Automobile Age* (Cambridge, Mass.: MIT Press, 1988), p. 25.

10. Braudel, *A History of Civilizations*. Braudel states, "the word 'industry,' before the eighteenth century—or rather, before the nineteenth—risks evoking a false picture. At the very most, then, there was what may be called 'pre-industry'" (p. 374).

11. Drucker, *Post-Capitalist Society,* p. 1.

12. Braudel, *A History of Civilizations.* Braudel writes of the Renaissance, "Its atmosphere was one of lively enjoyment, relishing the many pleasures of the eye, the mind and the body, as if the West were emerging from a centuries-long period of Lent" (pp. 347–48). See p. 344 for discussion on European confidence in human ability.

13. Brock Yates, "Hot for the Road: 100 Years of the Automobile in America," *Life Magazine* (Winter 1996). See pp. 19, 47.

14. Peter F. Drucker, *Managing for the Future: The 1990s and Beyond* (New York: Truman Talley, 1992). Drucker states, "Today's employed blue-collar worker in a unionized mass-production industry . . . working 40 hours a week earns about $50,000 a year—half in cash wages, half in benefits. Even after taxes, this equals . . . 25 times the worker's 1907 real income" (p. 132).

15. Drucker, *Post-Capitalist Society.* Drucker states that since "Taylor began to apply knowledge to work, productivity began to rise at a rate of 3.5 to 4 percent compound a year—which means . . . productivity has increased some fiftyfold in all advanced countries" (p. 38). Also see p. 38 for discussion on hours worked and car prices.

16. Yates, "Hot for the Road," p. 40.

17. Drucker, "The Theory of the Business," pp. 100–101.

18. The terms are taken from David Sibbet, "Seventy-Five Years of Management Ideas and Practice, 1922–1997," *Harvard Business Review* (September–October 1997).

19. Michael Hammer and James Champy, *Re-Engineering the Corporation: A Manifesto for Business Revolution* (New York: Harper Business, 1993), p. 13.

20. Ibid., p. 14.

21. Tarnas, *The Passion of the Western Mind.* Tarnas writes that "Man was [now] responsible for his own earthly destiny. His own wits and will could change his world. Science gave man a new faith—not only in scientific knowledge, but in himself" (p. 319). He states further that "the discoveries of the explorers gave the modern intellect a new sense of its own competence and even superiority over the previously unsurpassed masters of antiquity—undermining, by implication, all traditional authorities" (p. 226).

22. Ibid. After the discovery of Newton's Law of Gravity, people came to believe that Descartes's "deductive mathematical rationalism" (p. 280) of nature "as a perfectly ordered machine governed by mathematical laws and comprehensible by human science was fulfilled" (p. 270). At that time came the belief "that the quest for human fulfillment would be propelled by increasing sophisticated analysis and manipulation of the natural world, and by systematic efforts to extend man's intellectual and existential independence in every realm—physical, social, political, religious, scientific, metaphysical" (p. 281).

23. Drucker, *Post-Capitalist Society.* Drucker states: "Instead of the old-line capitalist, in developed countries pension funds increasingly control the supply and allocation of money. In the United States, these funds in 1992 owned half of the share capital of the country's large businesses and held almost as much of these companies' fixed debts. The beneficiary owners of the pension funds are, of course, the country's employees" (p. 6). Likewise see Special Report, *Time Magazine,* September 14, 1998, p. 22. *Time* states: "An unprecedented 43% of adult Americans are now invested in stocks, up from only 21% in 1990."

24. Peter Senge, *The Fifth Discipline: The Art and Practice of the Learning Organization* (New York: Doubleday Currency, 1990). Senge quotes Ray Stata: "the 'scientific management' revolution of Frederick Taylor took the traditional division of labor, between workers and managers, and gave us the 'thinkers' and the 'doers.' The doers were basically prohibited from thinking" (p. 350).

25. In explaining behavior, classical behaviorism believes that behind every response lies a stimulus that elicits it. Although Ivan (Petrovich) Pavlov (1849–1936) accepted the subjective elements of psychology, he felt "that it was not possible to deal with mental phenomena scientifically except by reducing them to measurable physiological quantities." John Broadus Watson (1878–1958), who dominated psychology in the United States in the 1920s and 1930s, claimed "that 'consciousness' is neither a definable nor a usable concept; that it is merely another word for the 'soul' of more ancient time." In a 1913 article he described psychology as "the science of human behavior, which, like animal behavior, should be studied under exacting laboratory conditions." Classical behaviorists concern themselves with measurable and observable data and believe that such things as ideas, emotions, perceptions, and feelings can be better handled in terms of stimulus response or as intervening variables. Likewise Burrhus Frederic Skinner (1904–90), who exercised a large influence on psychology in the United States, viewed "human behavior in terms of physiological responses to the environment." In part, classical behaviorism was a reaction to overt subjective introspection and, in keeping with the prevailing scientific approach,

looked at human behavior as mechanical. Although classical behaviorism has made great contributions to the understanding of human behavior, it is not by itself sufficient. (The quotations are from *The New Encyclopaedia Britannica,* 15th ed., 1998.)

26. Drucker, *Managing for the Future,* p. 172.

27. Brock Yates, "Hot for the Road: 100 Years of the Automobile in America" (*Life,* Winter 1996 Special) In the article "An American Love Affair," Yates writes, "They [cars] defined him in the class structure—better off than a Pontiac man, not as well off as a Cadillac man—and offered him instant identification on the social landscape" (p. 11).

28. Drucker, *Managing for the Future.* Drucker states, "Detroit is losing the younger ones and with them the future. Up to half of them buy 'lifestyle' cars—primarily non-Detroit cars. Income is, of course, still important. But where it was the determinant in automobile buying from 1920 until 1965 or 1970, it has now become a restraint" (pp. 172, 173).

29. Yates, "Hot for the Road," p. 100.

30. Flink, *The Automobile Age,* p. 292.

31. Ibid., p. 293.

32. Senge, *The Fifth Discipline,* p. 176.

33. Chart in *1990 Ward's Automotive Yearbook,* 52nd ed. (Southfield, MI: Ward's Communications, 1990), p. 260.

34. Ibid., p. 51.

35. Flinks, *The Automobile Age,* p. 336.

36. Drucker, *Managing for the Future.* On the effect of work rules and job restrictions in the building industry, Drucker states: "the crew working under work rules and job restriction needs two-thirds more people to do the same job in the same time" (p. 138). Drucker goes on to say, "But don't just blame the unions. Managements are equally at fault. One major reason for proliferation of work rules and job descriptions is the narrow focus on dollars per hour" (p. 140). As Drucker says, "But, then, conventional measurements available to both managements and unions also conceal the cost of work rules and job restrictions" (p. 141). Drucker similarly notes that Ford, GM, and Chrysler are burdened with about sixty job classifications, as opposed to three or five job classifications for Toyota in Freemont (p. 139).

37. Drucker, *Managing for the Future*. Drucker states, "Even after adjusting for their far greater reliance on outside suppliers, Toyota, Honda, and Nissan turn out two or three times more cars per worker than comparable US or European plants do" (p. 303).

38. Flink, *The Automobile Age,* p. 338.

39. Laurie A. Felax, The Harbour Report: Harbour and Associates, Inc. www. harbourinc.com, e-mail, November 9, 2001.

40. Senge, *The Fifth Discipline.*

41. Adapted from Gunther McGrath and Ian C. MacMillan, "Planning Discovery-Driven," *Harvard Business Review* (July–August 1995), p. 45.

Chapter 5

1. Harel van Wolferen, *The Enigma of Japanese Power* (Basingstoke: Papermac, 1989). See his comments on *wa,* the Japanese concept of harmony, p. 314.

2. Nancy J. Alder and Robert Doktor in collaboration with Gordon S. Redding, "From the Atlantic to the Pacific Century: Cross-Cultural Management Reviewed," *Journal of Management* 12, no. 2 (1986): 295–318. Alder, Doktor, and Redding describe culture as "collective maps" that serve to shape the way we think and what we do.

3. Boye Lafayette De Mente, *How to Do Business with the Japanese: A Complete Guide to Japanese Customs and Business Practices* (Lincolnwood, Ill.: NTC Business Books, 2nd ed., 1994). A Japanese president has two primary responsibilities, according to De Mente: "to watch over the harmony and spirit in his company and to make and maintain the necessary personal connections with other companies, associates, government agencies, banks and important clients" (p. 84).

4. T. Fujisawa, cofounder of Honda Motor Corporation, has said, "Japanese and American management is 95 percent the same, and differs in all important respects." Quoted in Alder, Doktor, and Redding, "From the Atlantic to the Pacific Century" (p. 295).

5. Gary Bonvillian and William A. Nowlin, "Cultural Awareness: An Essential Element of Doing Business Abroad," *Business Horizons* (November–December 1994).

6. Ibid., p. 44.

7. Ibid. Bonvillian and Nowlin cite Jean McEnery and Gaston Des Harnais's article "Culture Shock," *Training and Development Journal* (April 1990).

8. Ibid.

9. The sketch of Japanese history is adapted from "Japan: Early History," Social Studies Eight, an undated pamphlet in the author's collection.

10. Van Wolferen, *The Enigma of Japanese Power*, p. 322.

11. Yamamoto Tsunetomo, *The Hagakure: A Code to the Way of the Samurai*, trans. Takao Mukoh (Tokyo: Hokuseido Press, 1980). As told by Yamamoto, "Young people these days show propensities to become effeminate. Nowadays, good-natured, amiable, affable or gentle people are being talked much about as worthy men. This trend keeps everyone from being aggressive and bold enough in any undertaking."

12. Ibid., p. 5.

13. Ibid.

14. Ibid., p. 17.

15. Byron K. Marshall, *Capitalism and Nationalism in Prewar Japan: The Ideology of the Business Elite, 1868–1941* (Palo Alto, Calif.: Stanford University Press, 1967), pp. 10–11.

16. Jiro Gyu, et al., "Notes from the Frantic World of Sales," in Laura K. Silverman, ed. *Bringing Home the Sushi: An Inside Look at Japanese Business through Japanese Comics* (Atlanta, Ga.: Mangajin, 1995).

17. Francis Fukuyama, *Trust: The Social Virtues and the Creation of Prosperity* (London: Hamish Hamilton, 1995), p. 182.

18. Marshall, *Capitalism and Nationalism in Prewar Japan*, p. 57.

19. De Mente, *How to Do Business with the Japanese*. De Mente states: "Leading Japanese businessmen, on the other hand, automatically identify themselves as Japanese first and entrepreneurs second. Their guiding principles are (1) their overall responsibility to Japan, (2) their responsibilities to their employees, and (3) the need to be successful in business in order to fulfill the first two obligations. De Mente points out that "It is not smart to

play up profits when dealing with Japanese on a very high level. In the Japanese value system, it is far more effective to emphasize growth, market share, and permanent employment for more people—with profit potential tacked on somewhere near the end" (pp. 47, 123).

20. Van Wolferen, *The Enigma of Japanese Power.* See discussion pp. 395–98.

21. De Mente, *How to Do Business with the Japanese.* De Mente quotes Dr. Kazutaka Watanabe, who states, "we in Japan have discovered neither Man or Society. We are animal-like individuals who have been baptized in the philosophy of the nonexistence of 'I'" (p. 92).

22. Ibid. The term used is *kuse ga aruhito,* which literally means "a person who has habits," and as Joyce writes, this "by extension means anyone who is opinionated, individualistic, conspicuously aggressive or nonconformist in his manner of speaking or dress" (p. 148).

23. Ibid., p. 43.

24. Ibid., p. 50; van Wolferen, *The Enigma of Japanese Power.* According to van Wolferen, the *nemawashi* and the *ringi* systems can be used to impose compliance, diffuse responsibility, and stall action. See discussion p. 338.

25. De Mente, *How to Do Business with the Japanese.* Group consensus requires adjustment. De Mente states, "As the talk continues, the members feel each other out and gradually adjust their own views so that a consensus emerges" (p. 52).

26. Jiro Gyu, et al., "Notes from the Frantic World of Sales," p. 152.

27. De Mente, *How to Do Business with the Japanese,* p. 39.

28. Van Wolferen, *The Enigma of Japanese Power.*

29. Japan National Tourist Organization, *Make Friends for Japan* (Tokyo: Japan Convention Bureau, 1991), p. 57.

30. De Mente, *How to Do Business with the Japanese.* De Mente states, "When a man or woman is in a very high position in business, politics, entertainment, or any other profession in Japan, he or she is expected—forced is more accurate—to maintain a 'low posture toward the public.' That is, he must present himself as the humblest of creatures, deprecate his achievements" (p. 160).

31. Ibid., p. 85.

32. Rosalie L. Tung, "Managing Cross-National and Intra-National Diversity," *Human Resources Management* 32, no. 4 (Winter 1993): 461–77.

33. Ibid.

34. The analogy is adapted from Tsunehiko Ichijo, *WA (Harmony) for the World* (Kyoto: Koyo Shobo, 1993), p. 3.

35. Juzo Yamasaki, et al., "Diary of a Fishing Freak," in Silverman, ed., *Bringing Home the Sushi,* p. 42.

36. Ibid.

37. Van Wolferen, *The Enigma of Japanese Power.*

38. Ibid., p. 315.

39. De Mente, *How to Do Business with the Japanese.* See "Management by Intuition," p. 13.

40. This story was taken from Takashina Shuji, "The Aesthetic of *Suki:* Lessons from the Venice Biennial's Japanese Pavilion," *The Japan Foundation Newsletter* 24, no. 6 (March 1997): 20–24.

41. Ibid., p. 21.

42. Ibid., p. 23.

43. Ibid., p. 21.

44. *The Economist Intelligence,* "Japan," country profile 1997–98. The 1970s saw ups and downs, but according to *The Economist Intelligence,* from the mid-1950s to the '70s, the GDP annual growth average was 10 percent.

45. Ibid.

46. Shintaro Hori, "Fixing Japan's White-Collar Economy: A Personal View," *Harvard Business Review* (November–December 1993), p. 159.

47. De Mente, *How To Do Business with the Japanese.* De Mente states, "The personal nature of the business in Japan makes it extremely difficult for an outsider to break into the system. Commenting on the system, H. W.

Allen Sweeney, Executive Vice President of Yamazaki-Nabisco, said that it was not a distribution system but a social system and that anyone who ignored that essential fact was in serious trouble" (p. 202).

48. Paul Herbig, *Marketing Japanese Style* (Westport, Conn.: Quorum Books, 1995). See discussion on p. 77.

49. De Mente, *How To Do Business with the Japanese*. De Mente states: "Many Japanese manufacturers would like to break away from the old system and cut out as many middlemen as possible, but they are too tightly bound by personal ties" (p. 194).

50. Ibid. De Mente writes that the "cold, objective approach of the American business executive who hires and fires mechanically and whose primary concern is to make as much profit as possible is not only inhuman but morally sinful" (p. 107).

51. Hori, "Fixing Japan's White-Collar Economy."

52. Ibid. In talking about overhead efficiency, Hori "put the number of excess workers in these combined industries (services and manufacturing) at a minimum of 15% to 20% of the white-collar work force. If my estimates are correct across the economy as a whole, that means there are currently at least 5 million to 6 million redundant workers to be found in the Japanese industry" (p. 163). He notes that "To a significant degree, this extra level of cost due to poor white-collar productivity is 'subsidized' by Japanese consumers by way of premium prices" (p. 161).

53. Van Wolferen, *The Enigma of Japanese Power*.

54. Ibid. Although not discussed here, the 1990s Japanese financial crisis of nonperforming loans has much to do with the Japanese keiretsu cross-share holding system, excess patronage, and lack of system accountability for the efficient allocation of financial assets.

55. Hori, "Fixing Japan's White-Collar Economy," p. 160.

56. Ibid., p. 151.

57. Kenichi Ohmae, *The End of the Nation State: The Rise of Regional Economies* (New York: The Free Press, 1995), p. 49, exhibit 4–1.

58. Van Wolferen, *The Enigma of Japanese Power*. See p. 60 for a discussion on the effect of the Nokyo.

59. Hori, "Fixing Japan's White-Collar Economy," p. 172.

60. Hiroshi Tanaka, "Don't Cry, Tanaka-Hun!" in Silverman, ed., *Bringing Home the Sushi,* p. 139.

61. Ohmae, *The End of the Nation State.* See his discussion on "The Nintendo Kids," p. 35.

62. Li Genan, "The Rise of the Individual in Japanese Society and Its Impact: Trends Running Counter to Traditional Groupism," *The Japan Foundation Newsletter* 24, no. 6 (March 1997): 18–21. Genan states: "A recent survey found that some thirty percent of the young employees polled would be willing to switch to another company that offered better working conditions if the opportunity arose" (p. 19).

63. Ibid., p. 19.

64. See note 61.

65. Nancy Gibbs, "The Paradox of Prosperity," *Time,* December 29, 1997. Gibbs claims that "Americans are working 160 hours more each year than they did 20 years ago"(p. 63).

66. Genan, "The Rise of the Individual in Japanese Society and Its Impact." Genan writes, "Nevertheless, the swing toward individualism is making more rapid progress on the material front than it is on the Japanese psyche" (p. 21).

67. Eto Shinkichi, "Continuity and Discontinuity in Postwar Japan," *The Japan Foundation Newsletter* 23, no. 2 (September 1995): 1–5.

68. Tsushima Michihito, "The Japanese and Religion," *The Japan Foundation Newsletter* 23, no. 5 (February 1996): 1–5.

Chapter 6

1. Harel van Wolferen, *The Enigma of Japanese Power* (Basingstoke: Papermac, 1989), p. 314.

2. Paul Herbig, *Marketing Japanese Style* (Westport, Conn.: Quorum Books, 1995), p. 101.

3. Francis Fukuyama, *Trust: The Social Virtues and the Creation of Pros-*

perity (London: Hamish Hamilton, 1995). Fukuyama makes a distinction between high-trust societies and low-trust societies and presents a strong argument of how a sense of "reciprocal obligation" and "trust" exercises a large influence on corporate structure and operation.

4. Ibid., p. 84.

5. Ibid., p. 85.

6. Ibid. The Chinese history is an adaptation from Francis Fukuyama.

7. Gordon S. Redding, *The Spirit of Chinese Capitalism* (New York: de Gruyter, 1990).

8. Fukuyama, *Trust.* See discussion in Chapter 9.

9. Ibid.

10. Boye Lafayette De Mente, *How to Do Business with the Japanese* (Lincolnwood, Ill.: NTC Business Books, 1994). De Mente says: "As a group-oriented people, most Japanese find it difficult or impossible to act as individuals" (p. 93).

11. Ibid. About obligation, De Mente writes, "Good and bad were not abstract theories derived from some metaphysical heaven or hell. Actions and thoughts that did not disrupt personal relations were good—or possibly neutral—while anything that threatened disruption was bad" (p. 41).

12. Ibid. De Mente contends that Japanese businessmen believe that business "should be run as a huge family, with the president as both mother and father of the employees" (p. 42).

13. Ibid. De Mente states that to Japanese, an "executive who hires and fires mechanically and whose primary concern is to make as much profit as possible is not only inhuman but morally sinful" (p. 106).

14. James Ogilvy, "The Economics of Trust: A Lack of Trust Imposes a Tax on Both Organizations and Societies," *Harvard Business Review* (November–December 1995), p. 47. Ogilvy discusses Fukuyama's book *Trust: The Social Virtues and the Creation of Prosperity.*

15. Ito Shuntaro, "Universality in Japanese Thought," *The Japan Foundation Newsletter* 21, no. 6 (March 1994): 7.

16. Ibid.

17. Lu Zai Ling, ed., *A Collection of Mo Zi's Sayings* (Jinan: Qi Lu shu she, 1992). Mo Zi (468–384 B.C.), originally known as Mo Di, was a native of Lany of the state of Lu, present-day Tengzhou City in Shandong province. See note, p. 118.

18. Deborah Tannen, "The Power of Talk: Who Gets Heard and Why," *Harvard Business Review* (September–October 1995).

19. Ibid. The pilot story is on pp. 146–47.

Chapter 7

1. Steven E. Prokesch, "Competing on Customer Service: An Interview with British Airways' Sir Colin Marshall," *Harvard Business Review* (November–December 1995), p. 103.

2. Michael E. Porter, "What Is Strategy?" *Harvard Business Review* (November–December, 1996). Porter states: "Competitive advantage grows out of the *entire system* of activities."

3. Valarie A. Zeithaml, "Consumer Perceptions of Price, Quality, and Value: A Means-End Model and Synthesis of Evidence," *Journal of Marketing* 52, no. 2 (July 1988): 22.

4. Ibid., p. 5.

5. Thomas O. Jones and Earl W. Sasser, Jr., "Why Satisfied Customers Defect," *Harvard Business Review* (November–December 1995). Jones and Sasser state that serving the wrong customers "utilizes a disproportionate amount of the company's resources."

6. Jones and Sasser, "Why Satisfied Customers Defect," p. 91.

7. Bronwyn Fryer, "High Tech, the Old-Fashioned Way: An Interview with Tom Siebel of Siebel Systems," *Harvard Business Review* (March 2001). In his article Fryer claims that according to Claes Fornell, director of the University of Michigan Business School's National Quality Research Center and its American Customer Satisfaction Index, just a 1 percent increase in customer satisfaction can produce a 3 percent increase in market capitalization (see p. 120).

8. Prokesch, "Competing on Customer Service," p. 104.

9. Ibid., p. 106.

10. Ibid., p. 109.

11. Charles R. Weiser, "Championing the Customer British Airways Has Given Customer Relations a Critical New Mission," *Harvard Business Review* (November–December 1995), p. 114.

12. John Caspar, "The Smart Money," *Business in Vancouver* (1996). Caspar quotes Jane Handy, a public speaker.

13. Peter F. Drucker, "Looking Ahead: Implications of the Present," *Harvard Business Review* (September–November 1997), p. 22.

14. The American-style Keiretsu example is taken from an article written by Jeffrey H. Dyer, "How Chrysler Created an American Keiretsu," *Harvard Business Review* (July–August 1996), pp. 42–56. In his article Dyer discusses how "Chrysler transplanted Japanese-style supplier relations to the competitive soil of the United States" (p. 43).

15. Ibid., p. 43.

16. Ibid., p. 54.

17. Peter Drucker, *Post-Capitalist Society* (New York: Harper Business, 1993), p. 83. The 28 percent figure is from Nuala Beck, *Shifting Gears: Thriving in the New Economy* (Toronto: Harper Perennial, 1995).

18. Drucker, *Post-Capitalist Society*. Drucker states: "In knowledge work, and in practically all service, the machine serves the worker. The task is not given; it has to be determined" (p. 85).

19. Peter M. Senge, *The Fifth Discipline: The Art and Practice of the Learning Organisation* (New York: Doubleday Currency, 1990).

20. Francis Fukuyama, *Trust: The Social Virtues and the Creation of Prosperity* (London: Hamish Hamilton, 1995), p. 310.

21. "We Want You to Stay. Really," *Business Week,* June 22, 1998, p. 68.

22. Charles M. Farkas and Suzy Wetlaufer, "The Ways Chief Executive Officers Lead," *Harvard Business Review* (May–June 1996), pp. 110–22. Farkas and Wetlaufer present five approaches to leadership: (1) the strategy approach, (2) the human-assets approach, (3) the expertise approach, (4) the box approach, and (5) the change approach.

23. C. James Brian Quinn, Philip Anderson, and Sydney Finkelstein,

"Managing Professional Intellect: Making the Most of the Best," *Harvard Business Review* (March–April 1996). The article discusses the need for a central system as a means to improve performance, not to instruct. It states, "Field personnel connect with the center to obtain information to improve their performance, rather than to ask for instructions or specific guidance."

24. Nigel Nicholson, "How Hardwired Is Human Behavior?" *Harvard Business Review* (July–August 1998).

25. Durward K. Sobek, Jeffrey K. Liker, and Allen C. Ward, "Another Look at How Toyota Integrates Product Development," *Harvard Business Review* (July–August 1998).

26. Michael E. Porter, "What Is Strategy?" *Harvard Business Review* (November–December 1996).

27. Adapted from Thomas M. Hout and John C. Carter, "Getting It Done: New Roles for Senior Executives," *Harvard Business Review* (November–December 1995).

28. Ibid.

29. Michael E. Raynor and Joseph L. Bower, "Lead from the Center: How to Manage Divisions Dynamically," *Harvard Business Review* (May 2001).

30. Peter Drucker, *Post-Capitalist Society* (New York: Harper Business, 1993), p. 49.

31. Roger Dawson, *Roger Dawson's Secrets of Power Negotiating* (Hawthorne, N.J.: Career Press, 1995). See section 6, p. 211.

32. Daniel Goleman, *Emotional Intelligence: Why It Can Matter More than IQ* (New York: Bantam, 1995). See chapter 10, p. 148.

33. Richard Freeman of Harvard University and NBER said this in a lecture on the impact of profit-sharing plans on firm performance. Notes taken from Industry Canada, Micro, volume 8, no. 1 (Summer 2001), p. 7.

34. Ibid. Peter M. Senge, in talking about creative tension and what is needed for a "vision [to] become an active force," quotes Robert Fritz, who says, "It's not what the vision is, it's what the vision does" (p. 153).

35. T. J. Larkin and Sandar Larkin, "Reaching and Changing Frontline Employees: Frontline Supervisors Not Senior Managers Are the Opinion

Leaders in Your Organisation," *Harvard Business Review* (May–June 1996), p. 96.

36. Valerie Lawton, "Canadian Workers Feeling Low," Canadian Press article taken from the *Vancouver Sun,* May 30, 1998.

37. Senge, *The Fifth Discipline.* Senge describes a shared vision as "when you and I have a similar picture and are committed to one another having it" but warns that "Today, 'vision' is a familiar concept in corporate leadership. But when you look carefully you find that most 'visions' are one person's (or one group's) vision imposed on an organization. Such visions, at best, command compliance not commitment" (p. 206).

38. Henry Mintzberg, "The Fall and Rise of Strategic Planning," *Harvard Business Review* (January–February 1994), p. 111.

39. James C. Collins and Jerry I. Porras, "Building Your Company's Vision," *Harvard Business Review* (September–October 1996). Collins and Porras write, "You do not create or set core ideology. You *discover* core ideology" (p. 71).

40. Ibid. The marginal quotation is adapted from Ray Grigg, *The Tao of Zen* (Boston: Tuttle, 1994).

41. Steven E. Prokesch, "Unleashing the Power of Learning: An Interview with British Petroleum's John Browne," *Harvard Business Review* (September–October 1997), p. 147.

42. Ibid., p. 154.

43. Ibid., p. 162.

Chapter 8

1. The description and choice of words come from both the practitioners and the academy. See William L. Gardner and Bruce J. Avolo, "The Charismatic Relationship: A Dramaturgical Perspective," *Academy of Management Review* 23, no. 1 (1998): 32–58.

2. Daniel Goleman, "What Makes a Leader?" *Harvard Business Review* (November–December 1998).

3. Gary Hamel and C. K. Prahalad, "Competing for the Future," *Harvard Business Review* (July–August 1994). Quote from p. 124.

4. Jack Welch, quoted in "Today's Leaders Look to Tomorrow," *Fortune* (March 26, 1990), p. 30.

5. Gary Hamel, "Strategy as Revolution," *Harvard Business Review* (July–August 1996). Hamel gives ten principles that "can help a company liberate its revolutionary spirit and dramatically increase its chances of discovering truly revolutionary strategies." Hamel states: *"Principle 3: The bottleneck is at the top of the bottle.* In most companies, strategy orthodoxy has some very powerful defenders: senior managers" (p. 47).

6. Thomas M. Hout and John C. Carter, "Getting It Done: New Roles for Senior Executives," *Harvard Business Review* (November–December 1995), p. 136.

7. David A. Garvin, "Leveraging Processes for Strategic Advantage: A Roundtable with Xerox's Allaire, USA's Herres, SmithKline Beecham's Leschly, and Pepsi's Weathreup," *Harvard Business Review* (September–October 1995). Garvin states that "re-engineering experts report failure rates as high as 70%" (p. 80).

Carla Furlong on "Buzzword Management: Why 'Excellence' Programs Fail," *BC Business* (November 1994). Furlong writes, "Failure rates on TQM and re-engineering, for example, run as high as 80 per cent."

8. Ibid.

9. Nitin Nohria and James D. Berkley, "Whatever Happened to the *Take-Charge* Manager?" *Harvard Business Review* (January–February 1994). Nohria and Berkley quote a study that shows that more than 75 percent of managers are unhappy with the results of different programs. Nohria and Berkley blame the failure on "a lack of pragmatic judgment" by managers who adapt trendy management techniques as ready-made answers. Nohria and Berkley state that "instead of subscribing impulsively to fads, they must pick and choose carefully the managerial ideas that promise to be useful" and not fall for "the 'flavor of the month' syndrome" (pp. 129, 130).

10. Ibid. Nohria and Berkley write, "Most programs view companies as machines. But companies are more like organisms. If you do something to them, they react. And a program has to be fine-tuned constantly based on those reactions" (p. 134).

11. Chris Argyris, "Good Communication That Blocks Learning," *Harvard Business Review* (July–August 1994), p. 80.

12. Peter M. Senge, *The Fifth Discipline: The Art and Practice of the Learning Organization* (New York: Doubleday Currency, 1990). Senge

contends that nothing undermines openness more than certainty. Once we feel we have all the answers, thinking disappears.

13. Adapted from Raymond Ng, *Customers from Afar: Your Key to Serving Chinese Consumers* (Vancouver: S.U.C.C.E.S.S., 1996), p. 259.

14. Stephen R. Covey, *The Seven Habits of Highly Effective People* (New York: Fireside, 1989). Stephen Covey, in talking about empathic listening, stresses the need to "Seek first to understand." This, as Covey continues, "involves a shift in paradigm. We typically seek first to be understood. Most people do not listen with the intent to understand; they listen with the intent to reply. They're either speaking or preparing to speak" (p. 239).

15. Senge, *The Fifth Discipline*. Senge contends that holding your position does not mean being held *by* your position but rather being flexible enough to defend your point of view at an appropriate time.

16. Covey, *The Seven Habits of Highly Effective People*. Covey talks about five levels of listening: *ignoring* the other person, *pretending* to listen, *selective listening, attentive listening,* and *empathic listening.* Covey contends that it is only with empathic listening that one "gets inside another person's frame of reference" (p. 240).

17. T. J. Larkin and Sandar Larkin, "Reaching and Changing Frontline Employees," *Harvard Business Review* (May–June 1996). Larkin and Larkin quote a 1994 study by the Council of Communication Management that shows that 64 percent of employees believe that management is often lying.

18. Senge, *The Fifth Discipline*, p. 290.

19. David C. McClelland and David H. Burnham, "Power Is the Great Motivator," *Harvard Business Review* (January–February 1995), p. 126.

20. Ibid. "Above all, the good manager's power motivation is not oriented toward personal aggrandizement but toward the institution that he or she serves" (p. 129).

21. Ibid. "The better managers in the corporation also tend to score high on both power and inhibition" (p. 129). There is an interesting parallel between the results of modern research on the quality of leadership and ancient mythological heroes. Segal states that according to Joseph Campbell "the hero of a myth is heroic for two reasons. He does what no one else either will or can do, and he does it on behalf of everyone else as well as

himself" (Robert A. Segal, *Joseph Campbell: An Introduction* [New York: Penguin, Mentor, rev. ed. 1990], p. 33).

22. As an example, in sections 157 (LXV), 9 (III), and 112 (KLIX), the Tao Te Ching (translated by D. C. Lau) states that a leader "always keeps them innocent of knowledge and free of desire, and ensures that the clever never dare to act."

23. Morgan W. McCall, Jr., and Michael M. Lombardo, "What Makes a Top Executive," *Psychology Today* (February 1983).

24. The information on Bell is taken from Robert Kelly and Janet Caplan, "How Bell Labs Creates Star Performers," *Harvard Business Review* (July–August 1993).

25. Jeffrey L. Seglin, "The *Inc.*/Gallup Survey," June 1998, *Inc.*, p. 91. When workers were asked how work affected their lives and relationships, 62 percent said work enriched their professional life; 56 percent said it improved their intellectual life; 59 percent said it improved their personal growth. See p. 94 for additional data.

26. Peter F. Drucker, *Managing for the Future* (New York: Penguin Group, 1993). Drucker writes, "Leadership is a means" (p. 119).

27. The discussion of differences between leadership and management is a partial adaptation from Abraham Zaleznik, "Managers and Leaders: Are They Different?" *Harvard Business Review* (March–April 1992).

28. "Builders and Titans," *Time*, Canadian editions, December 7, 1998, p. 54.

29. Daniel Goleman in "Leadership That Gets Results" looks at six distinct leadership styles. Goleman's research indicates that authoritative, democratic, affiliative, and coaching styles provide the best climate and business performance. Although the coercive and pacesetting styles are appropriate for certain situations, on the whole they result in lower performance.

30. Robert Waterman, "How the Best Get Better," *Business Week* (September 14, 1987). Waterman writes, "They give up tight control in order to gain control over what counts: results" (p. 104).

31. Michael Fuller, with Alan Hobson, *Above the Bottom Line* (Toronto: Macmillan Canada, 1993).

32. Warren Bennis, "The Leader as Storyteller," *Harvard Business Review* (January–February 1996). Bennis calls leaders "pragmatic dreamers."

33. Nigel Nicholson, an evolutionary psychologist, suggests where—and why—managers may be working against our inner circuitry. "How Hardwired Is Human Behavior?" *Harvard Business Review* (July–August 1998), p. 146.

34. Cynthia Bloskie, "Leadership and Integrity," *Journal of Public Sector Management* (Autumn 1995), pp. 37–41.

Chapter 9

1. Samuel B. Griffith, trans., *Sun Tzu: The Art of War* (New York: Oxford University Press, 1971). Like many ancient classics, it is difficult to determine whether Sun Tzu himself wrote the material contained in it. The work is likely, as Griffith states, "a compendium of the teachings of an unknown Warring States strategist." Likewise, it is not known exactly when the book was written, but it is likely that the work was compiled during the Warring States, a period between 453 and 221 B.C. Some orthodox scholars date the Warring States from 403 B.C. See Griffith's introduction.

2. Ibid., p. 10.

3. Quoted in David Schiller, *The Little ZEN Companion* (New York: Workman, 1994), p. 152.

4. Michael Hammer and James Champy, *Re-engineering the Corporation* (New York: Harper Business, 1993). Hammer and Champy state: "Even Thomas J. Watson, Sr., the founder of IBM, fell victim to this common shortsightedness when he proclaimed that the world-wide demand for data-processing computers would come to fewer than fifty machines" (p. 85).

5. *Sun Tzu: The Art of War.* Sun Tzu states in military terms, "And as water shapes its flow in accordance with the ground, so an army manages its victory in accordance with the situation of the enemy" (p. 101).

6. Ibid., p. 40.

7. Ibid., p. 101.

8. Ibid., p. 43.

9. Ibid.

10. Ibid., p. 122.

11. Ibid., p. 149.

12. Ibid., p. 82.

13. Ibid. The quotes are adapted from statements 31, 32, and 33 on p. 84. Statement 31 says: "Therefore I say: *Know the enemy and know yourself; in a hundred battles you will never be in peril.*" Statements 32 and 33 are as quoted.

14. Ibid., p. 113.

15. Ibid. The first quote is from p. 152, the second from p. 113.

16. Ibid., p. 81.

17. Ibid.

18. Ibid., p. 112. Quote by *Ts'ao Ts'ao*.

19. Ibid., p. 104.

20. Ibid. The statement is an adaptation from p. 157: "There are six situations in which, without dividing, you must avoid attacking the enemy . . . where the superiors love their inferiors and their benevolence grows and spreads . . . where rewards are reliable and punishment is carefully considered."

21. Ibid. Precisely, "Now the method of employing men is to use the avaricious and the stupid, the wise and the brave, and to give responsibility to each in situations that suit him. Do not charge people to do what they cannot do. Select them and give them responsibilities commensurate with their abilities" (p. 94).

22. Ibid., p. 128.

Chapter 10

1. Daniel Goleman, *Emotional Intelligence: Why It Can Matter More than IQ* (New York: Bantam, 1995). In talking about optimism and its value for

college students, Goleman states: "It is the combination of reasonable talent and the ability to keep going in the face of defeat that leads to success" (p. 88).

2. Ibid. To do better in life, Goleman states, you need *"emotional intelligence,* which includes self-control, zeal and persistence, and the ability to motivate oneself" (p. xii).

3. Ibid., p. 34.

4. Denis Waitley, *New Dynamics of Winning: Gain the Mind-Set of a Champion for Unlimited Success in Business and Life* (New York: William Morrow, 1993), p. 21.

5. Helena Cronin, "The Evolution of Evolution," *Time* (Special Issue, Winter 1997–98), p. 73.

6. Goleman, *Emotional Intelligence.* See discussion p. 4, and explanation and diagram, p. 19.

7. Robert Wright, "The Evolution of Despair," *Time*, August 28, 1995, pp. 32–37.

8. Ibid., p. 35.

9. Goleman, *Emotional Intelligence.* See chapters 1 and 2 for a discussion of the limbic system and the neocortex.

10. Ibid. "The amygdala acts as a storehouse of emotional memory, and thus of significance itself; life without the amygdala is a life stripped of personal meanings" (p. 15).

11. Ibid. See discussion p. 20.

12. Ibid. See discussion in chapters 1 and 2. Of emotion and the rational mind Goleman states: "Still, the emotional and the rational minds are semi-independent facilities, each, as we shall see, reflecting the operation of distinct, but interconnected, circuitry in the brain" (p. 9).

13. Ibid.

14. Ibid.; "all emotions are, in essence, impulses to act" (p. 6).

15. Ibid., p. xii.

16. Ibid., p. 250.

17. Ibid., p. 237. Note: Linda S. Gottfredson, in making a case for "The General Intelligence Factor," argues that IQ scores are important predictors for both academic and life success. She states: "People somewhat below average are 88 times more likely to drop out of high school, seven times more likely to be jailed and five times more likely as adults to live in poverty than people of somewhat above-average IQ." See "Exploring Intelligence" (*Scientific American*, 1999). This issue of the magazine presents a diversity of viewpoints from different researchers on the definition of intelligence, on whether IQ represents a good measure of intelligence, and on its effectiveness in predicting outcome. Robert Stenberg (p. 12) believes creativity and practical intelligence need to be tested and that IQ testing by itself is a poor predictor of performance, especially as a forecast for later in life. Howard Gardner (p. 19) believes IQ alone as a measure of intelligence is not sufficient, and evaluations should include a number of other capacities such as personal, musical, spatial, and bodily-kinesthetic intelligence.

18. Goleman, *Emotional Intelligence,* p. 80.

19. Ibid.; "There is perhaps no psychological skill more fundamental than resisting impulse" (p. 81).

20. Waitley, *New Dynamics of Winning.*

21. Goleman, *Emotional Intelligence,* p. 83.

22. Ibid., p. 250.

23. Peter Salovey and John D. Mayer, "Emotional Intelligence," *Imagination, Cognition, and Personality* 9, no. 3 (1989–90): 185–211. Salovey and Mayer define emotional intelligence as "the ability to monitor one's own and others' feelings and emotions, to discriminate among them and to use this information to guide one's thinking and actions" (p. 189). Salovey and Mayer conceptualize emotional intelligence as: "a) appraising and expressing emotions in the self and others, b) regulating emotion in the self and others, and c) using emotions in adaptive ways" (p. 190).

24. Goleman, *Emotional Intelligence.* See discussion on empathy starting on p. 96.

25. Susan Johnson, with Hara Estroff Marano, "Love: The Immutable Longing for Contact," *Psychology Today,* March–April 1994, p. 34.

26. Harville Hendrix, *Getting the Love You Want: A Guide for Couples* (New York: Harper Perennial, 1990). Hendrix states: "As a child grows out of infancy, new needs emerge. . . . This is a stage of development referred to as the stage of 'autonomy and independence.' In this period the child has a growing interest in exploring the world beyond its primary caretaker" (p. 20).

27. To be born with emotions serves survival values. Without fear, we would advance toward dangerous predators, and without the need to bond we would lose the advantages offered by the group. Likewise, it seems, we are naturally curious, and at a given stage without prompting we start exploring. In the process we learn the needed skills for survival. One may ask whether this is learned or natural and which is more important. The debate on whether nature or nurture is most important has been ongoing for centuries. Are you born with a temperament, is intelligence mainly genetic or learned, and what about your personality? While the debate proceeds, most would agree the combined and interactive effects of culture, experiences, and emotional disposition shape and define the self. It seems we are born and all share a minimum core—fear, anger, sadness, enjoyment, and love—of emotions. It has been said by many that people seek pleasure and avoid pain. But how and what is sought is largely influenced by culture. Likewise, our emerging sense of time and space may be natural. But whether we put importance on time and complementarity or on space and cause and effect is largely dependent on our learned culture.

28. Robert Wright, "The Evolution of Despair" *Time*, August 28, 1995, p. 35.

29. Ibid.

30. In Japan, there is very strong emphasis on *Kaisho* for group solidarity. Japan's diagnostic system for emotional disorders includes a disorder called *taijin kyofusho,* a social phobia where individuals have an intense fear of being offensive to others. The marginal quotation by Leo Buscaglia is taken from Michael L. Fuller and Alan Hobson, *Above the Bottom Line* (Toronto: Macmillan, 1993).

31. Mont Redmond, *Wondering into Thai Culture* (Bangkok: Mont Redmond, 1998), p. 198.

32. Morgan W. McCall, Jr., and Michael M. Lombardo, "What Makes a Top Executive," *Psychology Today,* February 1983; Goleman, *Emotional Intelligence,* p. 113.

33. Ibid. Goleman writes, "the sense that you have nobody with whom you can share your private feelings or have close contact—doubles the chances of sickness or death." This must be taken seriously when you consider that, as Goleman observes, "smoking increases mortality risk by a factor of just 1.6, while social isolation does so by a factor of 2.0, making a greater health risk" (p. 178).

34. Waitley, *New Dynamics of Winning*. Waitley quotes his colleague Jack Canfield. See p. 150.

35. Stephen R. Covey, *The Seven Habits of Highly Effective People* (New York: Fireside Book, Simon & Schuster, 1990). Covey states: "But much of our current emphasis on independence is a reaction to dependence" (p. 50).

36. Ibid. "Life is by nature, highly interdependent. To try to achieve maximum effectiveness through independence is like trying to play tennis with a golf club—the tool is not suited to reality" (p. 51).

37. Roger Dawson, *Roger Dawson's Secrets of Power Negotiating* (Hawthorne, N.J.: Career Press, 1995).

38. Ibid. See section 8.

39. Ray Grigg, *The Tao of Zen* (Boston: Tuttle, 1994). The Zen saying in the marginal quotation is taken from Grigg. As Grigg states, "Closeness and distance are opposites. So are oneness and separateness. These opposites generate, define, and enhance each other" (p. 224).

40. Covey, *The Seven Habits of Highly Effective People*. Covey writes, "Between stimulus and response, man has the freedom to choose" (p. 70).

41. Grigg, *The Tao of Zen*. See discussion p. 289.

Index

measurable, 59; and the New Order, 74, 77
self, 3, 11, 18, 21, 49–50; civic self, 11, 52, 201–02; individual self, 11, 51–52, 203–4; religion, 50–55; spiritual self, 11, 50–51, 202–3; and emotional intelligence, 200–4; and leadership (*see* executives)
self-interest and economic principles, 111
shareholder, 130
Shintoism, 46–47, 92
Siebel, 136
Smith, Adam, 67
social cost, 200–4; civic, 201–2; individual, 203–4; spiritual, 202–3
social justice, 36–38
social network, 103
social obligation, 92, 103
Socrates, 59
specialization, 31–32, 68–70, 74
spirit, 24–28, 60
spiritual self, 11, 50, 202–3
sprint, 149
stumbling blocks, 165–73
suki, 100–2
Sun Tzu, 181–89; and managing, 187–89; understanding the situation, 184–85; and understanding yourself, 186–87
shinjinri, 107
strategy, 130–31, 181; and antiquity, 181–89
Supreme Court, U.S., 125
system, 7, 12–14, 19, 57
Szumann, Harold, 101

T
taijin kyofushao, 29
Tao, 43, 46
Tao Te Ching, 214

Taoism, 45–50, 52
tatemae, 98–100
Taylor, Frederic, 69, 74–75
te, 46
technology, 143
thinker/doer, 74, 164
3M, 177
Tokugawa Shogunate, 88–89
Toyota, 148
trade, 32
transparency, 7, 13–15
trust, 94
Twain, Mark, 8, 196

U
universal, 124–25

V
value-added, 134–37
vision, 16–17, 155, 178, 186
Voltaire, 60

X
xiao, 115

W
wa, 99–100
Waitley, Denis, 193–94
Welch, Jack, 144, 163
what/if, 109
Wheeler, John, 126
wisdom, 16, 20, 49
working knowledge, 142–44
world soul, 41–42, 51

Y
yin and yang, 123

Z
Zen Buddhism, 47–50
Zen sayings, 16, 29, 157, 213, 215

Donald Cyr has experience in the corporate world and has taught university courses for more than twenty years. Cyr is coauthor of *Marketing Your Product,* which is now in its third edition and available in six languages. He can be reached at globalthinking@donaldcyr.com.